THE LAST MRS. ASTOR

ALSO BY FRANCES KIERNAN

Seeing Mary Plain:
A Life of Mary McCarthy

More praise for

THE LAST MRS. ASTOR

"[A] gracious new biography."   —Cathleen McGuigan, *Newsweek*

"A gently revealing biography that does an especially good job of portraying Mrs. Astor before she was, well, Mrs. Astor."
                                        —Daniel Akst, *Wall Street Journal*

"Restor[es] Mrs. Astor to her throne."   —*Economist*

"In Kiernan's capable hands, [*The Last Mrs. Astor* is] more interesting than most novels about great fortunes being amassed and lost."
                                        —Thomas Mallon, *Commonweal*

"Enjoyable and flattering . . . an affectionate portrait of the poet and writer who really made her mark when she took over her husband's philanthropic foundation."   —*Publishers Weekly*

"An intimate and affectionate portrait of a woman who reinvented herself at age 56."   —Bob Minzesheimer, *USA Today*

"A concise and engaging look at the tiny doyenne of society . . . Ms. Kiernan's book is most valuable as a catalog of all the things that Mrs. Astor did for us."   —Hillary Frey, *New York Observer*

"A convincing case that [Brooke Astor] is a last of a kind."
                                        —Sheryl Connelly, *Daily News*

"*The Last Mrs. Astor* marks a fascinating era of American—and New York—history."   —Sarah Norris, *Chelsea Arts & Lifestyle*

"An engrossing and highly entertaining portrait of a remarkable life."
—*Camden Herald*

"Kiernan takes readers beyond the obvious . . . [she] never once wavers in telling the story, utilizing over five years of research and assistance from nearly 150 of Astor's friends. The result is authentic verbal clarity. Provocative, intelligent and atmospheric, this is a biography that every discerning admirer of Astor or the American spirit will embrace." —Elisabeth A. Doehring, *Press-Register* (Mobile, Ala.)

THE LAST MRS. ASTOR

A New York Story

Frances Kiernan

W. W. NORTON & COMPANY

NEW YORK ◆ LONDON

For information about permission to reproduce selections from this book,
write to Permissions, W. W. Norton & Company, Inc., 500 Fifth Avenue,
New York, NY 10110

Manufacturing by RR Donnelley, Bloomsburg
Book design by Dana Sloan
Production manager: Anna Oler

Library of Congress Cataloging-in-Publication Data

Kiernan, Frances.
The last Mrs. Astor : a New York story / Frances Kiernan.
p. cm.
Includes index.
ISBN 978-0-393-05720-1 (hardcover)
1. Astor, Brooke. 2. Socialites—New York (State)—New York—Biography.
3. Philanthropists—New York (State)—New York—Biography.
4. New York (N.Y.)—Biography. I. Title.
CT275.A847K54 2007
974.7'043092—dc22
[B]   2007002400

ISBN 978-0-393-33160-8 pbk.

W. W. Norton & Company, Inc.
500 Fifth Avenue, New York, N.Y. 10110
www.wwnorton.com

W. W. Norton & Company Ltd.
Castle House, 75/76 Wells Street, London W1T 3QT

1 2 3 4 5 6 7 8 9 0

For Howard Kiernan and Linda Gillies,
who made this book possible

CONTENTS

Contents

THE LAST MRS. ASTOR

INTRODUCTION

I first met Brooke Astor on January 7, 1999, when a friend brought us together for lunch at the Hotel Carlyle. The lunch was part business and part pleasure. Over the course of several years our mutual friend had gone from escorting Brooke Astor to parties to staying with her in the country. Although he was exactly fifty years younger than Mrs. Astor, the two of them were a perfect match. Both were funny and direct and quick to get to the heart of the matter. We were having lunch at the Carlyle because this friend, John Hart, believed I could help Mrs. Astor get the wonderful stories she told down on paper. A couple of years earlier, Mrs. Astor had officially closed the Vincent Astor Foundation, while I had recently finished my book on the writer Mary McCarthy. As John saw it, we were both at loose ends. Of course he didn't put it quite that way. The lunch was billed as a chance for two of his favorite people to get to meet each other. If anything came of it, that was all the better. But the point was to have a good time.

In preparation for the lunch John would have made sure to tell Mrs. Astor that I had worked for many years at *The New Yorker*. There was no need for him to tell me about Mrs. Astor. I'd been reading about her for years. In a crowd I could have picked her out with no difficulty. In Cincinnati or Detroit she might have gone unrecognized, but in New York she was famous.

Lunch was set for one and I made sure to arrive early. It was a typical first week in January. Outside, it was cold and gray, with a hint of snow in the air, but as I approached the steps that led down to the restaurant the first thing that caught my eye was an enormous spray of crab apple branches and quince. Once the maître d'hôtel learned I was part of Mrs. Astor's party, he ushered me to the best of four horseshoe-shaped banquettes that backed onto this extravagant tribute to spring. If I looked to my right, I had an unimpeded view of the entrance. Mostly I studied the menu, but occasionally I would glance up and see some well-dressed couple being led past me to a less desirable table.

At precisely one fifteen, Mrs. Astor entered the restaurant on the arm of John Hart. You couldn't exactly say she made an entrance, but when she appeared at the top of the short flight of stairs leading down from the vestibule, all eyes turned in her direction. Some of this had to do with the way the maître d'hôtel fussed over her ever so slightly as he grasped her free elbow to help her to the banquette. Part of it was what I think of as star power. And part of it was the way she was dressed. By the time John had gotten the three of us settled, with Mrs. Astor in the middle, I'd begun to covet everything she was wearing— the smart loden-colored felt hat, the pretty green silk blouse, the green windowpane-plaid suit, the triple string of gum-ball-sized pearls, the diamond starburst on her left shoulder, and the jade and diamond earrings that set off her green eyes. I had been prepared to admire her, but I hadn't been prepared to find her pretty or chic.

Photographs didn't begin to do Mrs. Astor justice. Part of what made her so attractive was the delicacy of her coloring. Part of it was the way she brought all her attention to bear on the person she was talking to. Part of it was the magic worked by charm. She was an accomplished seductress. That day, whether to please John Hart or for want of anything better to occupy her, she set out to seduce me. Nothing she said was especially witty or insightful. Indeed, I'm not sure I'd remember any of it if I hadn't written up some notes that same evening. But at the time everything she said seemed delightfully fresh and candid—remarkably so, when you considered that she was ninety-six years old.

That day, whatever Mrs. Astor ordered from the long menu, I ordered, too. I think it was a crabmeat salad. Neither of us paid much attention to our food. For one thing, I don't think she had much of an appetite: contributing to the stylish impression she made was the fact that she was impossibly tiny. For another, she had trouble hearing. John had made sure that I was seated on her right, by her good ear, but, even so, I had to speak up, and sometimes repeat myself, and she had to bend close to make out what was being said.

Mrs. Astor led off by asking about my time at *The New Yorker*. Then she asked me about my book, which was scheduled to come out the following year. The subject of my book seemed to interest her not at all, even though I had learned from Renata Adler that she had put up Mary McCarthy for the night when McCarthy's beautiful white Mercedes convertible had broken down near her place in Maine. The thought of two women so different—one known for her tact and good manners, the other for her sharp tongue—spending one night together conjured up all sorts of tantalizing possibilities. At one point I'd asked John Hart if I could talk to Mrs. Astor about that visit and word had come back that she had nothing to say on the subject. Mary must have stolen a toothbrush, her stepdaughter had joked. I tended to think nothing quite so dramatic had transpired. Mrs. Astor was of a generation that believed when you had nothing good to say you did best to keep your mouth shut.

At lunch that day Mrs. Astor did her best to put me at my ease, the way any experienced older person does with a younger person who is shy. When conversation flagged, she asked me another question. It was a method I myself had used many times. We talked again about *The New Yorker*, which had published three of her poems. Then we talked about her dear friend Brendan Gill, who had died one year before. I noted that she had been the only speaker at Brendan's big memorial who mentioned his wife. That made her laugh.

Mrs. Astor brought up someone we knew in common—an old friend of hers who had recently married a woman half his age. She made no bones about what she thought of his wearing jeans for the wedding ceremony and his going around beforehand saying he wasn't so sure he wanted to go through with the whole thing. That led her to talk about her terrible first marriage. She wondered why it hadn't left her embittered. She seemed bemused by that fact. She spoke of her honeymoon: of the groom's not having a dinner jacket so they could go down to the main dining room and of his going down alone to the bar only to come back drunk. But that was only the beginning. Some six months later when they were up in Maine she had terrible abdominal cramps and assumed she was having a baby, but when the doctor examined her he determined she was still a virgin.

She told me that the first American president she ever met was Harry Truman and her favorite was Ronald Reagan. On occasion the Reagans would have her down to stay overnight at the White House. He was fun and Nancy was *strong*. She said she'd gone down to the Clinton White House the year before to receive the Presidential Medal of Freedom. This led her to a discussion of Clinton's being caught in a lie about Monica Lewinsky. She was reminded of the time she'd been caught in bed by her mother with chocolate smeared on her face and had been foolish enough to try to deny it. Lying is not efficient, we agreed. You can't keep track.

She confided that she was hoping to go to St. Petersburg—to take a boat and go ashore to see all the palaces. It would be more pleasant that way. This reminded her of a recent visit abroad. She'd been staying with friends at Hatfield, one of the great houses of England, when she'd had the terrifying experience of finding herself locked out of her room late at night. She described waking and hearing dogs barking outside and wanting to let them in and slipping downstairs in her nightgown and having the door to her room shut behind her; finding no dogs when she opened the big front door and hearing the click of a timer as all the lights in the house shut off; making her way in the dark back up the stairs and down a long hallway and tripping and falling and banging her arm; finally calling for help and getting no response; and then crawling along the hallway until she was able to push open a door and let herself into an unaired room, where she wrapped herself in a rug for warmth and fell asleep, curled atop the damp mattress of an unmade bed.

It was amazing that we covered as much ground as we did, given that we were constantly interrupted. One after another, people came over to the table and greeted Mrs. Astor with the assurance of long-time friends. Invariably they made sure to tell her how well she was looking. One or two said something about not seeing her picture in the Sunday Styles section over the holidays. Sometimes they invoked the name of a mutual friend or an upcoming benefit. Always Mrs. Astor would lean forward and profess herself delighted to see them. Never did she show any sign of discomfort or confusion. Afterward, she would whisper to John and me, "I have no idea who that was."

After lunch, John and I walked Mrs. Astor home. In the restaurant Mrs. Astor had relied solely on his arm for support, but for the four-block walk to her apartment she used an ebony walking stick. Our pace was slow as we headed south down Madison Avenue with Mrs. Astor in the middle. There was no wind but the air felt cold and raw and unwelcoming. Over her suit Mrs. Astor wore a beautifully tailored loden coat and a honey-colored fur scarf so full and soft it could only be sable. A few people smiled as we passed but no one stopped. At one point, after we had walked a couple of blocks, Mrs. Astor paused to show us a gift shop where she'd found most of her Christmas gifts that year. Next door was a Christian Science reading room.

We were about to start on our way again, when a young woman

suddenly rushed out from the reading room and dropped to her knees on the sidewalk at Mrs. Astor's feet. Except for the fact that she was wearing no coat, she appeared to be a perfectly ordinary young woman. Before long, there was a cluster of people around us. Unfazed by the cold pavement or the gathering crowd, the young woman proceeded to tell Mrs. Astor how much she had always meant to her. Mrs. Astor leaned forward ever so slightly as if to better hear what was being said. Not once did she blanche or recoil or act as if this incident was in any way remarkable. When the young woman had finally said her piece, Mrs. Astor gently but firmly patted her shoulder and said, "Thank you, my dear."

It was like being with the Queen Mum or the Pope—at once totally out of the ordinary and totally in control. No mention was made of the incident. By the time we turned east toward Park Avenue, I was starting to wonder if our own parting might be in any way awkward. I needn't have worried. When we arrived at the entrance of her apartment building, Mrs. Astor asked how she could get in touch with me. Only as I was entering my address and phone number in her little red pocket diary did I realize that we had never once discussed the possibility of my working with her. As we said our good-byes, Mrs. Astor said what people say at such moments. Taking my hands in hers and looking me straight in the eye, she said that she had very much enjoyed meeting me and hoped to see me again soon. But then I thought I heard her say something totally unexpected: as she gave my hands one last squeeze, she seemed to say, "I think we're going to be *good* friends." Later I remember thinking, "Maybe yes. Maybe no." But walking home that day I had utter faith that we would be spending many happy hours together.

Three months passed without my receiving either a note or a phone call. Under different circumstances I might have been upset, but by then I knew that Mrs. Astor had no real need of me. On my way home, while I was still in her thrall, I had stopped at the New

York Society Library and checked out every book she had written. Putting her two novels aside for later, I read her two memoirs, *Patchwork Child* and then *Footprints*, in one sitting. By the time I finished these two memoirs, I realized that Mrs. Astor was a natural writer and accomplished storyteller and had already written quite eloquently about her life.

That seemed to be that. Occasionally, though, I'd recall our January lunch. In early 2000, with my own book finally out, I began thinking more seriously about Brooke Astor. Her life had truly been remarkable. If she didn't feel she had anything more to say about it, that didn't mean someone else couldn't try. The fact was, she had many of the same qualities that had appealed to me in Mary McCarthy. She was strong and resourceful and didn't mind taking time off from serious work to shop for a gift or give a dinner party. Although she'd sometimes had a hard time of it, she had very much enjoyed life. Like Mary McCarthy, she seemed to defy all reasonable expectation—to be someone who had no real predecessors or plausible successors. With no models to look to, she had been forced to improvise.

I had been charmed by Brooke Astor. But, more important, I liked and admired her. I also thought that at her best she was a surprisingly good writer. One problem, however, was that she herself had covered her early years so thoroughly. For a time I turned my attention to another project altogether. What brought Mrs. Astor back to mind again were the events of 9/11. As it became increasingly apparent how bad off the city was going to be—not only immediately but for years to come—I began to remember Mrs. Astor's description in *Footprints* of her work in the seventies, when New York was on the verge of bankruptcy. I began to think how much in need the city was of someone like Brooke Astor.

At that point it occurred to me that to give the full flavor of what Mrs. Astor was like I didn't need to cover her entire life in great detail. Instead, I could concentrate on the years she served as president of the Vincent Astor Foundation. From my reading I knew that it was through the Foundation that she'd been able to do as much as she had for the city. I also knew that she believed that it was through her work with the Foundation that she'd come into her own. In that respect, she had been a bit like another famous widow, her friend Katharine Graham, whose husband's death had catapulted her into a position of power.

Early on, two things were said to me that altered my thinking. First, David Rockefeller let me know in the kindest way possible that he didn't think I would have a book if I wrote only about the Foundation. Not long after that, Felix Rohatyn made a big point of telling me that Mrs. Astor may have been very visible during the seventies but she hadn't made any significant difference. I gradually came to agree with David Rockefeller. At the same time, I came to conclude that Felix Rohatyn and I had been talking at cross-purposes. He was talking about money and I was talking about a contribution that defied any assessment that placed a high value on results subject to measurement in dollars and cents.

In the end I decided not to limit myself solely to Mrs. Astor's philanthropy. Paul LeClerc, the head of the New York Public Library, gave me a title that sounded right for the book I wanted to write. Above all, it was Mrs. Astor who interested me—not merely her place in Astor family history but the prominent place she succeeded in making for herself as not just another Astor widow. My plan was to spend only as much time on the childhood as was necessary to show where she believed she had acquired the strength to first set out on a path of her own.

With the cooperation of Mrs. Astor and her son, Anthony Marshall, I began my work on the book in the fall of 2001, as Mrs. Astor was approaching her hundredth birthday. With the assistance and advice of Linda Gillies, who had served as director of the Vincent

Astor Foundation from 1974 until its official closing in 1997, I set about my research—starting with the Vincent Astor Foundation Records housed in the Rare Books and Manuscripts Collection of the New York Public Library and eventually moving on to the first of many interviews with friends and former board members, as well as fellow philanthropists and directors of nonprofit institutions that had benefited from Astor largesse. That November, when I met with Mrs. Astor for tea in her apartment, I soon saw that she was no longer quite the woman I had met almost three years before. For one thing, her hearing had grown much worse. Given her age, this was only to be expected. Whether it was owing to her inability to make out what I was saying or to a growing confusion, she didn't always respond to the questions I asked. That day I was caught off balance, but over the next few months I would learn to let Mrs. Astor take the lead and be rewarded with flashes of humor, candor, and good common sense.

When I sat down to write my book, the plan was to spend only as much time on Mrs. Astor's post-Foundation life as seemed necessary to tell her story—cutting off my narrative not long after her hundredth birthday. Over the following four years, as I worked on my book, Mrs. Astor slowly but surely faded first from Bill Cunningham's "Evening Hours" feature in the Sunday Styles section of the the the *Times* and then from public sight. Nonetheless, I continued to hear about her from one friend who continued to visit her regularly, and who, in the winter of 2005, suggested that I come along on the next visit. From what I could see that afternoon, Mrs. Astor's story was over, awaiting only her death to provide a quiet coda.

All this changed, however, on the morning of Monday, July 26, 2006, when the *Daily News* scooped its rivals with a front-page story announcing that Mrs. Astor's fifty-three-year-old grandson had quietly filed a petition in New York State Supreme Court to have his eighty-two-year-old father removed as Mrs. Astor's guardian and replaced by Annette de la Renta. After considering the petition, the judge had appointed Mrs. de la Renta, a devoted friend of Mrs. Astor, as temporary guardian and relieved Anthony Marshall of all responsibility for his mother's financial affairs, placing that responsibility, at least for the time being with JP Morgan Chase Bank. "Disaster for Mrs. Astor," the headline proclaimed. "Son forces society queen to live on peas and porridge in dilapidated Park Ave. duplex." Readers were promised "Stunning Court Allegations" inside. It seemed that, among other things, Anthony Marshall had been cutting back on his mother's expenses while paying himself $2.3 million per year to oversee her care. Over the next two weeks, as rival papers rushed to catch up, further shocking details were revealed. Once again Mrs. Astor was the talk of New York. But, no less important, she was being seen in a totally different light. A light that was not necessarily flattering or entirely to her advantage. While these revelations might elicit both outrage and sympathy, they had the cumulative effect of casting a shadow over decades of important contributions, threatening to permanently alter the way New Yorkers looked at the lady who had once reigned as de facto queen.

For almost five years I had been taking the measure of Brooke Astor. As I'd gone about my research, I had learned that Mrs. Astor was not exactly the woman I thought she was. That discovery was to be expected. For biographers it's part of the process. In this instance, it may have been hastened by the fact that my subject was still living and had reached an age where it was sometimes difficult for those close to her to reconcile her public image with what they saw in private. While the woman whose life had spanned virtually the entire twentieth century was terrific, she was not perfect. But, then, she never had been. It would be fair to say that Mrs. Astor was not always the dazzling charmer I met that day at the Carlyle or the glamorous philanthropist I discovered in articles written about her. Nor was she quite the blithe but resilient innocent of *Footprints*, who was blessed with two loving parents and also more than her fair share of good fortune. From the start she had worked hard to get where she was.

In her later years Brooke Astor made much of the fact that she came from an earlier, gentler time, when a gentleman was expected to wear white tie to a dinner party and a red runner was rolled out on the sidewalk to protect a lady's delicately shod feet. But that was only half the picture. And indeed, if asked, she might have been the first to admit it had never been the whole one. She was already in her mid-fifties when she took charge of her late husband's foundation—an age when even the most intrepid women of her circle were getting ready to replace their tennis game with golf, cut back on their cocktails, and look for satisfaction in the accomplishments of their grandchildren. For many years she managed to pull off the impossible—to balance a demanding job with an active social life, to hold on to her independence while making a place for romance—and for a time at least she was able to see to it that everyone was the better for it. Charm and luck played some part in this, but charm and luck can take you only so far.

One

THE UNION CLUB,
NOVEMBER 18, 1998

To receive, one must give.*

Brooke Russell Astor was not in fact the last Mrs. Astor. Just as four generations of Astor women bearing that name preceded her, at least two generations of Astor wives will survive her. Still, she promises to be the last Mrs. Astor to claim an exclusive right to the title. Only one of her predecessors, Caroline Schermerhorn Astor, managed to pull off such a feat. In their prime both women loomed large in the imaginations of their fellow New Yorkers. Both recognized that New York was a city that thrived on self-invention—a city where the cut of your suit could count for more than the place you came from. In the late nineteenth century, a meatpacking baron could get off the train in Hoboken and move into a Fifth Avenue chateau and immediately be treated as someone to reckon with. One hundred years later the chateau had given way to a luxury apartment but not much else had changed.

Great wealth made possible the power enjoyed by the two Mrs. Astors. A family name long associated with the city also played a part.

---

*This and all later epigraphs are from Brooke Astor's *Footprints*.

But, without the money or the name, the two Mrs. Astors would have made an impression. Both lived through times of great economic instability. Both viewed New York as a city under siege and were able to get other New Yorkers to see things the way they did. Both believed that by setting an example they had the power to make things right again. Both made their mark without Astor husbands by their sides and lived long enough to see their names count for more than their husbands' ever had. Yet no two women could have been less alike.

Caroline Schermerhorn Astor, born into an old New York family that claimed descent from the first Dutch settlers, believed that in marrying an Astor she was marrying beneath her. Caroline Astor was neither beautiful nor amusing and owed much of her position as Queen of New York Society to the lavishness of her entertaining, the costliness of her gowns, a strong sense of mission, and a self-appointed court chamberlain by the name of Ward McAllister, who shared her passionate desire to maintain certain well-defined standards. Delighted to act as her gatekeeper, McAllister was soon treating her every prejudice as gospel and spreading the word to a world that proved surprisingly eager to listen to what he had to say. "Why, there are only about four hundred people in fashionable New York society. If you go outside that number you strike people who are either not at ease in a ballroom or else make other people not at ease," he confided to a reporter in 1888, putting a fine gloss on an exclusivity that some might mistake for snobbery.

Word had it that four hundred was precisely the number that could easily be accommodated by Caroline Astor's ballroom. Some said it was the number that could fit into the ballroom at Delmonico's. Either way, the result was the same. By proudly limiting her entertaining to select members of long established New York families, the first Mrs. Astor not only buttressed her position as the sole arbiter of New York Society but also effectively barred the door to the next wave of meatpackers.

This much publicized standard for social acceptability guaranteed the first Mrs. Astor lasting notoriety. It wasn't long, however, before this same standard ceased to be a practical model for any New York hostess intent on putting together a gathering where the guests had some hope of enjoying themselves. Indeed by the end of Caroline Astor's reign, she, too, was beginning to make room for guests she might once have dismissed as unsuitable. Running into the decorator Elsie de Wolfe, she confided that she was about to have one of those new "Bohemian" parties everyone was talking about. When asked whom she was inviting, she responded, "Why, Edith Wharton and J. P. Morgan."

Brooke Russell Astor, who married Caroline Schermerhorn Astor's grandson, would never have made it through the first Mrs. Astor's door. At the time of her predecessor's death in 1908, she was all of six years old. Although she had not been born rich, she saw no reason to hide this fact. She was not connected to an old New York family and betrayed no twinge of regret about it. She made use of the Astor name, along with the Astor money—often for her own purposes but frequently for the benefit of those less fortunate than she was.

Like the first Mrs. Astor, she was always turning up in the pages of the city's newspapers. Unlike the first Mrs. Astor, she could be found outside the Society section. And, unlike the first Mrs. Astor, she felt no need to have anyone speak on her behalf. Words came naturally to her. And while she, too, cherished certain long held beliefs and lived by certain long held standards, she made it a point always to refrain from passing judgment. If she harbored serious reservations about her celebrated predecessor, she never gave voice to them in public. Her interests were diverse, her friends wide ranging. An invitation to one of her parties guaranteed a good time.

On November 18, 1998, ninety years after the first Mrs. Astor's death, Brooke Russell Astor was presented with the Edith Wharton

Achievement Award for the "Complex Art of Civilized Living," named for one of her predecessor's bohemian dinner guests. Edith Wharton, like Caroline Schermerhorn Astor, had been born into Old New York Society. Indeed, through her father, Edith Wharton was related to the Schermerhorns, while on her mother's side her antecedents were, if anything, even more distinguished. Unlike Caroline Astor, she had broken with that insular world and gone on to carve out a comfortable but productive life for herself. The award named in her honor was to be presented at the Union Club, at a black-tie dinner whose main purpose was to raise money for the restoration of the Mount—the lovely summer home Wharton had built in the Berkshires with royalties she'd earned from her writing and later had to sacrifice because of heavy losses incurred by her feckless and unfaithful husband Teddy and their subsequent divorce.

The Union Club was in many ways the perfect setting for this particular occasion. Edith Wharton's father had been an early member, as had Caroline Astor's, back when it had been located on lower Broadway, at the corner of Great Jones Street. Founded in 1836 by a small group of conservative Protestant merchants and lawyers, the Union Club was proud to claim for itself the title of New York's first social club. In 1887, the year before Ward McAllister made his famous pronouncement, the club's reputation had become so firmly established that one society chronicler felt free to assert, with no qualifications, that membership "implies social recognition and the highest respectability."

Not everyone seems to have agreed. Ten years earlier, some younger members, finding all that respectability more than a little stifling and the current standards for membership more relaxed than was commensurate with true "social recognition," had started up the even more exclusive Knickerbocker Club, where they saw to it that the card games were livelier and the food was vastly better. A century later, the card games had ceased to be an important factor but the characters of both clubs had changed very little. Brooke Astor herself favored the Knickerbocker, where she enjoyed a widow's privileges and made frequent use of the ladies' dining room for cozy lunches or quiet dinners with friends. Although neither club admitted women as full members, women were by no means barred from their doors.

Two hundred tickets had been sold for the dinner at the Union Club, which since 1933 has made its home in a handsome limestone building at the northeast corner of Park Avenue and Sixty-ninth Street. Most of the men and women who paid for those tickets would have agreed that "civilized living" was very much what Brooke Astor was about. Whether it was a "complex art" she practiced . . . well, that was another matter. Some might have said that "civilized living" was second nature for her. Or even bred in the bone. Others might have begged to differ, pointing out that what appeared to be effortless was in fact the product of enormous discipline. But what exactly was "the complex art of civilized living" supposed to mean?

As it happened, the award's unlikely title was not fine-sounding nonsense. Nor was it an oxymoron. The words were Wharton's own and could be found in her memoir, *A Backward Glance*, written toward the end of her life, when she was beginning to recall her early years in the city with something approaching affection. After describing the succulent dishes prepared by Mary Johnson and Susan Minneman, the family's "two famous negro cooks," she had gone on to write with no hint of irony: "I have lingered over these details because they formed a part—a most important and honorable part—of that ancient curriculum of housekeeping which, at least in Anglo-Saxon countries, was so soon to be swept aside by the monstrous regiment of the emancipated: young women taught by their elders to despise the kitchen and the linen room, and to substitute the acquiring of University degrees for the more complex art of civilized living."

Had she actually read those words beforehand, Brooke Astor— who had no college degree to boast of and appreciated the importance of setting a good table—would have been pleased to see that Wharton actually named the family's two Negro cooks and made note of the stylish way they dressed. But she would also have recognized immediately that for most young women living in the last decade of the twentieth century a return to such a past was not by any stretch of the imagination possible or even desirable. For even a reasonably privileged young woman the cozy picture Edith Wharton held up as a model for civilized living would seem like an unattainable pipe dream. Or something requiring the drive and energy of a Martha Stewart. But for virtually all the young women Brooke Astor had met as president of the Vincent Astor Foundation—women who asked for nothing more than a bed to sleep on and a chance to earn a decent wage— Edith Wharton's words would make no sense whatsoever.

Unfortunately, that night Brooke Astor had neither the time nor the desire to search out that puzzling sentence and ponder its meaning. In any case, she was not being honored for her knowledge of Edith Wharton. Or for her many years devoted to public philanthropy and many private acts of generosity. She was just expected to be gracious in accepting this new honor and to add luster to an occasion where her name on the program was guaranteed to sell seats.

This would be only the second time that the Civilized Living Award was given. The first time had been two years earlier, when Letitia Baldrige, the White House social secretary under the Kennedys, received the award for advocating the complex art of civilized living in her well-regarded etiquette books. Brooke Astor was to be honored because she herself practiced this art. Two other awards were to be given that night. Louis Auchincloss was to receive the Henry James Award, for his achievements as a writer, and Lady Bird Johnson was to receive the Landscape Preservation Award. The Civilized Living Award was to be presented by Charles Ryskamp, while Louis Auchincloss's award was to be given by Elizabeth Barlow Rogers. Unfortunately, Lady Bird Johnson was too ill to accept her award in person. Lady Bird, like virtually everyone else on the program, was not only an old friend of Brooke Astor but also someone she had worked with happily at some point in the past. Schuyler Chapin, whose grandmother she had known before he was born, was to serve as master of ceremonies.

For dinner that night Brooke Astor wore a long black gown and her prized emerald necklace. As always, she had taken care to dress for the occasion. She liked to say that people expected it of her—which was true—but it also seemed doubly important to look her best now that she was older, and especially important after all that she had been through in the past few months. The year had started off well, in January, with President Clinton's presenting her with the country's highest honor, the Medal of Freedom—an honor he had also bestowed on David Rockefeller, making it possible for the two of them to fly down together with a small group of friends the day before and celebrate with a special dinner at a good Washington restaurant. In April, she had flown, with some of the same friends, to the Dominican Republic, to visit Oscar and Annette de la Renta—a visit where she could count on her host's dancing with her long into the night.

"At ninety-five in the sun, she still puts others in the shade," Suzy had written in her May society column in *W* magazine, taking note of Brooke Astor's presence in the glamorous party of guests celebrating the completion of the new house that Oscar de la Renta had built. But then, in June, leaving a big celebration at the Museum of Natural History, on her way to her car, Brooke Astor had slipped on the sidewalk and broken her hip. Before long, she was receiving guests wearing full makeup and looking none the worse for the experience. And by August she was back summering in Maine, swimming and taking the dogs for walks on her property while astonishing her nurses with the speed of her recovery. Still, the fall had shaken everyone around her, so that she was now forced to carry a cane always and to remember to slow down to make effective use of it.

The plan was for Charles Ryskamp, an old friend who had worked closely with Brooke Astor as head of the Morgan Library, to pick her up at her apartment on Park Avenue and Seventy-third Street and help her down to her car. Later, he would recall how during the short drive south she began asking him if she might have known Edith Wharton during the years when she was married to Buddie Marshall. Immediately he had tried to tell her why he thought this was highly unlikely. "'Brooke,' I said, 'You are an Anglophile, not a Francophile, and you wouldn't have visited Edith Wharton in France, where she was living at that time. I don't know how you could have seen her in Lenox.'" He had explained to her that by the time she was living in the Berkshires, Edith Wharton was dead. And for the moment at least his response seemed to satisfy her.

In the ballroom, Brooke Astor and her escort were seated at a table with Jock and Elly Elliott, whom she had known since they were a young couple back in her *House and Garden* days, and the writer Roxana Robinson and her escort, Ashton Hawkins. Roxana was a new friend she saw primarily in Maine, but Ashton was someone she had known long before he became general counsel for the Metropolitan Museum of Art. Here, too, she was surrounded by friends. And when she held the black cane close against the black of her skirt, it turned out to be scarcely noticeable. Later, no one would remember that she had even been carrying it.

At the beginning of the evening, Brooke Astor had asked Stephanie Copeland, the director of the Mount and organizer of the event, if she could possibly speak last. On the program the award for civilized living was listed first, but Stephanie Copeland had no choice but to say yes. Because she was seated at a table nearby, Copeland had occasion to observe the guest of honor listening to what the other speakers were saying, deciding what to say when her turn came. Later, she recalled that when it came time for Charles Ryskamp to walk up to the podium to present the award for the Complex Art of Civilized

Living, he could be heard to comment, "I'm not really sure what that means." That was the first unexpected turn the evening would take.

At their table that evening Charles Ryskamp had Brooke Astor on one side and Marian Frelinghuysen on the other. Marian Frelinghuysen, it seemed, had actually met Edith Wharton. At the age of five she had been taken to see "Cousin Edith" at her house outside Paris. While Ryskamp was busy holding up his end of the conversation with Marian Frelinghuysen, Brooke Astor was deep in conversation with Ashton Hawkins and Roxana Robinson. Finally, the time came to present the awards. "I was perhaps the seventh person to speak," Ryskamp would later say. "All the others had gone on forever. You can't do that. I cut my speech short. Maybe it was a couple of sentences."

When she got up to the podium, Brooke Astor was facing an audience that had already had one speech too many. The first thing she did, according to Ryskamp, was to ask the audience how many of them had *read* Edith Wharton? Immediately several men's arms shot up. "The wives looked shocked, and you could see the arms start to go down," he recalled. "Then Brooke asked, 'How many of you *knew* Edith Wharton?' Marian's arm started to go up, but already Brooke was saying '*I knew* Edith Wharton!!'" Having secured her listeners' undivided attention, Brooke Astor then went on to describe her brief friendship with the great writer and touch on recent experiences related to their meeting. She spoke of historic houses and their perils. Inspired by this topic, she told the story of being lost at Hatfield. "By the end the audience was standing and cheering," recalled Ryskamp.

Roxana Robinson, too, remembered the evening vividly. At the table, Brooke Astor asked Ashton Hawkins and Roxana when Edith Wharton died, and Roxana said she believed it was 1937—several years before Brooke Astor and her second husband bought their house in the Berkshires. Then, when it came her turn to speak, Brooke Astor gave a very moving speech about knowing Edith

Wharton, liking her, and the two of them sharing an interest in dogs. "When Mrs. Astor said, 'Edith Wharton loved her dogs—she was so cozy and we had such a good time,' Ashton and I tried not to laugh," recalled Roxana. "But the audience swallowed it whole. Everybody cheered. They loved it. You could hear the whole room thrumming with excitement."

"At the beginning, even though she was so bright, Brooke's speeches were written out and then she added a little something," Ryskamp reflected, looking back at the turn the evening had taken. "She added a little something because the speeches didn't entirely get at what she had to say. Now she had to ad-lib. She wasn't able to read a prepared talk. But the spark was still there."

"She had them in the palm of her hand," recalled Copeland. "Her visiting with Edith Wharton was of course impossible. Wharton hadn't been living in Lenox in years."

As it happened, there may have been some reason for Brooke Astor to believe she had met Edith Wharton. Or at least to experience some confusion with regard to that point. Two decades earlier she had written that owing to the fact that her mother spoke so vividly about the great writers and artists she had met, it was hard sometimes to be sure whether she herself had spent time in their company. "Did *I* meet Maurice Rostand? Had *I* known Saint-Gaudens, and did I have tea with Edith Wharton?" She thought not, but even then there had been some uncertainty. With time it would have become more difficult to tell where memory left off and her mother's stories began.

"Nothing was said after Mrs. Astor returned to the table," recalled Roxana Robinson. Of course there was little one *could* say. And by then the party was breaking up. But for Roxana Robinson and Ashton Hawkins the evening was far from over. Suddenly there was a crash and there was blood all over Ashton's head and blood on the sleeve of her dress. Where had all this blood come from? Roxana, who had been struck on the back of the head, had no idea. It took a while to understand that someone—perhaps a passing waiter—had tripped over a wire, toppling a heavy speaker that was positioned high on a nearby pole. In the midst of all this excitement Brooke Astor was being quietly ushered from the ballroom by Charles Ryskamp. By the time anyone thought to look for her, she was nowhere to be seen.

Roxana wet napkins with iced water to clean some of the blood from Ashton's head and managed to get him into a cab and take him seven blocks north to the Lenox Hill Hospital emergency room, where someone immediately checked him out to see that his case was not urgent, and then left them to find two vacant seats in the reception area and wait their turn. The bleeding hadn't stopped, but it was beginning to slow, and they were still waiting when Jock and Elly Elliott showed up, apologizing for the delay. Elly Elliott had lost a bracelet on Lexington Avenue and they had been trying to track it down.

"Ashton and I told them to go on home," recalled Roxana, "but they insisted on waiting. Everywhere you looked there were typical emergency room patients and here you had two men in boiled shirts." There were no nurses or doctors where they were waiting. No one to ask how long it would be before Ashton could be seen by a doctor. There was a middle-aged guard at a desk behind a screen who was in charge. At about two A.M. the phone rang and he answered. After a few minutes of conversation, he asked if there was an Ashton Hawkins in the room. Mrs. Vincent Astor wanted to make sure he was all right. "How she knew where we were I'll never know," said Roxana. She may have checked with all the local emergency rooms. Or it may have simply been a lucky guess. Elly never got her bracelet back but Ashton got seen by a doctor not long after that. It was typical Brooke."

At the Union Club that night, Louis Auchincloss managed to contain himself, although on the way out he did mutter something to Anna Glen Vietor, a cousin of Brooke Astor's beloved second husband. "As the two of us left together he said, 'There's Brooke, typically remembering a lot of things that never happened,'" Anna Glen Vietor would later recall.

But a few days later, when he spotted Charles Ryskamp at the Knickerbocker Club, Louis Auchincloss felt no need to keep his voice down. "In the men's dining room there were ten men eating and a voice booms out," recalled Ryskamp. "'Brooke had no cause to say that. She never knew Edith Wharton. Why did she say that?'" In fact Louis Auchincloss believed he knew why his old friend Brooke had said that and he credited it to no more than the confusion that can accompany extreme old age.

Roxana Robinson, who had no idea why Brooke Astor had said that, knew only that the evening had been transformed. "It was like the Queen of England's saying 'I put my blessing on all of you. I knight you. Carry this with you.'"

Charles Ryskamp, who had no wish to start up an argument in the men's dining room of the Knickerbocker, did not get into a long discussion with Louis Auchincloss then or later, but begged to disagree with him. He credited Brooke's saying that to something ingrained and long apparent in her nature. "She said that to make them happy."

Two

THE PATCHWORK
CHILDHOOD, 1902—1919

I had the priceless advantage of being an only child.

All her life Brooke Russell Astor tried to see to it that those around her were happy. And, more often than not, she succeeded. First, because her own nature tended to be sunny. Second, because she was prepared, if necessary, to make an extra effort. Finally, because as long as she could remember, she had known how to please those she cared about. On occasion there were failures. But if she failed, it was rarely for want of trying.

Always she believed she had been blessed with the happiest of childhoods. As an only child she had never had to compete with any brothers or sisters for her parents' affection. To the abundant love she had received from both parents Brooke Astor credited her ability to steer a steady course in the face of serious assaults, an abiding faith that, whatever happened, all would come right in the end, and a long-standing conviction that everyone she met was worthy of serious attention.

To be an only child can provide an enduring sense of security. On the other hand, it can also result in a heightened sense of one's own importance. "Don't get beyond yourself," the young Brooke Astor was warned early on. For all that the love she received was strong and abundant, it was never unconditional. She was expected to abide by certain rules. To tell the truth. To work hard. To stretch her mind. To take advantage of the circumstances life offered. And, no less important, to take the needs of those around her into consideration. If rules are fair, they need not seem onerous. For Brooke Astor those set by her parents soon became second nature.

Certainly to be an only child can be a mixed blessing. By providing a heightened sense of the child's own importance, it can make any disruption to this secure family setting doubly disturbing—if only because the child may feel some responsibility for whatever is going wrong. What made life on occasion difficult for the young Brooke Astor was the undeniable fact that while her parents might agree on many things, they not only possessed very different natures but had been raised to subscribe to very different standards of behavior. Inevitably there were clashes. Or at the very least there were cracks in the united front they presented. To smooth over these fissures called for the skills of a diplomat. To be on guard for them called for the highly developed senses and quick reflexes of a practiced double agent.

Roberta Brooke Russell was born on March 30, 1902, in Portsmouth, New Hampshire, a not particularly prepossessing fishing port, situated on the narrow wedge of land that separates Massachusetts from Maine, where her father—a graduate of Annapolis and a captain in the United States Marine Corps—happened to be stationed at the time. The new baby had been named for her maternal grandmother, but early on she would drop the "Roberta"—sometimes admitting to it and sometimes claiming that she had been the first "Brooke." Her parents, Captain John Henry Russell Jr. and the former Mabel Howard, had been married for a little less than a year.

John Henry Russell, twenty-nine at his daughter's birth, was the son of a career naval officer raised in Maryland who had been a mem-

ber of the first graduating class at Annapolis and then fought with distinction on the Union side during the Civil War. Perhaps owing to
the vicissitudes of a military life, the war hero had married late. After
a long career in the service of his country, he had retired to California
as a rear admiral. To his third child and only son he had left a small
house he owned in Washington, D.C.

For the young Brooke Russell, her father's parents would always
remain upright, irreproachable, and so remote as to be barely distinct.
Both were dead by the time their son married. The only time the
retired rear admiral would take on any life for his granddaughter was
when she heard the story of how he tried to see to it that his son did
not follow in his footsteps and make a career in the navy. With no
backing from his father and no California billet at Annapolis available, John Henry Russell Jr.—showing already the stern stuff he was
made of—appealed directly to President Grover Cleveland for an
appointment.

While her father's family would always remain shadowy figures,
the young Brooke had ample time to observe her mother's family at
close hand. Three months after his daughter's birth, John Henry
Russell received orders to report for sea duty. The Howard family,
too, had a house in Washington—one that was more solid and imposing than the house inherited by their daughter's new husband. There
Brooke would live with her mother until his return.

For an alert child the Howard family presented a fascinating study
in contradictions. Brooke's grandfather, George Howard, had emi-
grated as a young man from England and trained as a lawyer, while
her grandmother, born Roberta Brooke McGill, fancied herself a
member of the Southern landed aristocracy. As such, she harbored a
healthy respect for wealth and position. Making do with such money
as her husband gave her, she prided herself on a well-managed household. Her pretensions and overfondness for creature comforts were at
least partially redeemed by her ability to tell a good story. For a

daughter she might be difficult. But for a granddaughter she was, more often than not, a source of delight.

George Howard had literary ambitions as well as a law practice sufficiently successful to keep his family in some comfort. At one point he was working on a study of crime and criminals in Great Britain. On the other hand, his wife's primary ambition seemed to be that her four daughters marry well—that is, better than she herself had married. In this she bore a certain resemblance to Mrs. Bennet in *Pride and Prejudice*. Unlike Mrs. Bennet, she had a son—whose future seems scarcely to have concerned her. Owing to her husband's unfortunate midlife conversion to Catholicism, her four daughters had been sent as boarders to an Academy of the Sacred Heart outside Philadelphia. There they received a firm grounding in the French language and a fine education that did nothing, for a time at least, to alter the girls' fundamental agnosticism or their healthy appreciation of the great importance to be placed on a sizable fortune.

For Mabel Howard to marry John Russell was to fly in the face of her manifest destiny. A career in public service was never going to make this serious and irreproachable young man rich. But Mabel Howard wasn't getting any younger and there were no serious suitors in the offing. In the end love triumphed. She was the first of the four sisters to marry.

When John Russell received his orders in June 1902, there was no thought of his wife's taking up residence in the little house he had inherited. New babies require care and attention. The Howard women were delighted to help look after little Roberta Brooke while welcoming Mabel back to the fold.

For three years Roberta Brooke Russell enjoyed all the pleasures and prerogatives that are considered the just due of a first grandchild. If her mother was only one of many kindly figures attending to her needs, she was the one who read aloud to her from Rudyard Kipling's *The Jungle Book*. If there were conflicts or recriminations in this household dominated by women, she was never aware of them. If there was no father present in her life, there was more than sufficient love. And when, after some three years, her father returned for good, it was love at first sight. "Little Woman," he called her, much to her initial delight and enduring satisfaction. What the other woman in John Russell's life made of this first meeting there is no way of knowing. That her husband and daughter took to each other immediately must have seemed a promising beginning. If Mabel had cause for jealousy, her daughter seems to have entertained no such possibility—even in retrospect, some sixty years later.

Brooke Russell Astor would go on to write most eloquently about her childhood, first in great detail in *Patchwork Child* and then in the opening pages of a second book, *Footprints*. Blessed with what can seem to be total recall, a keen eye for detail, a love of words, a feeling for the shape of a narrative, and a gift, not unlike her Grandmother Howard's, for telling a good story, she would offer her readers a memorable account of a childhood that bridged three continents and two worlds.

By the time she wrote her first memoir there were very few people in a position to contradict her. Nonetheless, as late as the spring of 2005, Anna Glen Vietor would say that she had a friend with a family member who had been minister in Peking at the time the Russells were there and go on to add, "According to my friend, Brooke highly exaggerated her Peking experience. She never moved in those diplomatic circles." One year later, Louis Auchincloss, who had admired the book and even given it a blurb, would speak with some amusement about his dear friend Brooke's trying to disguise her age during all the important events in her memoirs and of his teasing her one time about how she must be a lot older than she was letting on if she actually witnessed the funeral of China's infamous Dowager Empress, who died in 1908. "Why, I must have seen it as a babe in my father's arms, " Brooke had said with a laugh, not about to be thrown off her stride by a mere date.

A child's perception of events is not necessarily accurate and in the course of writing her memoirs, Brooke Astor's memory played the usual trick of telescoping some incidents and drawing out others. For instance, she believed she had lived in China for four years when in fact it had been three at most. She also believed that she had witnessed the funeral of the Dowager Empress, marked by all the pomp and pageantry of a rapidly vanishing feudal world, long before her father arranged for certain Peking notables to witness a demonstration of one of the wonderful new flying machines the American military had ordered from the Wright brothers. In fact both events had probably taken place more or less at the same time. If anything the funeral had come later. Progress is not necessarily orderly. And the modern and feudal can occasionally overlap.

By the time she wrote the second book, there was virtually no one alive from her early years and even her first marriage. She might call the second book "an autobiography," but, like the first, it was highly subjective and gave no precise dates for any important events in her life. In both books she was—among other things— fudging her age, taking care to systematically pare away two years, if not more. (For something like an accurate chronology, one has to rely on the dates to be found in the register of her father's personal papers assembled by the Marine Corps and published in 1987.)

Brooke Astor's first memoir was published in 1962, when she was still finding her way as president of the Vincent Astor Foundation and was hardly a household name. The second came out in 1980, when she was famous. The first, which depends on well-shaped dramatic narrative, can be seen as the work of an aspiring novelist. The second—which starts off with a string of aphorisms that in less skilled hands might come across as pronouncements—is more guarded about some aspects of her childhood, particularly her experience with boys.

It would be fair to say that the young Brooke Russell's sheltered early years came to an end when John Henry Russell gathered up his little family of two women and carried them off with him—first to nearby Annapolis, where he stayed two years and was promoted to major; then to Hawaii, where he remained one year; and then to Panama, where, soon after completing his first year, he was bitten by a rabid dog and was rushed, along with his terrified wife and daughter, to New York for treatment. For the next two years John Russell and his family lived in Newport, where he had been assigned to the Naval War College. And then, when his daughter, Brooke, was eight years old, he was assigned to head the guard for the American legation in Peking.

By giving the young Brooke Russell no time to forge close friendships with children her own age, the constant reassignments that characterize a career officer's life threw her into the company of servants and adults. With servants she did well when they were kind or sympathetic. But, like most young children, she was helpless in the face of a nurse who abused her. With adults she tended to fare better, but even here there were occasional missteps—one of which took place in Panama, when she unwittingly betrayed her mother to a neighbor by innocently parroting her mother's observation that the rockers on the woman's porch made her home look like a "summer boardinghouse." At the time of this gaffe Brooke was five years old.

From early on, her dogs and her dolls served as the child's most satisfying companions. The dolls could be packed up and shipped, but with each move the dogs would be left behind. Inevitably she would find her way below stairs to the cooks and maids and to the gardeners and butlers. While this may have contributed to the remarkable ease she showed in the company of members of all classes that she displayed as an adult, it had its drawbacks, depending once again on the character of the servant she was thrown in with.

Given all this upheaval, it is not surprising that by the time she arrived in Newport the six-year-old Brooke Russell had trouble sleeping. To pass the time, while sleep persisted in eluding her, she would sometimes tell herself scary stories. One night, though, the storytelling got out of hand, terrifying her so thoroughly she later woke from a light sleep to discover she was all alone in their Newport house, with neither her parents nor her nurse anywhere within the reach of her voice. Not daring to go back to bed, she curled up in her blanket at the top of the front stairs, to make sure that her parents would rescue her when they returned.

In *Patchwork Child* the story of the Panama gaffe has the feel of a much told anecdote that has taken on the polish of a set piece. This second story, on the other hand, feels painful and raw. To be able to write about what happened suggests a certain distance, but this waking nightmare can only have heightened the horror some ninety years later, when she found herself alone in the dark, locked out of her room and lost in a long corridor at Hatfield, one of the great houses of England—a corridor that was not nearly as long or as wide as her telling might lead a listener to believe.

Brooke Astor lived in China from the time she was $8\frac{1}{2}$ years old to the time she was $11\frac{1}{2}$. Always she believed that her early life helped forge her character, while giving her a perspective very different from that of the average American child of her time. Particularly her years in Peking. For one thing, there was the one summer she spent with her mother in the Temple of One Hundred Courtyards, a Buddhist monastery in the Western Hills, where the priests taught her to think of each tree and rock as more than just another object. In her nineties, when she added an introduction to her first memoir, she wrote: "They told me that everything in nature was as much alive as I was.

Every tree and every flower must be respected and you must let them know that they—and particularly a venerable tree—must be given real love, a touch, and a happy word. . . ."

But every bit as important was the ritualized and at times frenetic social life that took place within the Legation Quarter. In 1962, she wrote: "It was an Edwardian life in an eighteenth-century atmosphere. For me it was the normal grown-up world. I sensed intrigue around me but it was masked in discretion. I heard talk that I did not understand and I saw things that made no sense. . . . As a result, I became quite sophisticated but absurdly innocent—a rather ridiculous combination."

Carefully choosing her words, she contrasted her two parents— saying they were like oil and water, before touching on the crux of her dilemma: "Mother was mercurial, fascinating, and intellectual. Father was steadfast, stern, and endlessly compassionate and loving. With these two totally dissimilar characters, how could life be simple for me?" There is one incident dramatized at some length in both *Patchwork Child* and *Footprints* that illustrates the difficulty of being the child of John and Mabel. The incident is said to have taken place in China and a 1913 diary entry included in the second version of *Patchwork Child* suggests she was eleven years old. The entry is succinct: "Mother and Father quarelled [*sic*] at lunch, and then remained cross. So, I told Father to go over to the K.T. Club, so as to see Mother. Father is like a snail without a shell without Mother." The K.T. Club was not a real club, but simply a place where one of the younger diplomats kept open house at cocktail time, and it would not be mentioned the second time she told the story, in *Footprints*, where the account would be pared down and Mabel would seem less cavalier.

The quarrel apparently started at a small family lunch where the three of them were celebrating her parents' anniversary. In the midst of this special occasion Mabel made the mistake of asking her husband if he loved her as much as ever and then, when he replied that of course he loved her, going on to ask him if he had ever been irritated with her. The total silence that greeted this question led Mabel to rush from the room in tears and shut herself up in her bedroom, leaving both Brooke and her father visibly upset, although he assured his Little Woman that all would soon be right again. But that night, when her father returned from work, the door to the bedroom remained closed. Only when Brooke interceded on his behalf, did the door open a crack, giving him an opportunity to sweep his wife into his arms.

For the moment everything was put right again. But the child who had served as peacemaker was already beginning to understand the fragile nature of this reconciliation. In *Patchwork Child* she simply told readers she then went off to spend the night with her dolls, but this incident was soon followed with another charged exchange when Mabel received a gift from one of her gentleman friends and John, clearly displeased with all the tokens of admiration she had been receiving, particularly from some of her foreign admirers, let her know: "[S]ome American men don't like to have these foreigners hanging on their wives' hands and kissing them. One thing leads to another." When Mabel seemed to be taken aback, he informed her that he was not talking about himself and assured her, "I know you would never have your head turned by these ridiculous 'je ne sais quoi' young men." In *Footprints*, when her mother was long dead, Brooke Astor did not bother with a comic scene. Instead, she rounded off the reconciliation at the bedroom door with a bittersweet coda. Her mother, she wrote, never again asked her father if he had ever been irritated with her, knowing full well the answer she would get. Her flirtations continued to cause him pain, but he did his best to hold his tongue. On the other hand, faced with a direct question, "even at the risk of breaking his heart, he could not tell an untruth."

Mabel Russell was an unrepentant and incorrigible flirt, who had no intention of changing her ways but also had no desire for her daughter to follow in her path. "Do as I say, *not* as I do," she told the young Brooke. But the effect Mabel had on men was not something a daughter could easily ignore. At her best, Mabel could be counted on to add a dash of gaiety and high spirits to any social gathering. She was the one who saw to it that all three Russells, with no real claim to such a position among the American diplomatic community, were soon at the center of British and French legation life. By sheer dint of her determination she made herself "the Belle of Peking."

It is clear, though, that, despite the writer's many protestations to the contrary, she much preferred her father. And, without question, he adored her. If John Russell could be stern and unbending, he was also fair. If he demanded much of her, he was also prepared to reward any serious effort on her part. He bribed her to start learning the Chinese language by promising her any pet she wanted. By the end, she had acquired a pony, a donkey, five hedgehogs, and three dogs. He always took seriously what she had to say. By nature he was serious. But he was not without humor, his daughter was careful to point out, calling him "a merry saint." He was a merry saint who liked women and respected them. Because he respected the two women in his life, he also expected a great deal from them.

Although Brooke Astor would always claim that her mother, too, adored her, one has the feeling that Mabel's gaze was often directed elsewhere. Whenever the child managed to capture her mother's attention, the results were, at best, mixed. For Mabel, Brooke wasn't pretty enough. Or accomplished enough. And her taste in friends was definitely disappointing. They lacked chic. At the small school Brooke attended at the British legation with the sons and daughters of diplomats, her closest friend was the poorly dressed daughter of an American missionary. For Mabel, this plain little girl, blessed with a great gift for telling bloodcurdling stories, had nothing to recommend her.

Mabel Russell's taste in stories was far more refined and cosmopolitan than her daughter's friend's. Like her British-born father, she had literary aspirations—although she herself had no desire to sit down in a quiet corner with pen and paper. Instead, she chose to preside over the Peking version of an international salon—one frequented by attractive men and women from the French and British embassies as well as the occasional American. She was also a founding member of a book group. And, to provide additional diversion, she helped organize elaborate costume parties for both legation adults and their children. In Peking, with a house full of servants and a rate of exchange that favored the dollar, it didn't matter that she and her husband weren't rich. They were privileged nonetheless.

But privilege and the walls of the Legation Quarter could not protect the young Brooke Russell from brushing up against the violence of this turbulent period in Chinese history. Leaving a friend's house one winter afternoon later than was wise, when the sky was already darkening, she and her amah were warned that there were "bad men" about. Hurrying home in their rickshaws, they soon found themselves in streets where men and women were scurrying for cover and the few remaining merchants were hurriedly closing their shops. It was then that she came upon a sight she would never forget: "Down the middle of the road were tripods and hanging by their pigtails from these tripods were severed heads." What made it all the more horrible were the "staring" eyes and "great bloody cords [that] hung from their necks." Just when she felt trapped in a "nightmare" worse than any bloodcurdling tale her best friend could concoct, there came a group of soldiers from the British legation sent out to search for them and see them safely home to their own compound, where there were sandbags barricading the entrance and Marines "at the ready."

What was going on here? The child had no idea. Twelve years after the massacres of the Boxer Rebellion, violence was again erupting in the streets of Peking. Within a couple of days all was back to normal. But later she would conclude that this incident must have taken place at the moment when China's first president assumed power and the boy emperor was "relegated to the background." Without question, Brooke Astor was in China at a pivotal moment in that country's history. It was her belief that Henry P'u-i, the boy emperor—who was soon to be deposed entirely and then later set up as a puppet of the Japanese in Manchuria and then eventually reduced to a pathetic tool of the Communists—was the little boy she sometimes sat next to at legation parties.

The Dowager Empress Tz'u-hsi, who had been the de facto ruler of China for decades, had installed the two-year-old P'u-i as emperor before her death in 1908 and named her niece as the new Dowager Empress. In the autumn of 1911, in the face of increasing violence, the Dowager Empress Lung-yü agreed to P'u-i's abdication on the condition that the Imperial family would be able to continue living in the Forbidden City and would retain all its titles and assets. Then in 1912, after another eruption of violence, the Empire was abolished, making way for a less autocratic government.

Major John Russell had arrived in Peking in November 1910, in time to observe the fall of the Ch'ing dynasty and witness the birth of the Republic of China. In all likelihood Henry P'u-i was not the little boy Brooke Astor remembered from legation parties who liked so much to fly his kites. But turmoil in the streets there surely was. And the funeral Brooke Russell witnessed was for the Dowager Empress Lung-yü, who died in 1913, only a few months after handing over all that remained of the boy emperor's power. In her diary for that year, Brooke wrote, "I think that she was poisoned, although they say she had dropsy."

It is surely this funeral—an impressive vestige of a world that was rapidly crumbling—which an eleven-year-old Brooke Russell witnessed standing on her own two feet, near the end of what was no more than three years in China. In July 1913, Major John Russell received orders to report to Washington. Although there was a most welcome delay, while his replacement was sent off for additional training, the family eventually had to pack up their possessions and prepare to make their way home. For the daughter of the family this meant leaving behind her first close friend and her parents' first serious home and saying good-bye to her pony, Ginger, to her beloved dog Gyp, and to Number One Boy, the wise and sympathetic majordomo who saw to it their household ran smoothly and also found time to answer any question she had.

Always Brooke Astor believed that it was during her years in China that she learned to value the solace to be found in the natural world. To respect other cultures. To treat her servants as equals. To believe that every man and woman was worthy of at least a moment's close attention. To make the best of any social engagement, however dreary. To value the hours when she was left to her own devices. To rely on her dogs for company and affection. To read books for entertainment and not merely for lessons. And to keep a diary, however sporadically.

Coming at a point in her life when she was old enough to take the measure of those around her, the years she spent in China played an important part in the formation of her character. Not only did she find herself in an exotic setting she found immediately sympathetic but she was placed at the very center of a potentially explosive family drama. Over the course of three years she had a chance to observe, at close hand, her mother and father making a life together. This had never happened before and it would never happen again.

On the way to China the Russell family had rushed directly to Peking as quickly as possible given the constraints of ocean travel, but once Major Russell received his new assignment, their return to Washington was more leisured, with stopovers in Singapore and Hong Kong and a voyage through Suez before winding up in Paris and London—for shopping and sightseeing. In Paris Brooke had the pleasure of getting one new outfit and seeing her mother fitted for a stylish French wardrobe. In the British capital Brooke had her new

French purse snatched, but, despite this unfortunate incident, it was London that she preferred. "I like the English," she wrote in her diary. Later, during a quick stop in New York, her mother would order her four more dresses she thought appropriate for a schoolgirl. Of New York Brooke wrote: "It's not as nice as London."

When the Russells returned to Washington in 1914, they finally moved into the little house that John had inherited on the corner of De Sales and Seventeenth streets. Almost immediately John Russell left for Philadelphia, to prepare for duty in Mexico, but by this point Mabel was more than capable of setting up a well-run household on her own.

The house that Mabel's husband had inherited was a pleasing "cream-colored brick . . . with a New Orleans-type grilled porch, a little garden with flowering bushes, and a brick path which ended at a little iron gate." Across the street was a convent with a lovely garden. There was space for Brooke to have her own bedroom with "darling little windows" and also a tiny sitting room. With the help of a few good pieces of old furniture, along with Mabel's pretty slipcovers and curtains and a constant infusion of fresh flowers and books, it soon became a place any woman would be happy to call her own. To keep this new household running smoothly, Mabel had nothing like the large staff she had grown accustomed to, but she did have two Negro servants as well as a French maid paid for by her mother.

Rather than seeming cramped, the little house felt cozy. Particularly for a young girl who liked having pretty things around her. Furthermore, it was quite near the Howards' far grander residence and also within easy walking distance of Dupont Circle and Miss Madeira's School, a school for select young Washington ladies that Mabel felt would be best suited for finishing her daughter's education. Unfortunately, before being admitted as a student at Miss Madeira's, Brooke was going to have to prepare for its demanding curriculum at some less distinguished center of learning.

This year or so of preparation was something Brooke Astor would never bother to mention in her memoirs, but she did confess to it during an interview in 1997 with two Madeira alumnae, who had on record the fact that she had attended the school for two years, 1916 and 1917. Although Miss Madeira's was within walking distance, Brooke's first school required that she take a trolley, accompanied always by the French maid she shared with her mother. For Brooke, the constant presence of the maid at her side was a source of no little discomfit as were the outfits her mother had bought for her in Paris and New York. When the other girls her age were starting to dress like young ladies, she was being dressed as a child—a European child with prim collars and cuffs and high-laced shoes to keep her ankles slim.

At this first school, Brooke was placed in the sixth and seventh grades. "Some of the girls laughed at me today," she wrote in her diary. "They say I speak queerly. I didn't cry." At this new school she did not make friends easily, no doubt owing in part to her foreign ways but also owing to the fact that she looked much younger than she actually was. Then, too, she had always been more at ease with adults than she was with children her own age. In Peking her failure to be popular with her schoolmates hadn't mattered so much. There, where she was very much a part of their family of three, she could always count on "getting a cozy worm's-eye view of all that went on." But after she and her mother returned to America "there was a complete severance." Her mother had her life and she was expected to develop a life of her own. Having failed to do this, she was falling back on the company of her dolls.

For Mabel Russell, any difficulties stemming from her daughter's new wardrobe were hardly a source of embarrassment. If anything, to have a young-looking daughter could serve only to make her look younger—something that in her new life was hardly undesirable. Although Mabel felt a need to keep her daughter's life within strict bounds, she felt no such need when it came to her own. Almost immediately after her husband's departure, she began devoting herself not only to renewing old friendships but also to getting to know the best of the new people who had arrived during her absence, always making sure that her social calendar was full. If she was without a husband to accompany her, that didn't seem to discourage her. And indeed there were not a few men happy to take John Russell's place. As long as these relationships were innocent, no one in Washington—certainly not the Howards—seemed inclined to object. And they *were* innocent, Brooke would later assure her readers.

Mabel Russell's love of reading had long predated her stay in Peking. She had always enjoyed the company of intelligent and well-educated men and one of the friendships she resurrected from the past was a former schoolmate who was a relation of the writer Henry Adams. In this case it worked to her advantage to usher her only child across the threshold of this new life she was making for herself. "She told him that she had a daughter whom she was trying to educate and would he, a man who knew so much about education, deign to see the child," Brooke Astor later explained. The great man invited Mabel's daughter to join him for lunch at his home with a few of his friends. "But the conversation was mostly highly political and I was unable to understand a word," she noted. She fared better once the other guests took their leave and she joined her host and her mother's friend in the study, where her mother's friend began to play old songs on the clavecin and the great man set about putting her at her ease—"drawing me out and talking to me, as though I were grown-up, a fact that I appreciated." Although later she would be unable to recall a single thing Henry Adams said that day, she would remember his kindness, his collection of "fantastic drawings by 'a man called William Blake,'" and the fact that "[h]e was a small man and the low sofas and chairs had been made to his measure."

But most of her social outings were less rewarding. Once a week the French maid walked with her to Miss Hawks's dancing school, where the boys showed no wish to have anything to do with her. Much to her mother's horror, she was turning out to be a "wall-flower." Some of this seemed to be owing to the shapeless velvet dresses she wore and some of it to the fact that she had no idea what to say to boys her own age. Clearly they had no interest whatsoever in savoring any choice bits she had managed to glean from a recent gift her mother had given her, a two-volume edition of Walter Pater's *Plato and Platonism*. "[W]hat I had to say seemed to bore them, and they were always calling over my shoulder to someone else," she later recalled.

At the same time that Mabel was giving her daughter something of no practical use to her, she was taking away something quite dear to her. One day, Brooke returned home from school to discover that her mother, having decided that the time had come for her only daughter to put such childish things behind her, had confiscated all her dolls and given them to the Salvation Army. Rather than wait at home to break the news herself, she had gone about her business, leaving it to the French maid to explain what had taken place.

If it had not been for the Howards, Brooke Russell's new life in Washington would have been very thin gruel indeed. Once a week after school she would lunch with her Granny and then stay on, happy to sit by a nice fire and talk. Sometimes she would get to sleep over. At the big house on N Street she was always treated as someone worthy of attention. Her grandfather would read aloud to her from Poe or Conan Doyle. Her Granny might be "a money snob" but she was also good fun. Her dream was for Brooke to become a Southern belle. But the way things were going there seemed little chance of her ever being a great success with boys. "I can smell them but I can't talk to them," Brooke confided to her Granny, who nonetheless continued to hold out hope for her.

By the time Brooke Russell finally did start at Miss Madeira's School, she was getting to know some of the daughters of her mother's friends and also making friends on her own. At Miss Madeira's, where classes were held in a row of five small yellow town houses backing onto an alley, she was no longer an outsider but welcome to take part in the convocation that always began the school day, where prayers were recited and Miss Madeira herself said a few heartening words. And she was soon part of a select group of girls that formed a literary club called Facio, which put out its own little magazine, finally providing her with a place to share the stories and poems she liked more than ever to write. She was delighted with the Latin she was beginning to take, with the teachers, and with the school's indomitable founder, who strode through the halls in her sagging long skirt and tennis shoes—a figure she found inspiring, even though her mother made it a point to let her know she did not share her enthusiasm. Later she would say, "I worshipped Miss Madeira. We all did."

Once again Brooke Russell had fresh material for her diary. She was being invited to parties and even to a friend's house to stay over and when she was invited to a dance at another friend's house she was able to cajole her Granny into buying her a new dress more like the ones the other girls were wearing. By the time she was fourteen, she had also developed a crush on Morton Hoyt, the younger brother of the glamorous poet Elinor Wylie and the older brother of a schoolmate. A brilliant but troubled young man, he had dropped out of Yale and was back living with his family with no gainful employment other than sitting with her on a bench near Dupont Circle and talking about ideas and literature. "I was way out over my depth, but not since I had first learned to spell had such an exciting thing happened to me. . . . I could have stayed on that park bench forever," she later wrote. For Morton Hoyt she was more than willing to stretch her mind. Or to stretch it sufficiently to hold his attention. Inspired by hearing him read from Aristophanes' *The Frogs* in its original language, she was soon wondering aloud whether she shouldn't start learning Greek. In the meantime, she read *Anna Karenina* and Dostoyevsky. And, like any self-respecting girl in love, she filled countless pages with fevered poems of her own composition—poems that owed not a little to the Romantics, whose work she was just coming to know.

Had her mother been less occupied with her own intellectual affairs she might have been alarmed. As it was, Brooke was soon receiving her first phone call from this young man without Mabel's raising any strong objections. It seemed he needed to talk to her privately. Emboldened, she invited Morton Hoyt for tea and enlisted a friend of her mother to help see to it that the tryst she was planning was not interrupted. What Morton wanted to tell her was that he was planning soon to leave for the South of France—news that gave a bittersweet flavor to the occasion. "[Y]ou have been the only real interest I have had in Washington," he confided at one point, upon which she asked if she could read him one of her poems. Then, as they were about to part, he behaved like a hero out of a romantic novel, holding her in his arms and kissing her right on the lips.

It was not Morton Hoyt, however, who left Washington that summer. John Russell, now a lieutenant colonel, asked that his wife and daughter join him in the Dominican Republic, where he had been placed in charge of the northern province.* Whether this request was in response to a report on his daughter's activities or whether another more troubling De Sales Street flirtation had come to his attention, there's no way of knowing. But his request couldn't have been more timely. Romance was taking its toll. Brooke would later write: "Knowing I was no beauty, I wished to dazzle by my mind

---

*Although a sovereign nation, the Dominican Republic, then popularly known as Santo Domingo (its capital), was occupied by U.S. troops from 1916 to 1924.

and spirit. It was hard work and I slept so badly that Mother had to call in a doctor. . . ."

In Santiago de los Caballeros, during the summer of 1917, a fifteen-year-old Brooke Russell had a chance to catch up on her sleep and to acquire, in the company of a group of young Southern lieutenants, some skill at juggling more than one heated romance. Before long, there was very little time for reading and not much space for Morton in the pages of the diary she now had every reason to keep. The community she and her mother found themselves in lacked the sophistication of the Legation Quarter in Peking but there were Spanish lessons to attend and long rides in the country and band concerts every night on the plaza. Few, if any, Dominican girls her age were permitted to come to the Americans' many parties and dances and she had the field to herself from August until mid-October, when her mother decided it was time for her to return to school—this time as a boarder—while Mabel rented out the De Sales Street house and returned almost immediately to the Dominican Republic. Later Brooke wrote, "I had been told nothing of it, and I wept bitterly when the subject was first broached."

Worse, she would not even be returning to Miss Madeira's. Instead, her mother was placing her as a boarder at another local school for young ladies, Holton-Arms. It would seem that some officious staff member at Miss Madeira's had insisted, in the headmistress's absence, that if Brooke wished to return to her old school she would have to prepare for the College Boards. Mabel had no intention of sending Brooke to college. Indeed she had been none too pleased by her talk of studying Greek or by all her feverish reading of the previous spring. She had no wish to have a bluestocking for a daughter.

In her old age, Brooke Astor would say, with no hesitation, "I hated Holton-Arms." The plan was for her to stay until Easter, but, as it turned out, she lasted only a few months. The most memorable event of her stay was a fight with her roommate over who had the right to wear a beaver hat they had both agreed to share—a fight that ended with Brooke on the floor and the hat's being torn so badly it was rendered unwearable. "I lay on the floor with the brim in my hand while Audrey had the crown. It was indeed the decision of a Solomon!" In this sorry outcome there was a valuable lesson not entirely lost on one combatant, but there was also one immediate benefit: "The upshot of this incident was I was moved to a room of my own. It was one of the few single rooms, and was tiny, but I could close my door and give myself up to daydreaming without interference."

When Brooke Russell left Holton-Arms that spring at the age of sixteen, her school years came to an end. To make a home for her daughter, Mabel returned to Washington, leaving her husband, by now a full colonel, to fend for himself in Latin America. Mabel continued to see no reason for her daughter to go on to college and here for once she and Brooke's Granny were in total agreement. There might be art classes and some tutoring for a bit more polish, but that was to be the extent of her preparation for life. For the moment, she was left with little to do but perfect her tennis and her watercolor painting, continue her reading, persist in her daydreaming, and wait for a suitable husband to appear.

Within a year, the wait had ended, thanks in part to a friend Brooke had made at Miss Madeira's. When this friend became too ill to attend her brother's Princeton senior prom as his date, Brooke was asked to fill in at the last minute. When Mabel demurred—saying the child was too young and, in any case, had no suitable gown to wear—an enterprising aunt offered up one of her own gowns to be altered and the friend's mother promised to act as chaperone.

The first time a seventeen-year-old Brooke Russell set foot on the Princeton campus, the die was cast. At her first college prom, while dancing to the music of Meyer Davis with all the young men who had placed their names on her sick friend's dance card, she met a graduating senior with striking blue eyes by the name of John Dryden Kuser. The president of one of the Princeton debating societies, the managing editor of the *Daily Princetonian*, the head of the New Jersey Audubon Society, and the possessor of a red Stutz Bearcat, Dryden Kuser had a passionate interest in a branch of philosophy she had never heard of and a total recall for lines of highly regarded, albeit to her mind boring, poetry by Wordsworth, Longfellow, and Tennyson. To her inexperienced eyes he appeared to be a perfect gentleman and, more important, he appeared to find everything she had to say of great interest.

Many of the things her dance partner had to say sailed right over the young Brooke Russell's head. And the less than appealing qualities she couldn't help noticing seemed, on balance, not to matter all that much. From the very start she felt that there was a special bond they shared. He might quote dull poetry, but he did have an excellent memory. Furthermore, until Princeton he had never been sent away to school but had, instead, been educated at home by a succession of tutors of varying quality. "He seemed almost another patchwork, like myself," she later wrote.

Dryden Kuser, too, seemed to sense a special bond. What might appear to be nothing more than a chance meeting rapidly developed into a long-distance love affair. After starting off with the gift of an enormous bunch of violets and a beautifully bound copy of *The Oxford Book of English Verse*, he was soon moving on to frequent letters and phone calls. Before long he was inviting her to come visit his parents' mansion in Bernardsville, twenty-five miles north of Princeton. Not since the days of Morton Hoyt had she been treated to such single-minded attention. And, on the face of it, this new man in her life appeared to be eminently more suitable than her first great love: among other things, he was the son of a self-made millionaire. If the name Kuser struck Brooke and her family as funny, and if the house of this self-made millionaire seemed both ugly and forbidding, these things gave her only a moment's pause. She was, after all, Roberta Brooke Howard's granddaughter.

Having done nothing more than agree to help out a friend's brother, a seventeen-year-old Brooke Russell found herself with an ardent suitor blessed with parents who soon proved to be no less ardent in their pursuit of her. When Dryden Kuser asked for her hand in marriage and Mabel protested that her daughter was too young, his parents made the journey down to Washington in their own private railroad car in order to persuade her. The private car alone was persuasive. But the Kusers were prepared to strengthen their argument with the promise of a generous marriage settlement.

Having overcome an initial aversion to the name Kuser, the Howard family was soon delighted with the proposed match. Before agreeing to the marriage, Mabel Russell apparently saw no reason to take time to launch even a halfhearted investigation of this suitor so eager to marry her daughter. Nor did she see fit to consult with her husband. Instead, she wrote him of their daughter's marvelous good fortune, presenting the upcoming marriage as a fait accompli.

Soon plans were under way for an elaborate Washington wedding, with eight ushers and eight bridesmaids and two clergymen presiding. Howard family money was pooled to provide Mabel's daughter with a nice silver dinner service and an elaborate trousseau. If, at the time of her marriage, Mabel's daughter was neither as young nor as innocent as she would later have readers believe, she was too young to understand that it was perhaps unwise to bear too much in mind the happiness of family members who were not themselves going to have to live with the rich young man they regarded as such an eminently suitable choice for her. At the same time, she was too young to have acquired the sort of experience that might have suggested that this rich young man could prove to be serious trouble. The same cannot be said of her mother, however. Or of her grandmother and aunts.

In her two memoirs Brooke Astor was reasonably circumspect. But later, when she was in her nineties, she began telling friends or anyone who seemed at all sympathetic that when her father finally made it home from Latin America for the wedding and saw what his wife had done, he was furious. Had he been living in Washington, he would never have agreed to his daughter's marrying into the Kuser family. But of course by the time he arrived home, it was too late.

Three

MRS. DRYDEN KUSER, 1919–1929

> Mother used to quote a French proverb, "What is inno-
> cence in a girl of eighteen is ignorance in a woman of
> thirty."

On April 26, 1919, Roberta Brooke Russell married John Dryden
Kuser at St. John's Episcopal Church, on Lafayette Square, across
from the White House. The bride wore a plain white satin gown,
with a square neck and long sleeves, while her maid of honor and
eight bridesmaids were outfitted in flowing green chiffon dresses and
large leghorn hats trimmed with apple blossoms. Their outfits, like
her own, had been chosen by her mother, but to the bride's eye theirs
were undeniably "prettier." The one piece of jewelry she wore to the
ceremony was a striking sapphire necklace, a gift from the Kusers,
that nicely complemented her sapphire engagement ring.

If the bride's wedding attire was not entirely to her liking, the
service at St. John's was all she could have hoped for. Presiding at the
ceremony were the rector of St. John's and the bishop of Washington,
who had been enlisted by her godmother, soon after her return from
China, to oversee her religious education. Although neither of her
parents had any use for organized religion, they had been persuaded
by her godmother that she would benefit from formal instruction.

John Russell's father had been on the vestry at St. John's and he himself had attended church there as a boy. So it was at St. John's that Brooke had been confirmed and then gone on to regularly attend Sunday services. For her, the Book of Common Prayer and the traditional Episcopal hymns and liturgy had become an enduring source of pleasure, while in no way superseding all she had learned from the Buddhist priests at the Temple of One Hundred Courtyards. If anything, her new faith seemed to reinforce the solace she was able to find in the natural world.

Thanks to the efforts of the bride's mother, the reception for the Russell–Kuser wedding was treated as an important Washington social event. Attending, along with the bride's friends and family, were some of the more glamorous friends Mabel Russell had made there in recent years. Not only did Alice Roosevelt Longworth deem it worth her while to put in an appearance, but also Mrs. Perry Belmont, newly arrived from New York. Neither President Wilson nor his wife could be found on the list of guests, but the current president was by no means a stellar member of Washington Society and in any case the Russells had always been staunch Republicans.

Brooke Russell had never had a debutante year. But at her wedding reception, with the cream of Washington Society in attendance, she could be said to have officially come out. With champagne flowing and music once again provided by Meyer Davis, she had little to do but smile and greet all the guests who were there to wish her well. If her dress was not something she herself might have chosen, she could not fault her sapphire necklace—at least not until she took note of the stunning impression made by Mrs. Belmont's long ropes of perfectly matched enormous natural pearls. Something she could hardly fail to do once a mischievous Alice Longworth informed her, "You are competing with Mrs. Belmont, Brooke."

While the wedding came close to living up to the rosiest of expectations, the ten-day honeymoon at the Hotel Greenbrier, in

West Virginia, was an unqualified disaster—beginning with a rough overnight journey on an uneven rail bed, during which, in the confines of their specially reserved drawing room, the newlyweds discovered that they had come to this marriage with very different expectations. Dryden had naturally assumed this flirtatious young girl had some notion of the facts of life. As it happened, she didn't. Whenever her mother or her friends tried to broach the subject, she had made it abundantly clear she had no wish to listen. This was not her idea of romance. Briefly the Howards had wondered whether the bride and groom might be too young to start a life together, but Granny Howard had taken the more optimistic view that this would give them a chance to grow up together. On the journey from Washington to White Sulphur Springs, it became clear to the bride at least that this was not likely to happen. "Dryden was oversexed and completely inexperienced, and I was hopelessly ignorant and unprepared in any way for this great adventure," she later wrote. To be more accurate, Dryden had a great interest in sex, while she had yet to discover that there might be good reason to also take a serious interest in this subject.

The pretty nightgown the bride wore that first night was only one of many lovely gowns and dresses in the elaborate trousseau that had been carefully packed for her stay at the Greenbrier. Although the atmosphere was still strained as the new couple settled into the large suite that had been reserved for them, the bride could at least look forward to an evening in the gracious public rooms downstairs, dining and dancing in one of her pretty new dresses in the company of their fellow guests. Of course Dryden had never been much of a dancer—something that might have warned her. That is, if she'd had any idea what she was being warned against. Now that she did have some idea, she was inclined, by training and instinct, to try and make the best of it.

Unfortunately, the groom's valet had forgotten to pack his dinner jacket, and gentlemen were not permitted in the hotel's dining room without one. Young ladies were not permitted in the hotel's bar in any attire. The newlyweds were going to be forced to dine alone in their suite. Dryden's way of preparing for their first solitary dinner was to head downstairs to the bar for a few fortifying cocktails. For the entire length of their stay he persisted in resorting to this measure, returning in no state to make the best of their quiet dinners together and in no way remedying the unfortunate impression he had made on their wedding night.

By the end of this benighted honeymoon, the bride had taken the measure of her new husband, but the implications of what she had discovered were not something she was capable of understanding or even imagining. "I was no longer ignorant, but I was still innocent," she later wrote. The young couple's next stop was the Russell house in Washington, where Brooke immediately rushed into her father's arms and burst into tears. By the end of the Washington visit, there was no mistaking these for tears of joy. At one point she found time to take her mother aside and ask why she hadn't prepared her for what was going to happen. "I tried to," Mabel responded, "but you didn't want to listen to me." Looking back in her old age, Brooke Astor could only acknowledge that this was true.

When Dryden Kuser had courted the young Brooke Russell, he promised her a smart sports car of her own to drive, along with a house of her own, where she would have a free hand in choosing the way it was decorated and where, no less important, she would be free to have as many dogs as she wished. The Kusers—much taken with this old-fashioned young woman who dropped a pretty curtsy upon being introduced to them and who bore no resemblance to the fast young women their son had been seeing—had backed up his promises with additional promises of their own.

Sad to say, the sports car would have to wait until the new bride acquired a driver's license. And the dogs would have to wait until she was installed in the lovely new home she had been promised. For the moment, the young couple were to move back to the Kusers' house in Bernardsville, to take up temporary residence in the gloomy apartment Dryden had occupied before their marriage, whose one redeeming feature was its spacious private sitting room.

As the new bride took her leave of her parents, her one consolation had been the promise that she could always come stay with them. Within a month, however, her father had been posted to Haiti, with orders to take charge of the regiment of Marines stationed there. Her mother immediately chose to join him, leaving Brooke totally dependent on her new husband's family. All told, her parents would remain in Haiti eleven years, eight of them with John Russell serving as High Commissioner, a position that involved his reporting to both the War and State Departments.

For the first summer of their marriage, the young Kusers made the best of it in the oversized and overstuffed mansion Colonel Anthony Kuser had built on his expansive and ever expanding Somerset County property. "Colonel" was an honorary title, owing nothing to any military prowess but a title he enjoyed using nonetheless. While the two generations of Kusers could not be said to be living cheek by jowl, they could not entirely avoid one another. Large as any house may be, there is usually only one dining room. And while Dryden and his wife were free to spend their days playing golf and tennis at the Somerset Hills Country Club, Colonel Kuser expected the young people to return promptly each night to take their customary places at the family dinner table.

That first summer, for want of anything better to do, Dryden's new wife had ample time to observe the couple who had worked so hard to secure her hand for their son. Her mother-in-law, the proud daughter of U.S. Senator John F. Dryden, a founder of the Prudential Insurance Company, struck her as strongly resembling Queen Victoria in both her ideas and her person. Like Queen

Victoria, Susan Kuser was passionately devoted to her husband. The only other object of her affection seemed to be her daughter, Cynthia, fourteen years younger than Dryden and still being tutored in the nursery. Colonel Kuser, who presented an imposing and, on occasion, terrifying figure, was no Prince Albert, but he was no less devoted to his wife. His one competing passion was for ornithology—which had led him to underwrite an expedition to India headed by William Beebe, curator of birds at the New York Zoological Society in the Bronx, to conduct a definitive study of the pheasant. Eleven years later, with the Colonel's backing, Beebe had produced a beautifully illustrated four-volume monograph regarded even today as one of the Zoological Society's great treasures, and which immediately earned the Colonel and his family a place of honor at the society's annual spring garden party.

Of Dryden's two parents, the Colonel was his new daughter-in-law's favorite. But her initial fondness for him did not stop her from seeing him clearly. He was a bully, who didn't hesitate to shout at his employees or throw his weight around. Furthermore, he always believed he was in the right. "The arrogance of big money is one of the most unappealing of characteristics, and it goes very deep," she later wrote.

While the Colonel's shouting might produce immediate results with his staff, the same could not be said for his son. If anything it had the opposite effect. Although his father had strongly encouraged Dryden's early interest in birds, by the time Dryden married he had broken all ties with the Audubon Society. Even though his father made it clear that a split of champagne ought to be more than ample for pre-dinner cocktails, Dryden saw no reason to limit his alcohol intake, although at this point he did try to keep it secret. And when his father let it be known that it was time for Dryden to find a full-time job, Dryden persisted in leading the life of a gentleman of leisure, subsidized by a generous monthly allowance and the occasional emergency supplement.

If the Kusers had counted on their son's maidenly new bride to exert a stabilizing influence, they were soon disappointed. Dryden's idea of making the best of a bad bargain was to revert to his old habits—to drink more than was good for him, to vanish for long periods of time, and to show up late for family meals when he bothered to show up at all. Colonel Kuser's response was to deduct a hundred dollars from his son's monthly allowance for every minute he was late for dinner. The trouble was, when Dryden stumbled in long past the hour he was due, everyone at the table, including the Colonel, was subjected to the company of a loud and angry young man, more inclined to talk back than to show any sign of remorse. Later Brooke concluded that, if anything, the Kusers' plan to provide their son with a "model of piety and devotion" had backfired. "I am afraid, the very qualities they liked in me were Dryden's undoing. I literally drove him to drink. . . ."

That fall, Colonel Kuser tried a new tack, by renting a furnished house for the young couple in Princeton, where he had secured his son a job as a vice president at Lenox China. Once he was back in the town where he'd enjoyed something of a success, Dryden made contact with old friends in Princeton and New York and Brooke invited friends up from Washington. Dryden's friends were definitely more worldly than his wife's. During quiet moments, when Dryden was at the office, Brooke had the company of the dog she had been promised, a handsome Airedale she named Sandy McTavish. Faced with a husband who was increasingly abusive, the new bride, blessed with an unlimited budget, resorted first to tears and then to the comfort provided by chocolate, creamy desserts, and any delicious carbohydrate-laden food she could lay her hands on. The following May, when she left Princeton for good, to return with Dryden to Bernardsville, she weighed ten pounds more than he did.

At least there was to be no repetition of the boredom, the lack of privacy, and the dismaying dinner table scenes of the previous summer. Colonel Kuser had made plans to set forth with his entire family for a grand tour of the great cities of Europe, a tour that his daughter-in-law would remember: for the Colonel's being roundly cheated by the factotum hired to secure him the very best food and accommodations the Continent had to offer; for the Colonel's tips, which were so low Dryden had to scurry behind him and leave extra coins; for the unabashed xenophobia of the Colonel and his family; and for Dryden's humiliating and reckless flirtation with the wife of an attractive couple they linked up with in France during the one week she and Dryden were left to their own devices. Her fondest memory was of the entire Kuser entourage sporting surgical masks to ward off infection as they navigated the canals of Venice in their gondolas.

This was the last trip to Europe she and Dryden would make with the Kusers, but not the last of the journeys they would make as a couple. There would be winters in New York, passed in furnished town houses rented for them by Dryden's parents; summer visits to Bar Harbor, Maine; a scouting expedition to Palm Beach to secure one of the area's major houses for the Colonel to purchase; and subsequent stays in the magnificent oceanfront mansion they actually managed to find. All of these journeys would be made in circumstances that might be called luxurious but all were colored by Dryden's drinking, his ridiculing her in front of his friends, his flagrant womanizing, and his resorting to physical abuse whenever words failed him.

A sugarcoated version of this troubled marriage later appeared in Brooke Astor's first novel, *The Bluebird Is at Home*, set in the 1920s but published in 1965. Here a young couple, living in a lovely New York town house given them by the husband's fabulously wealthy parents, find happiness only after the wife discovers that the husband is cheating on her and decides to take matters into her own hands. First, she complains to her father and mother, who happen to be in Washington, where her father is about to be made assistant secretary of state. Her parents urge her to leave her cheating husband immediately. Realizing she is not yet ready to give up on her marriage, she lies and tells her parents that she is pregnant. Luck is with her. She returns home to find that her husband's mistress has gone back to her previous lover. Trusting to her husband's vanity, she makes it clear she knows he has cheated on her, but blames herself for his straying. Then, by resorting to a no-holds-barred seduction, instead of her customary tears and reproaches, the wife wins her husband back. For the moment at least, the future looks promising. The wife has learned her lesson. All that remains is for her to confess to her parents that there won't be a baby—at least for the moment.

For Mrs. Dryden Kuser, there was no such reconciliation—although there was a baby. Dryden's parents' response to the news of their daughter-in-law's pregnancy was to finally give the young couple a place of their own—a mansion on a parcel of land the Colonel had recently acquired, off in a remote corner of his property—along with a generous budget to paint and furnish this new home. While the renovations were in progress, Dryden and his wife traveled first to Palm Beach and then to New York, where they settled into a rented town house on East Ninety-fourth Street.

Dryden's response to his wife's pregnancy was to continue to yell at her and abuse her. If anything, her condition seems to have enraged him further. In *Footprints*, published in 1980, Brooke Astor did not go into details, but in the introduction to a revised edition of *Patchwork Child*, published in 1993, she revealed that when she was six months pregnant Dryden broke her jaw. By then the Kusers, too, were angry with her—for refusing to have the baby delivered at home by their family doctor and insisting, instead, on seeing a New York doctor with an affiliation at a small private hospital.

It was around this time that the Russells made a trip up from Haiti. John Henry Russell had not been made assistant secretary of state but he had been named High Commissioner and Ambassador Extraordinary by President Harding, and then promoted to brigadier general. While he returned to his post in Port-au-Prince, Mabel stayed on for several weeks at East Ninety-fourth Street—long enough to show their daughter a good time and to see her safely delivered of a healthy ten-pound baby boy.

Looking back in *Footprints*, Brooke Astor made it clear that once her son, Tony, was born, everything changed for her. "He was perfect! And what's more, I would never be alone again. We were two." If these words sound like those of any teenage single mother today, her next words seem to echo those of some concerned social worker or counselor: "if I were to be responsible for another life I had to become someone myself." Whether or not this sense of mission was owing to a heart-to-heart talk with her mother or advice she had received from some other quarter, a very different Brooke Kuser returned to Bernardsville and took up residence in her newly renovated home.

Around this time two things happened. Dryden inherited a large trust fund from his mother's father, Senator Dryden, which meant that he and his wife had a larger income than they'd ever enjoyed before. In addition, Brooke came into some money of her own, thanks to a robbery the previous year when the entire Kuser household had been chloroformed while thieves made off with their valuables. Instead of replacing her beautiful sapphire necklace and ring, she had taken the insurance money and used it to make her new home more to her liking, tearing down a two-story porch and replacing it with both a pretty terrace off a downstairs sitting room and a sunny balcony off her bedroom.

"Whether my taste is good or bad, I must make the nest my own," she later wrote. And in fact her taste was not bad at all. By using bright chintzes, fresh paint, and some pretty furniture, she did her best to create the perfect setting for her new Bernardsville life—a setting she intended to stock with fresh flowers and a smorgasbord of current books, much the way her mother had when she was growing up. To help tend this nest of hers she had ten in staff to keep the house in order, along with three gardeners and two chauffeurs outside. She also had a smart-looking car of her own.

She would never be the adoring wife of *The Bluebird Is at Home*, but she did find better ways of dealing with her husband's drinking and infidelities than tears and reproaches. In time, she learned she fared better if she simply went her own way. In Bernardsville and then in New York and Palm Beach, she began to acquire friends of her own. She knew how to please when she set her mind to it. Older people, like her Granny, tended to look upon her kindly. And she had absorbed many lessons during those years when she had been quietly observing the Belle of Peking.

Before long, she, too, was having flirtations, despite the fact that one of the first of them had taken an unfortunate turn. Flattered by the attention paid to every word she uttered by a much older best-selling author named Joseph Hergesheimer, she had accepted an invitation to join him for a weekend at his cottage on Cape May and to bring along her husband. This weekend got off to an unpromising start when she and Dryden arrived in her new sports car to discover there was no dinner to speak of, just a drunken cocktail party. It soon degenerated into farce when she woke from a sound sleep to find her host squeezing a hairy leg into her narrow bed, prompting her to fling on her clothes and flee into the night, while her husband lay passed out down the hall.

"[Y]ou certainly couldn't have thought it was your mind that interested me," Hergesheimer had shouted at her after she pushed him out of bed. But by then she'd heard a lot worse from her husband. During a game of bridge at the country club Dryden had been known to throw a hand of cards and the rest of his drink in her face when she made the mistake of trumping his ace.

If she was chastened, she remained unbowed. After Tony was born, she had not only begun to go to church again but to make friends with some of the older and more settled wives in the community. Through one of her new friends she found her way to an editor at *Vogue*, whom she was able to persuade to let her start a monthly books column in the form of a blithe and newsy letter to "Anne." Soon she was also writing for *The Pictorial Review* and even getting paid real money for it—earning $600 for a piece on whether women dressed for men or for other women.

By then she herself had begun to pay special attention to the way that she dressed. She liked pretty clothes and used some of the money she made to augment her allowance. Moreover, she had begun to put her stylish new wardrobe to good use—and not just for the benefit of the women she knew. She was attracting serious admirers more attractive than Joseph Hergesheimer. In New York City, she would sometimes meet one of these new men in her life for lunch in the pretty Japanese garden at the Hotel Ritz or stay on for an evening of dinner and dancing on the Ritz Roof. If she was not quite the Southern belle her Granny had hoped for, she was hardly a wallflower. Not limiting herself to flirtatious notes or glances, she confessed in *Footprints* "sometimes I received, and sometimes I gave, a kiss."

Her own flirtations made it easier to tolerate Dryden's increasingly flagrant affairs. And for a time it made it possible to try to help him once he made an effort to finally strike out on his own. When Dryden began to take an interest in politics—running first for assemblyman for Somerset County and getting elected, and then going on to run for state senator—she joined him on his campaign trips and did her best to play the devoted wife. If he wanted to follow in the footsteps of the grandfather who had seen fit to leave him a substantial sum of money, she was not about to stop him. Even more than the candidate himself, she enjoyed meeting the various people who welcomed him as he traveled around the county solidifying ties and getting out the vote. Afterward, though, when she realized "Dryden seemed to have guaranteed every bad loan in the county," she began to have second thoughts.

It wasn't only Dryden's political career that was costly. Alcohol had always been a problem, and as his drinking spiraled out of control, so did his gambling. No longer content to gamble at bridge he would have several stiff drinks for lunch at the club and then go out and bet $2,000 on each hole he played of golf. On a bad day he could return home owing $36,000. Even with a generous monthly stipend it became difficult to make ends meet without constant infusions of cash from the Colonel.

"Only by being curious and interested in people and learning to give, can one grow," she later observed. If nothing else, taking an interest in other people can provide some much needed diversion. And what begins as a conscious effort can in time become habit and go on to become second nature. While her husband added politics to his other pursuits, she managed to keep herself entertained. Not only was she writing for money, but, in a modest way, she was beginning to take an interest in philanthropy—joining the boards of both the Virginia Day Nursery and the Maternity Center Association of New York.

She was also seeing to it that she would never again be heavier than Dryden. She watched her diet. At the Somerset Hills Country Club she played golf and tennis. On autumn weekends, she had taken up "beagling," a form of hunting where the quarry, a rabbit, is pursued by a band of men and women and their pack of dogs, and where pursuit is always on foot and requires nothing more from these men and women than a willingness to risk inclement weather, a reasonable amount of stamina, a healthy dollop of enthusiasm, and the sort of hearty appetite that can make short work of an ample late afternoon tea.

Soon she had graduated to the role of "whipper-in," where her chief responsibility was to run along the fringes of the pack, keeping the beagles in line. While performing this task, she wore a smart khaki skirt and gaiters, with a little cap and a fitted green jacket with metal buttons, thereby combining her new interest in fashion with her new fondness for exercise. It was in this capacity that she met an attractive and wonderfully engaging stockbroker who belonged to a hunt in neighboring Mendham—a new friend she could count on to listen to her troubles or share a good time.

Before long, she was branching out from Bernardsville—not only hunting in Mendham but joining a select exercise group that met in Far Hills, at the home of one of the not so much older wives in the area who had taken a great shine to her. "Mrs. Pierrepont did more for me than anybody out in Far Hills," she would later joke. "At her exercise class we all had to do the 'elephant walk.'" But the most important thing Natalie Pierrepont did for her had nothing to do with a ridiculous fitness routine she later enjoyed making fun of. The first morning she walked into her hostess's large dining room, there on the floor, by the long French windows, was a little boy kicking and screaming. "Pay no attention to him. He does it all the time," laughed her hostess. Jackie, the naughty little boy first discovered in the throes of a "temper fit," would grow up to become one of her dearest friends.

At this point in her life, though, it was her own little boy who most concerned her. "The greatest thing in my life was Tony," she later recalled. Certainly from the moment she brought him home with her, she liked to think of him as being at the very center of the new life she was making for herself in Bernardsville. Of course like most mothers of her generation and social class who could afford it, she left his day-to-day care to a nurse and then a nanny and eventually to a governess. But always she tried to make it a point to be home by late afternoon, to read to Tony, and to be with him while he was eating his dinner, the way her own mother had. She loved her Tony for his sturdy legs—

perfect for kilts, his Scottish nanny said—and for his round, rosy face. And she delighted in taking him for long drives in his little goat cart. But she could not, by any means, be said to be occupied with tending to his every need.

Still, she felt a special responsibility for her son's well-being. Particularly since neither his father nor the Kusers seemed to feel any such responsibility. The Colonel and his wife never showed much interest in the little boy. "As for Dryden, he was not interested in Tony at all," she wrote. Tony had been named after the Colonel. But for all that he was the first grandchild in the Kuser family, no one seemed to think Anthony Dryden Kuser warranted special consideration. Mrs. Kuser's gaze remained focused on her daughter, Cynthia. And Colonel Kuser seemed to regard his grandson as nothing more than another member of an increasingly costly and unfailingly disappointing household. Why this was so, the writer couldn't say. Or didn't care to. Certainly the Kusers' response was nothing like what she had experienced during her own childhood. For one thing, it meant that Anthony Dryden Kuser might be an only child but he was never blessed, the way little Roberta Brooke Russell had been, with a cocoon of unconditional love to fall back on when his mother was absent or preoccupied.

Some things in the marriage had changed for the better, but one thing remained the same. Dryden continued to depend on his father for money. And the Colonel continued to treat his son and daughter-in-law as errant children, summoning them to the morning room at his mansion, either separately or together, in order to call them on the carpet—upbraiding them for the latest thing they had done to disgrace the family and then threatening to cut off all funds. Those times when Dryden was particularly awful to her, Brooke understood she could not look for help from the Colonel. Nor could she look to her parents. They were more than happy to have her come join them for a long stay in Port-au-Prince or meet them for a holiday in France with Tony.

And they always saw much to admire in Tony whenever they visited. But that was the extent of the support they could offer her.

By 1929, she had been staying in Bernardsville longer than she'd stayed in any place before. There were many things she liked about the life she had made there for herself. She might be slighted or dismissed by the Kusers, but, thanks to them, she led a life steeped in every possible comfort. Later, she would describe her circumstances as being far more luxurious than anything she ever experienced again, even as Mrs. Vincent Astor. Perhaps if she had seen someone waiting in the wings eager to provide her with a spanking new life, she might have seen things differently. But there was no such person hovering anywhere near. Later she would say that sometimes it seems safest to stay with the devil one knows. But safety can seem especially attractive when there is no second devil in the offing.

No matter how bad things got with Dryden, she never seriously considered a divorce. There was the ensuing scandal to consider. Divorce had yet to become an everyday occurrence. And there was the equally pressing consideration of what she would do for money. For all the early talk of a financial settlement, there was no document to back this up. Long ago the Kusers had ceased to think of her as a good investment. It was clear she could not expect her parents to support her in the style her husband's family was keeping her. Indeed it was far from clear that they could support her at all.

Just when it seemed as if this increasingly strained marriage of hers would limp along for at least another decade, suddenly in the early winter of 1929, while resting in Palm Beach, an ailing Colonel Kuser was diagnosed with cancer of the neck. By early April, he was dead. Driving back in the car from his father's funeral, Dryden suddenly found the courage to ask for something he had apparently been wanting for some time. There was a new woman in his life whom he very much wanted to marry—a marvelous horsewoman who coincidentally had just left her husband.

Later, Brooke Astor would write, "One must never take for granted a husband, a wife, a lover, one's children, one's friends, or even one's looks." She had good reason to know this. Much to everyone's surprise—including his long suffering wife's—it was Dryden who had asked for a divorce. Although Dryden's desire to put an end to their marriage came with no warning, his wife had no choice but to take this shock in stride. And it wasn't long before she had recovered her balance. Certainly it helped that this marvelous horsewoman was known to have a voice like a crow. Well into her nineties, Brooke Astor never tired of saying to friends, "Every day I should fall on my knees and thank God for Vieva Perrin."

Four

CHARLES MARSHALL, 1929–1952

My mother used to say, "Nothing is so dangerous as boredom." It certainly kills marriage and romance.

Once Dryden Kuser decided to end their marriage, his wife was not about to put any obstacles in his path. It was agreed that she would be the one to ask for a divorce. A divorce in New Jersey was out of the question, if only because that November Dryden was up for reelection. To avoid any scandal beforehand, she agreed to postpone her trip to Reno, Nevada, until late autumn. In return, Dryden's mother financed a quiet separation, making it possible for Brooke to move to the city, into a suite at the Savoy Plaza, bringing with her Tony and his severe but nonetheless devoted French governess, Madame Grumeau. In November, after Dryden was safely returned to the State Senate, his wife set off with her little family for Reno. To fulfill Nevada's residency requirement, she took a small bungalow, barely large enough to accommodate a household that included not only Tony and Madame Grumeau but also her Pekingese, Pushkin, and Tony's canary, Goldie. By this time Madame Grumeau had unbent sufficiently to become something more than a paid companion and had taken on a role partaking of aspects of adviser, confidante, and surrogate mother.

Just how much advice Madame Grumeau felt free to dispense is another matter. Certainly there was need of sound counsel. By some strange turn of events, living in the bungalow next door to Brooke Kuser and her little family was her first great love, Morton Hoyt—seemingly married to Tallulah Bankhead's sister, Eugenia, better known as "Baby." With Morton Hoyt next door to keep the furnace of her little bungalow going and to provide some much needed amusement, the new Reno arrival could consider herself fortunate. Certainly it helped make the long winter months pass more pleasantly.

In *Footprints*, when describing this odd coincidence, Brooke Astor gives no indication that there was any prior contact with Morton Hoyt. Nor does she indicate that Morton had eloped with Baby back in 1917, at more or less the time of her own abrupt departure for the Dominican Republic. At the time of the elopement Baby had been sixteen, one year older than Brooke Russell. Possibly Morton Hoyt had been embroiled in two simultaneous flirtations. Or perhaps he was a serial flirt. But, given this seductive college dropout's penchant for young girls, Mabel Russell's removing her daughter from the scene seems, in retrospect, sensible, prescient, and deliberate.

All the Bankheads could do was see to it that Baby's marriage was annulled. But there was no keeping the lovers apart. In 1920, after a big Bar Harbor wedding, they moved to New York and then to Paris, remaining together until 1928, when Baby got a divorce—only to remarry and immediately divorce Morton in 1929. All told, they were married three times. Morton's drinking was a factor, just as it was in the marriage of his friend Scott Fitzgerald. Toward the end of Brooke's stay in Reno, Baby left with some young man for Honolulu. Her departure seems scarcely to have troubled her neighbor—either at the time or years later. But, then, there were many things the author of *Footprints* felt no need to question or explain.

For all that it bills itself as an autobiography, *Footprints*, like

Patchwork Child, is a memoir. As such it is highly subjective—sometimes extremely vague about crucial events in the author's life and occasionally misleading when it comes to chronology. For instance, in telling the story of her terrible first marriage—a story that would bring tears to her eyes when reading aloud certain passages more than seventy years later—Brooke Astor has Tony's birth take place at the end of her second year with Dryden Kuser. This would be 1921. Or, at the very latest, 1922. But Anthony Dryden Kuser, was actually born in the spring of 1924, five years after his parents were married—when, according to *Footprints*, she had been doing her book reviewing and beagling for at least one year. Life often tends to be complicated, with fits and starts and no clear narrative line. As pure storytelling, cutting out those three years prior to Tony's birth makes sense—if only because it provides the writer with a straight and simple narrative arc: with the birth of her child, the very young Mrs. Dryden Kuser recognizes that the time has come to grow up and then goes on to lead an independent life, with book reviewing and beagling and the occasional flirtation.

But it also happens to make sense in terms of the author's own personal narrative. The independent life Mrs. Dryden Kuser was leading during the five years prior to Tony's birth may well have given her husband and his parents cause for reflection, particularly since Tony, as a chubby infant and toddler, did not much resemble his father, an unfortunate failure on his part that would be rectified only after he became an adult—not quite soon enough to reassure the Kusers or any concerned Bernardsville onlookers.

There is every reason to believe that Tony's father was Dryden Kuser. I, for one, regard Tony as Dryden's true son. But for years there were rumors about Tony's paternity—rumors sufficiently widespread that the author of *Footprints* could hardly have been unaware of them. The most persistent rumor identified her subsequent husband as being Tony's father. After all, such things had been known to happen in even the finest of families. (Indeed it was said to have happened in her third husband's family, not once but twice.) The chronology of *Footprints* neatly ruled out that possibility, while simultaneously ruling out virtually all other likely contenders for the role of Tony's father.

It would be fair to say that when the author of *Footprints* writes, "I never knew why Dryden timed his decision for that moment. I wonder now why I never asked him," she is being more than a little disingenuous. In marriage certain things are best left unsaid, particularly when one party is known to have a terrible temper. It is likely that she never asked Dryden because she already had good reason to suspect that her husband's decision to divorce her at this particular moment owed something to his being aware that in her role as whipper-in for a nearby hunt she had developed a close friendship with a fellow beagler by the name of Charles Marshall—the attractive and marvelously sympathetic stockbroker who resided nearby in Mendham.

In just about every way Charles Marshall was the opposite of Dryden Kuser. Red haired and stocky and eleven years older than Dryden's wife, he was admired by everyone who knew him. He was thrifty and responsible and hardworking. Every weekday he commuted by train to the city, where he earned his living on Wall Street as a partner at Butler, Herrick and Marshall, a well-regarded brokerage firm headed by Arthur Butler, the husband of a cousin of his. Known to his friends, of whom there were many, as "Buddie," he did not have the Kusers' money but he did have a sister-in-law married to Vincent Astor and a glamorous sister married to Marshall Field III, heir to a great Chicago fortune.

Over the course of three generations the Marshalls had become firmly established members of New York Society. In 1816, Captain Charles Marshall, Buddie's grandfather, had joined with three partners to found the Black Ball Line and immediately assumed an important role in the city's growing maritime industry. The Black Ball Line kept to a schedule, with two ships at sea, plying the waters between New York and Liverpool. The ships carried only light cargo, primarily gold, and passengers, and passed each other in the ocean, some sixty miles apart. Whether they were full or not, they set sail on time. The idea of this thrilled the newspapers. It was revolutionary. Before long, Captain Marshall wisely bought out his three partners.

Never rude, always considerate of others, Charles Marshall could hold his own in any company. He was what is called "a man's man," but he was also much liked by women. At Yale he had been a classmate and friend of Cole Porter. In every respect, save for one, he was perfect: he was married with two children, one of whom—Charles Jr., known as Peter—was said to be "not quite right." In *Footprints*, Brooke Astor did not even hint that there was any problem with Charles Marshall's son. But she was careful to describe their friendship as romantic but chaste. Sixteen years later, however, in an unpublished interview with Eileen Simpson she confided that she and Charles Marshall had actually been having an affair. Either way, there was little hope that a man like Charles Marshall would leave his wife, now or ever. Not when it meant leaving behind two children, one of whom required special care.

In divorcing Dryden Kuser, Brooke Astor had asked only for custody of Tony and a desk Mrs. Kuser had given her on her twenty-first birthday. It had not occurred to her to ask for money. In the end, for all the talk of settling a large sum upon Dryden's bride, there had been no prenuptial agreement. She had simply assumed that in return for postponing the divorce until after Dryden was reelected, the Kusers would repay the favor. At the time of his death, in April 1929, Colonel Kuser's substantial fortune had been evaluated for tax purposes, but, unfortunately, thanks to the crash of the stock market several months later, the Colonel's fortune was no longer what it had once been. By the spring of 1930, when his former daughter-in-law returned to the Savoy Plaza, after a spring stay in Santa Barbara and a side trip to the Grand Canyon, the Colonel's estate owed more in taxes than it possessed in assets.

With no alimony and no savings to speak of, the new divorcée found herself in serious trouble. Fortunately, her parents returned at this point from Haiti. Thanks to one of her older friends from Bernardsville, she was introduced to an excellent lawyer. Thanks to the intercession of her father and the able advice of this new lawyer, an agreement was reached whereby she received a settlement from Dryden's mother, whose fortune remained considerable. This settlement was sufficient for her to take a relatively modest two-bedroom apartment overlooking Gracie Square and to completely renovate and decorate this apartment with the help of a young Billy Baldwin, while keeping three Scandinavian servants plus Madame Grumeau.

Although the new divorcée's father was happy to step in when she needed him, he was not prepared to give her free rein. As a married woman, she had enjoyed a protective coloring. Living on her own, she could afford no hint of scandal—particularly if that scandal involved a gentleman believed to be happily married. Her father insisted that she cut off all contact with Charles Marshall. Fortunately, she was not lacking ways to distract herself. The New York of 1930 was very different from the city she had first encountered as a young woman. During the course of her marriage, even friends a generation or two older had begun accepting the manners and mores of the jazz age, thinking nothing of dropping by at a fashionable speakeasy or ordering up some liquor from a local bootlegger and giving not so much as a second glance to some pert flapper in a short skirt.

If Brooke Kuser's skirts had not been among the shortest, they had definitely crept up above her knees. After the crash of the stock market, as hemlines began to fall again, there was still plenty of opportunity for anyone looking for adventure. Certainly for any twenty-eight-year-old divorcée who was attractive and curious and had a lovely new apartment perfect for entertaining. For all that she had never chosen her newfound independence, she soon learned how to make the most of it. Before long she was enjoying a life not necessarily more rewarding than the one she had been living in New Jersey but one that was definitely more carefree.

Her first year on her own, she continued to frequent the salons of some of the city's more lively grande dames, particularly those where she was likely to meet writers and artists and theater people. Accustomed to going to parties without Dryden, she had no difficulty striking out on her own. If there was a small literary salon that seemed at all welcoming, she was happy to join it. Her mother had taught her many things, both by example and intention, including the importance of keeping a stack of books by her bed—not only fiction and poetry, but history and philosophy. It wasn't enough for a book to be diverting, it must also offer something fresh or unexpected. A different way of seeing the world. When a passage she read sailed right over her head, this didn't stop her, just as it didn't stop her when she couldn't quite follow the discussion at some literary gathering. No one seemed to notice—or if they did, they never held it against her. Brimming with curiosity and eager to learn from all the new people she was meeting, she could be counted on to help make a party jell.

For the most part the new people she was meeting were very different from the ones who had taken her up in Bernardsville. In the circles she now traveled in, she came upon relatively few churchgoers, businessmen, or club women. Soon she was spending time with such luminaries as Somerset Maugham, Osbert Sitwell, Aldous Huxley, and Glenway Wescott. At the apartment of Mrs. Nathaniel Potter, who presided over a salon at her home on East Seventy-second Street, she met Mrs. Potter's handsome nephew John Sargent and the critic John Mason Brown, both of whom would go on to become close friends, with John Sargent becoming a frequent escort and eventually the publisher of *Footprints*. It was during this period that she was first introduced to Clare Brokaw, the stunning *Vanity Fair* editor who would go on to marry Henry Luce and eventually be a winter neighbor of hers in Phoenix. Always she liked to suggest that if there was no competing with the ravishingly beautiful Clare Brokaw she couldn't have cared less, mostly because they attracted very different men. "[T]he men I liked quite often did not like her."

Now that she was being courted by both men who were eligible and those who were not, she was beginning to have second thoughts about sex and see "that after all it might be a rewarding experiment." Through two friends who did business in London she was introduced to several delightful Englishmen who happened to be in the city, at least three of them starring in successful Broadway plays. She was soon spending time with the likes of Noël Coward and Herbert Marshall and also with Brian Aherne who was starring with Katharine Cornell in *The Barretts of Wimpole Street*. Later, she would have memories of happily waltzing with a young Cecil Beaton at a friend's grand apartment, with Beaton looking particularly dashing in white tie and tails so long they practically touched the floor.

Her second year as a divorcée, she used her new freedom to study writing at Columbia's School of General Studies—first taking a class with a successful author of popular fiction and then a class where everyone was required to write a full-length play. For this second class she wrote a drawing-room comedy with a special actor friend in mind, giving her a perfect opportunity to let him see it and then enlist his advice as she embarked on a series of revisions, before finally putting the play in a drawer for good. In *Footprints*, the actor friend remains unnamed but it is more than likely that it was Brian Aherne, whose name she buried in a long list of glamorous new acquaintances. Young and handsome and about to go off to Hollywood to act in movies, Brian Aherne became more than a glamorous acquaintance, eventually assuming a featured role, if not quite a starring one, in her own personal drama—playing the part, at least in retrospect, of one of the great loves of her life.

The United States might have been slipping into a serious economic depression, but this seems to have had little effect on the life
the new divorcée was leading. Between her classes and flirtations, her
days were becoming increasingly crowded. Nonetheless, before setting off again at night she did her best to make sure to be home to
spend time with Tony: "[T]o read to him at suppertime and listen to
his prayers when he went to bed."

As she came to gradually accept the loss of her lovely Bernardsville
house and all the friends she had made while living there, she discovered that this new life she was leading suited her quite nicely. How it
suited Tony was another matter. Her son was almost six at the time of
the move to the city. He was leaving behind all of his friends and was
starting school for the first time at Buckley, where many of his classmates had long ago met at a birthday party, at the park, or through
some family connection.

Madame Grumeau saw to it that at least some things at Tony's
home remained the same, but she could not ensure that Tony's mother
was there as much as he might have liked her to be. More often
than not, it fell to Madame Grumeau to escort Tony to school and
then pick him up in the afternoon. Or to make sure that he finished
his homework before going to bed. By his second year in the city,
it was clear that his mother was enjoying her classes at Columbia
more than he was enjoying his studies at Buckley. The most his
mother seemed prepared to do to rectify this was to make sure to
provide a supportive presence at certain school occasions—such as
the 8:30 A.M. performance of a little drama about George
Washington, where Tony had been assigned the nonspeaking role
of the cherry tree.

Although the new independent life Tony's mother was leading had
much to recommend it, this life was a source of some concern to her
parents, who believed they could predict the direction it was taking
her. "If you stay out in the rain, you will get wet," her mother warned.

Just when both her mother and father were beginning to have serious cause for concern, her amusing and adventurous single years came to an end.

If General Russell had been putting into effect some calculated or time-tested strategy when he insisted that his daughter cut off all relations with the married man she had been seeing—a man he happened to like and admire—he could take great satisfaction in the result it produced. Having spent two years with no hope of contacting the lively and engaging fellow beagler he'd fallen in love with, Buddie Marshall was ready to admit defeat. In spite of everything he stood to lose by this decision, he chose to divorce his wife and marry Brooke Kuser.

Among Buddie Marshall's friends and associates, divorce was gradually becoming more widely accepted—if not necessarily more welcome. Within his own family he had recently seen an easing of long-standing prohibitions. Two years earlier, when the Kusers were parting, his sister Evie, after giving birth to three children, had obtained a divorce from Marshall Field III—receiving a million-dollar settlement, touted in newspapers everywhere as record breaking. Buddie Marshall could not afford to be as generous as Marshall Field, but by the terms of his divorce he agreed to give up all claim to his two children and take nothing from the marriage other than his father's books.

Quietly, Buddie Marshall also agreed to support his wife, Alice, and their children should his wife remarry, and to continue to provide some means of support for Alice even after his death. In *Footprints*, Brooke Astor never comes out and says this directly, but alludes, instead, to the fact that such unfair and, ultimately, highly punitive arrangements were sometimes made by men divorcing their wives. This arrangement stood in marked contrast to the settlement the lawyers at Carter, Ledyard, and Milburn had managed to secure for her. By that settlement, once she remarried she would forfeit her right to any alimony, although she would continue to receive child support. The forfeited alimony would go into a trust for Tony, to become his to do with as he wished when he turned twenty-one.

She should consider herself fortunate to receive an offer of marriage from a man like Buddie Marshall, Brooke's father told her. Then, to drive home his point, he added, "I could die happy knowing that you were married to such a man." But by accepting Buddie Marshall's proposal of marriage, she would be giving up financial independence as well as all the freedom she had been enjoying. Of course this was only to be expected. But the agreement that Buddie Marshall had made would eventually have drastic implications.

For the time being, though, all she could see was that Buddie Marshall had given up just about everything that was dear to him in order to marry her. She was well aware that such a sacrifice demanded something in return. She wanted to make him happy and to be worthy of his love. "I wanted to be the perfect wife," she later wrote, and then added, "Of course no one can be perfect, and I am among the frail ones in life."

On April 19, 1932, Brooke Russell Kuser and Buddie Marshall were married in a quiet ceremony at her Gracie Square apartment, standing before its tall living room windows, overlooking Carl Schurz Park. In attendance were both of the bride's parents and their friends Mr. and Mrs. James Dunn; the groom's sister, Evie; his senior partner, Arthur Butler; as well as the bride's son and his governess. Divorce might be a fact of modern life, but that did not mean the church had to look kindly upon it. Once again it was an April wedding, but this time—instead of two Episcopal priests, one of whom was a bishop, presiding—the bride had to make do with a liberal-minded Presbyterian minister willing to read from the Episcopal service.

Charming as the bride's apartment was, it was not really large enough to comfortably accommodate another adult. Nor was it quite grand enough for a couple who had every reason to assume they would be taking their place as members in good standing of established New York Society. Fortunately, a large penthouse apartment had become available for purchase at 10 Gracie Square, just down the street. While its future occupants were on their honeymoon, some renovations would be completed, with separate quarters provided on the penthouse roof for the bride's seven-year-old son, fitted out like the cabin of a ship.

Leaving Tony and Madame Grumeau behind in her old apartment, while taking along the housemaid to serve as her personal maid, the new Mrs. Charles Marshall boarded the *Bremen* immediately after the service and set off with her new husband for a leisurely tour of Europe. She was thirty years old, no longer the ignorant young girl who had boarded a train for White Sulphur Springs, but, despite some evidence to the contrary, she persisted in believing in romantic love, just as she believed in the necessity of honoring an obligation. She was not by any means ignorant, but in some important ways she appeared to remain innocent. Most people would say it was part of her charm.

The newlyweds' first stop was Paris, where they remained just long enough to dine with Cole and Linda Porter, before heading south to Italy and then on to London, to Grosvenor Square, where Buddie Marshall's mother welcomed them with a wedding gift of a small blue Rolls-Royce limousine. Buddie's mother couldn't have been more different from Dryden's, whose gifts to her daughter-in-law had been very much in the spirit of two pieces of advice she'd given: first, to inspect her servants' rooms every Monday and make sure to check their bureau drawers; second, to never give away an old coat, because coats always come back into fashion.

Mrs. Marshall, who had begun living on her own in London even before her husband's death in 1912, was amusing and attractive and loved nothing better than to show those around her a good time. Her granddaughter Peggy would have a lasting memory of her popping into the Grosvenor Square nursery to say good night to Peggy and her brother, when Peter was still tiny, and trying to stop the little boy's crying by making faces and then, when that failed, shaking her beaded dress, until suddenly there was a clatter, as all the beads came loose, so that the next thing Peggy knew there was Peter laughing like crazy while her grandmother was standing in nothing but her underwear. Instead of being upset, her grandmother was laughing, too. That was the way she was—full of gaiety and high spirits.

The following fall, the new couple finally moved into their renovated penthouse, with its terraces overlooking the river and its enormous double-height living room, which promised to provide ample space for Buddie Marshall as well as a gracious background for all the entertaining they planned to do. Although for a time the new Mrs. Charles Marshall did her own shopping in her blue Rolls-Royce and kept a strict account book, that was the extent of her serious housekeeping. There was a large staff of servants, tall bouquets of fresh flowers, beautifully served, well-prepared food, and a chauffeur for the little limousine. All in all it was a glorious life—hard to make vivid, in retrospect, if only because great contentment, like great charm, remains hard to capture on the page, forcing the author of *Footprints* to resort on occasion to lists. Fortunately, there were some articulate observers present to capture the spirit of those years.

The circles the new Mrs. Charles Marshall now traveled in were less bohemian than they had been when she was on her own, but they were also far grander than they had been when she was Mrs. Dryden Kuser—especially those frequented by her sister-in-law, Evie. Buddie's recently divorced older sister was known to be high-handed and imperious, but she seemed delighted to take Brooke under her wing, introducing her to friends, inviting her to dinners and parties, while bossing her around. "Evie was very beautiful, but also terrible; we used to call her 'Poison Evie,'" Louis Auchincloss, who for many years was Evie's son's best friend, would recall. "Brooke was the life of her parties. She was bright and fun. When she bubbled with laughter, it was contagious. I used to describe her as Freya, who kept the gods young when they were all old and boring. Had she accomplished nothing more than that, it would have been enough."

Not only Buddie's sister and mother but all the Marshall cousins seemed delighted to see Buddie married to a woman who made him happy. Anna Glen Vietor—whose mother was Buddie's cousin as well as being the wife of Buddie's senior partner at Butler, Herrick and Marshall—was fourteen years old at the time of the wedding, but already a keen observer. "It was a still pond, that little circle," she would recall. "Brooke moved into the circle and it was a great thing for Buddie. She introduced him to a whole new group of people. Theater people. Literary people. It was fun. My father was thrilled when Buddie married Brooke."

One of the reasons the Marshall relatives may have taken to her so quickly was that they felt no great loyalty to her predecessor. Born Alice Huntington and raised with her older sister, Helen, in one of the grand houses of the Hudson Valley, Alice Marshall was in almost every way her successor's opposite. "Buddie's first wife considered herself to be terrifically good-looking and she always took care of herself," recalled Anna Glen Vietor. "There she'd be resting on a chaise longue, conserving her strength for the moment when it was time to go out."

Writing about the breakup of her first marriage to Dryden Kuser, Brooke Astor wrote, "A woodpecker never attacks a sound tree." The same could be said of the Marshalls' marriage. Their daughter, Helen, who was known as Peggy, was thirteen at the time of the divorce. She was old enough to understand that although there was never a harsh word or raised voice in their house, there had been cause for serious strain. For one thing, her mother had insisted that the children be raised in the country, the way she had been. "It was hard for my father going back and forth those long hours on the train," Peggy would later say.

And then there was additional strain put on the marriage by the birth of their younger child, always called Peter—who would be described by his loving sister as "handicapped" or "delicate" or "not able to live a full life." It was her belief that at Peter's birth something happened that "tipped him a little bit." Anna Glen Vietor was less tactful: "Peggy's brother was retarded. Almost always he was sent away to institutions." Louis Auchincloss, who met Peter only once, put it this way: "He looked like Buddie, but there was something not quite right." That "something" remains hard to pin down. In his last years, he lived in an apartment at Fountain House, a New York organization that provides counseling and subsidized housing for the mentally disturbed. In their records he is diagnosed as "schizophrenic."

Given that Buddie Marshall was leaving behind a child whose condition was at best "delicate," his response to the new son in his life had to be complicated. "Buddie was fond of him, but it must have been hard when his own son was languishing," said Anna Glen Vietor. When the newlyweds moved into their penthouse it turned out that there was room for everyone but Madame Grumeau. In *Footprints* we are told that Buddie wanted the governess to go because he believed that she was spoiling Tony, who, under her influence, was becoming jealous and rude, particularly to his mother.

Surely, Madame Grumeau, like Tony, felt excluded from all this newfound happiness. And, no doubt, her departure did nothing to make life better for him. Nor did the little cabin all by itself up on the roof where, in his mother's words, Tony "cheerfully survived" all the childhood diseases, including whooping cough, as well as appendicitis. Or the fact that Madame Grumeau was replaced by a Scottish nursery governess. On the other hand, Tony finally had a father who paid attention to him. Although Buddie Marshall was fair, consistent, and attentive, he was not easy on Tony. When Tony's grades at Buckley continued to be disappointing and Brooke wondered whether it would be a good idea to send the boy off to boarding school, Buddie immediately took her up on this, seeing to it that a place was found for Tony at the Harvey School in Westchester, which took boys ages eight to twelve.

His first winter at the Harvey School, Tony ran his sled into a tree, rupturing his spleen and one kidney and nearly dying in the local hospital. Unable to return to school that term, he was tutored at home for many months. Subsequently Tony stayed briefly at several schools, including Groton, Buddie's alma mater. Always his grades were disappointing. His last school was Brooks. This treatment was not intended to be unduly harsh. Nor would it have been regarded as such by any of his stepfather's contemporaries. He may have been sent away to school slightly earlier than some boys his age, but he was receiving the same sort of schooling that Buddie Marshall had been given. If there was a model, it was the English public school system. Its rigors and also its privileges reflected the conventions of what was coming to be regarded as "Old Money," the closest America came to having an aristocracy.

It would be wrong to say that Brooke Marshall was a bad mother. But owing to the pressures, distractions, and diversions of her new life, she was an erratic one. At those times when Tony's life was threatened, his mother remembered just how much she loved him, but ordinarily her son's welfare was not foremost on her mind. Although her concern for Tony was very real, it was far from consistent. Louis Auchincloss, with one brief anecdote, would suggest its limits: "My mother and father went back with Brooke one time on the train from Groton. Brooke was in tears. So sorry to leave poor Tony. One cocktail and the tears disappeared, like a brief spring shower."

To suggest that Tony's life was pure misery would also be wrong. For one thing, he enjoyed long summers with his mother and stepfather at the Castello, a castle situated on a rocky promontory over-looking the harbor of Portofino—a romantic spot that Brooke had sought out during her honeymoon, having recently read of it in a novel called *The Enchanted April*. Discovering that the Castello was available for rent, the Marshalls took a ten-year lease. A staff came with the castle, but they had to provide additional furniture and linens and dinnerware and also pay for those months when the Castello stood vacant. To help cover expenses they turned to Evie, who was delighted to assist with the decorating and also to share the rent, receiving in return the exclusive use of the place for the month of August.

The family's first summer at Portofino, Tony was joined by both Peggy and Peter, who came with an Irish nurse to look after him. Of the three children Tony was the youngest. In *Footprints* Brooke Astor describes Peggy as "a darling girl whom I grew extremely fond of." Peter is described as "also a dear" but "delicate." The reader is told that the nurse who took care of him was rude and impolite to her, which is the reason Peter was never asked back again. Peggy, whose mother kept her in little red slippers and dresses suitable for someone much younger, was a girl her stepmother must have recognized immediately. "I got on very well with Brooke," Peggy later recalled. "She was very good to me. She would question me about my life. She was always laughing, making everyone around her happy. She made my father very happy, always. It was wonderful living there with her."

At the Castello Tony spent the summer after his sledding accident convalescing and working with a tutor to make up the months of school he had missed. In the summers everything fell into place for the extended family. Here once a year they and their guests would gather for a strictly scheduled but leisurely interlude, where the hours seemed to stretch longer and the days seemed somehow fuller. Mornings would begin with a brisk two-mile walk before everyone sat down at eight o'clock for a light breakfast on the terrace; followed by letter writing and any personal tasks that had to be tended to; and then on to some more strenuous task, such as a swim in a nearby cove or a game of tennis at the club in Rapallo; followed by lunch and a siesta and possibly more tennis or a visit to the little port at the foot of the hill, with perhaps a stop at the local café; and then back to the Castello for dinner on the terrace, beneath the stars.

The Castello was indeed enchanted and the Marshalls, unlike the characters of the novel, could look forward to enjoying many years there. Buddie, who had to be in New York for business, could stay only a limited number of weeks, but soon his wife was extending her stay, so that she was sometimes in Europe from late spring well into the fall. In August, when Evie took over the castle, Portofino made an ideal jumping-off point for exploring other parts of Italy and then driving on into Germany and Switzerland, to visit friends or hike in the mountains.

Over the course of the seven summers she spent at the Castello, Brooke Marshall got to play tennis with a boorish and bare-chested Ezra Pound at the club in Rapallo and also have tea with the far more congenial Max Beerbohm. But for all that her new life seemed to be carefree, she had to take into account the fact that Buddie tended to be thrifty by nature and many of their friends were a lot richer than they were. In the early years of the marriage, however, there was enough money for all the things that really mattered. Just as there were enough distractions to obscure, or consign to the background, Hitler's brownshirts on the streets of Munich or Mussolini's turning his attention from the timetables of the Italian railroads to empire building in Africa.

Hitler's invasion of Poland on September 1, 1939, followed by England and France's immediate declaration of war, brought to an end any hope that all would be well again and also brought to an end their long summers in Italy. The Marshalls happened to be in Switzerland when the news came, prompting them to set off at once

1. Caroline Schermerhorn Astor, the first Mrs. Astor

2. Mabel Russell and toddler Brooke

3. Mabel Russell in Peking

4. John Henry Russell, commandant of the Marine Corps

5. Brooke at home in Peking, with her dog, Gyp

6. Mr. and Mrs. Dryden Kuser in Venice, on their first trip to Europe

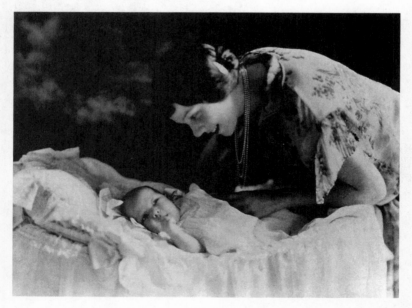

7. Mabel Russell in middle age

8. Brooke with her infant son, Tony

9. Buddie Marshall as
a young man

10. Brooke Marshall

11. Brian Aherne

12. John Jacob Astor
IV at a costume ball

13. Vincent Astor in full
uniform during
World War I

14. Helen Hull, the first
Mrs. Vincent Astor

15. Minnie Cushing,
the second Mrs.
Vincent Astor

16. Vincent Astor
walks the dog, 1938

17. Janet Rhinelander
Stewart

for Portofino, to pack up a few things and then head for France. Leaving behind all their household possessions, they boarded the Rome–Paris express and then scrambled to find safe passage to New York on one of the ships already booked to capacity.

The outbreak of war in Europe led to, or coincided with, further changes in the Marshalls' lives. In 1934, a trusted member of Butler, Herrick and Marshall had failed to make good on a sizable loss of money. They had returned from their first summer at the Castello to deal with the consequences. Two and a half years after their first trip to Europe, Buddie's marvelous mother had died of cancer. Now, they returned from Europe to find that they could no longer afford to keep a limousine and chauffeur or a grand penthouse apartment. A decision was made to make their main residence a house in the country and to buy a more modest apartment farther downtown, on Sutton Place.

From the moment his daughter accepted Buddie Marshall's proposal of marriage, General Russell had welcomed him into the family. In 1934 John Russell had been appointed by President Roosevelt as commandant of the Marine Corps, an appointment that stipulated he be promoted to a three-star general, a promotion subject to approval by the Senate. This promotion was not universally popular, resulting in a debate on the Senate's floor. He was accused by his enemies of having behaved in a cowardly fashion back in 1914, when he commanded a regiment stationed in Mexico. Unfortunately, he had enemies in high places. In *Footprints* Brooke Astor takes credit for setting the record straight. Rather than behaving like a coward, her father had actually been a hero, and, with the help of one of *her* friends in high places, she found newspaper clippings to bear this out.

John Russell was able to retire later that year, at the age of sixty-four, with the title of commandant. After settling briefly in Arlington (like living at a cemetery, with all those military funerals to attend, he complained) he moved with his wife to Coronado, still a separate small island reached by ferry from San Diego, where Brooke would visit on occasion and where he wrote a column as a military analyst for the Copley syndicate. In 1940 and 1941, when the war made the Castello no longer viable for them, the Marshalls took a summer place nearby—affording time for Tony to finally get to better know his grandfather, to come to value his ideas and opinions, and then, eventually, to seek ways to earn his respect.

In 1941, not long before America entered the war, the Marshalls found a stucco house to buy in Tyringham, a Quaker village in the Berkshires, not far from Lenox. The setting was lovely and by the time Brooke was finished with this house, she had turned a dark and undistinguished dwelling into a light and airy country villa, complete with beautifully landscaped grounds and one of the area's first swimming pools. There was a caretaker on the property, and, as the war dragged on, some of this property was given over to a victory garden. At one point, until they fully appreciated the implications of what they were doing, the Marshalls tried raising pigs, only to have Brooke develop a strong attachment to the hapless runt of one of their first litters.

From the start one appeal the house had for Brooke was that in the summer there were many theater people living in the area. She soon had almost as many friends as she'd had in Bernardsville, thanks in part to her nearest neighbor, Mrs. Palmer, whose husband's family had been in the area for some time. In winter there were about 250 or 300 people, but there were about four times as many during the summer. If there was any fun to be had, Brooke Marshall was at the center of it. One of her closest friends was the widow of the playwright Sidney Howard. Every day the two of them would talk on the phone. The problem was they were talking on a party line. To make sure there was no eavesdropping, Brooke began speaking in French. For instance, when Brooke needed to ask how much to tip the volunteer fire department at Christmas, she would ask, "*Combien pour les pompiers?*"

When they first moved to Tyringham, Brooke was worried about Tony's not doing athletic things. He was a bit overweight and she enlisted Mrs. Palmer's son, Gilly, who was a year younger than Tony, to play tennis with him. She also persuaded her best friend, Mrs. Sidney Howard, to have the foreman at her farm hire Tony for the summer—only to have the foreman fire Tony after a couple of weeks, saying he was "hopeless."

Tony wasn't "hopeless," but he wasn't happy with the way his life was going. He was "a wretched student," his mother wrote in *Footprints*, and disliked school. From the start he had been unhappy at Groton but for a while things had seemed better at Brooks, until there, too, he began doing badly, dropping almost to the very bottom of his class. By the summer of 1942, when he was entering his senior year, there was some question as to whether he would graduate. Now, more than ever, he had come to admire his grandfather. In a gesture that owed not a little to this admiration, Tony quit Brooks that December and enlisted in the Marine Corps. With the war on everyone's minds, he had made up *his* mind to join the fight. At the same time, he made up his mind to change his name officially to "Anthony Marshall," a gesture that can be seen as a reverse form of adoption— a simple enough act but one that would lead to subsequent confusion, with most people assuming that at some point Buddie Marshall had legally adopted Brooke's son and given him his name. This indeed was something even his Marshall cousins would come to assume, although his stepsister, Peggy, would point out that this couldn't be true and he was really Tony Kuser.

At the time, both Tony's grandfather and his stepfather were touched by what he had done. His grandfather went so far as to see to it that the headmaster at Brooks gave him a diploma, so that he would not be prevented from going to college later. His stepfather did not take the natural step of legally adopting him, although he may have considered it. Of course there were those rumors to be considered.

But there was also the more pressing question of his son, Peter. Any guilt that was involved here could only have been compounded by the fact that Buddie's father had left a generation-skipping trust. Although Buddie was currently receiving regular interest payments from this trust, the principal would be divided among his two children at his death. Any legal adoption of Tony might result in this substantial sum of money being divided three ways, instead of two, and thus reduce the amount of money to be inherited by his own children—money that was going to be needed to help care for Peter.

If nothing else, when Tony changed his name and enlisted in the Marines, he was hoping for a fresh start. He was also taking charge of his life. His mother, too, was making some changes in her life—contributing to the war effort by working as a Gray Lady at Halloran Hospital, on Staten Island. This volunteer work called for her to get up at dawn five days a week and to take a bus, a subway, and then a ferry to Staten Island, where she would work long hours, frequently returning home after dark. At Halloran her assigned task was to wheel a cart loaded with books to the wounded soldiers in the wards and to sometimes read aloud to them, but it soon involved listening to their problems, of which there were many, especially as their stay at the hospital dragged on. Halloran specialized in paraplegics, many of them so gravely wounded that the ships bringing them to the hospital arrived under cover of darkness so as not to alarm nearby civilians.

Although Brooke tried to keep her tone lighthearted, as she saw these badly wounded men being left to lounge about, unshaved and ungroomed, in their bathrobes and pajamas, she noted how demoralized and depressed they eventually became. And, as she watched the fiancées and old girlfriends and even close family members stop by less frequently and then cease to visit entirely, she saw the terrible consequences of this wholesale desertion.

Thanks to her father, Brooke Marshall was a dyed-in-the-wool old-fashioned patriot. She was proud of her country and proud of these men she was helping take care of, many of whom had sacrificed their futures fighting for their country. Not least of all, she was proud of her son for enlisting. But, in the spring of 1945, when she learned that Tony was taking part in the battle being waged at Iwo Jima, she became terribly frightened. "Brooke was nervous as hell," recalled Louis Auchincloss. "I was there one day when she had a letter that she hardly dared open. Evie, who acted like she was boss with everyone, said, 'Brooke, open it. Open it up this minute.'" By this time Brooke was so desperate for news of Tony that she'd had her father pull strings in Washington to find out whether or not her son was alive. As it turned out, Tony had survived, although she later learned he had been wounded in the leg, earning him a Purple Heart.

When the war ended, instead of returning home and going on to college, Tony stayed on in the Marine Corps. For two years he served on Guam as a second lieutenant and battalion adjutant, and then retired in 1947 as a captain. Having given up on a military career, he decided to enter college. By then most soldiers had been back for some time, taking advantage of the GI Bill, so college admission wasn't as simple as it had once been. Thanks to his mother's pulling some strings, however, Tony was able to enter Brown as a freshman even at this late date, and even though he had not completed his course work at Brooks.

Proud of what her son had accomplished, Brooke Marshall had resolved to stop nagging Tony and urging him to do better—particularly since that had never seemed to work anyway. Relations between mother and son seemed to have grown smoother until Tony proposed marriage to Elizabeth Cryan, a freshman at Pembroke, the sister school to Brown. When his mother urged him to put off the wedding— at least until he and this young woman had both finished school—he would have none of it. As it happened, Brooke didn't much care for Elizabeth Cryan. Moreover, she feared that her son and this Pembroke freshman were too young. This fear of hers no doubt owed something to her own unhappy first marriage. Given the way she felt, it was just as well that when her son did marry Elizabeth Cryan, he didn't return to New York. Already Ivy League colleges, like Brown and Yale, had become important recruiting grounds for a newly formed federal agency. Upon graduating, Tony went with his wife to live in Washington, where he had been offered a job in government or, rather (as he would inform readers of the Playbills of two Broadway plays he later produced), where he had been offered a desk job with the CIA.

Like many of his classmates at Brown, Tony had benefited from the GI Bill to help meet his tuition, but he now had a small trust fund of his own. Tony was twenty-three and past the age when he was legally free to take possession of the alimony payments held in trust for him—payments that had been building up since his mother's remarriage. Now Dryden Kuser stepped in and tried to block this, declaring that by taking his stepfather's name Tony had forfeited all right to Kuser money. Ex-wives can be expensive and Dryden, well past his second marriage, was not about to give up any potential source of income. But thanks once again to sound legal advice, Tony's mother was able to fight Dryden off.

While Tony's prospects seemed better than they had ever been, Buddie Marshall appeared to have a good deal less money than he'd had before. At the end of the war, when most businessmen seemed to be reaping enormous profits, Buddie seemed, at best, to be treading water. To keep up with inflation, further economies were in order. But no major changes were necessary, at least for the time being, thanks to his wife's taking a paying job at *House and Garden*. She'd been hired by Albert Kornfeld, the magazine's new editor, in 1946 with a mandate to help breathe some life into this rather sleepy Condé Nast publication.

As the magazine's features editor, she was soon coming up with ideas for articles on how to set a table or serve a buffet dinner in a world where young housewives could no longer count on a staff of well-trained servants to help them out. More important, she was getting her wealthy friends to open up their houses to the magazine's photographers. In time she was able to persuade Henry du Pont to let the magazine photograph the beautifully restored eighteenth-century rooms at Winterthur for the first time and to get young Osborn Elliott and his new wife to talk about how to make the best of an odd assortment of wedding presents. Using her not inconsiderable gifts of persuasion, she also got her old love Brian Aherne to agree to be photographed with his wife serving friends an informal dinner on their terrace. This set of photographs suggested, among other things, that informal dinners were not only becoming perfectly acceptable but were positively chic.

Her sister-in-law Evie, now married to the architect Diego Suarez, provided her with rooms to photograph, as did her friends the Joseph Pulitzers in St. Louis. Linda Gillies, who would one day serve as director of the Vincent Astor Foundation, remembers as a child hearing an aunt say she was letting *House and Garden* photograph her Sutton Place dining room "because Brooke needs the money." When all else failed, Brooke made use of her own homes—using shots of the Tyringham study, with its lovely paneling stripped from the walls of their old penthouse, or the brand-new small studio, where Buddie was devoting many weekend hours to caring for, and rebinding, the handsome first editions he had inherited from his father.

As an editor at *House and Garden* she was able to come to work wearing a smart hat and suit and to keep her little dog tucked beneath her desk. But she was also terribly busy—organizing the photo shoots, coordinating temperamental photographers with stylists, and making sure that everyone arrived on time. Unfortunately, Condé

Nast editors did not earn large salaries—the assumption being that they were doing this primarily for their own amusement.

In 1949 Buddie Marshall's senior partner, Arthur Butler, died, naming Buddie, twenty years his junior, as executor of his family trust. With this death Buddie Marshall lost a valued friend and adviser and the firm lost a valuable asset. Increasingly Buddie seemed to be under pressure—tired, distracted, not quite himself.

"Buddie Marshall was a most attractive man," Louis Auchincloss would later say. "He was modest and easygoing, but firm. He stuck by what he believed." Certainly he stuck by his wife. In *Footprints* Brooke Astor credited Buddie Marshall with giving her the self-confidence to enter any room without worrying about what everyone there thought of her. He was firm. And he was smart, though he tended to stay in the background, watching. Always he worked hard, but he played hard as well, hunting with friends on their plantations in the Carolinas, taking anyone up on the offer of a good game of golf or tennis. For many years he had been an active member of the Brook Club as well as its president. But for all that he was a man's man, he clearly liked women. And they liked him in return.

In *Footprints* Brooke would write about how not long after she became Mrs. Charles Marshall, back when they still had the blue Rolls-Royce, she overheard a fellow guest at a dinner party regaling Buddie with tales of her unhappy marriage, and then suggesting the two of them meet downtown at lunch the following day so she could get some further advice from him. Perhaps seeing hints of her own early history with Buddie, she cut short any possibility of a lunch, by immediately confronting Buddie in the limousine on their way home and, just to show how serious she was about this, pitched her Cartier wedding ring out the car's window. She wanted to make it clear that she was not about to tolerate a repetition of her marriage to Dryden Kuser. A new ring was purchased and certain ground rules had been established. But it was understood that Buddie Marshall would always be sought out by women. "No one wants to be married to someone else no one wants." The moral of the tale, she added, was this: "Be cautious."

The moral of the tale can be read several ways. Cautious about what exactly? Cautious, meaning discreet? After the war, when she and Buddie were apart more frequently, owing to the traveling she had to do for her job, and also to the fact that she was no longer free to accompany Buddie on some of his winter hunting trips, her definition of caution seemed to have grown more flexible. At least according to Evie Clarkson, her summer neighbor in the Berkshires and a fellow Condé Nast employee, who would say most emphatically, "Brooke had affairs at the time she was married to Buddie Marshall. A man I knew offered to take her home after a party. She asked him in, the way you do, for a drink. Then she eagerly led him to her bed. 'But your husband,' the man said. She let him know that didn't matter."

Certainly she was attractive to men, even those who had no idea of having an affair with her. Younger men found her especially appealing. Thomas Hoving, who was a teenager when his father and stepmother moved to the Berkshires during the war, would recall the joy of having her as a neighbor, "I remember going over there for lunch with my parents, and Brooke and I bonded immediately. She was total perfection. At fifteen I could clip a car from the garage and drive over and chat with her. She was nice about my adolescence—funny and gay."

Louis Auchincloss, who was at law school with Evie's son when he first met Brooke during the war, would declare, "Brooke was the most attractive woman I've ever known. She was never beautiful, but she was radiant and charming. There was nothing highfalutin about her during the *House and Garden* days. She always did things well, but this was when she did things the best. Her parties then were better than anything she did later. Funds were by no means unlimited. It took management. In life you do better with a challenge. In the Buddie Marshall years she was in her heyday."

It may have been her heyday, and the challenge may have put her on her mettle, but there was no getting around the fact that funds were increasingly limited. Through her position at *House and Garden* Brooke Marshall had access to various high-profile decorators—one of whom, Dorothy Draper, offered her a job in 1950 that kept her off the masthead of the magazine for a year—a year she dropped from any later discussions of her work life, perhaps because she couldn't make it sound as if she were simply working for Dorothy Draper as a lark. This new job, which permitted her to continue keeping a little dog under her desk, seems to have involved, at least on the occasion of a visit to St. Louis, her engaging in a bit of public relations for the firm. There she gave a long interview to the *St. Louis Post-Dispatch*, a paper owned by her friend Joseph Pulitzer, where she discussed Dorothy Draper's plans for bright and attractive low-income housing, emphasizing how, simply by lifting its occupants' spirits, cheerful and comfortable surroundings could provide the springboard for a better life—thereby introducing an idea that she would later refine and develop once she had funds at her command to implement it.

Whatever happened with Dorothy Draper, the following year Brooke Marshall was back with Kornfeld at *House and Garden* and continuing to put a good face on a life that was not quite as carefree as it had once been. She and Buddie continued to take summer vacations in Europe, although they never returned to the Castello. One of their great summer pastimes was hiking in the mountains, going from hut to hut with nothing but a knapsack. Now that Buddie was getting older, however, he sometimes had difficulty breathing. And, after eating a large black sausage for dinner one night, he had a painful attack of indigestion unlike anything he'd had before.

In *Footprints* she would say that by the early fifties Buddie had begun talking about planning for the future. Also about making changes in certain provisions he had once made for her. By late November 1952, she said, he was talking about how he had papers he was planning to go over with his lawyer immediately after the Thanksgiving holidays. All this talk could have been prompted by the death of Arthur Butler. As his old partner's executor, he had wills very much on his mind. Or it could simply have been prompted by the fact that he had reached an age when, witnessing the deaths of those around him, he had begun to have intimations of his own mortality.

For Brooke, a source of great sadness in the years after the war had been her father's failing health. The man who had embued her with a strong sense of the importance of discipline—whom she could always count on for sound advice as well as unstinting love—had been having problems with his heart. In the late winter of 1947, she had managed to make it to San Diego in time to be with him for a few weeks before he died. That March, General Russell was buried with full military honors and laid to rest on a quiet knoll within the grounds of Arlington, the very place he'd been fleeing when he moved with his wife to California some ten years before.

One night when they were alone together, shortly before he died, her father had confided to Brooke that he didn't mind dying but was worried about what would happen to his wife. "Who will look after her?" he asked. Brooke promised that she would. "Thank you, Little Woman. I know that you will," said her father, making her responsible for the care of a woman who proved to be less independent than anyone could have predicted. And also leaving her with a second family member to fret over.

With Tony's life apparently on track, Brooke's mother now became her primary concern. After Mabel failed to find a comfortable place on her own in Coronado, she helped move her mother east, to Norwich, Connecticut, where Mabel settled into an apartment within easy reach of Tyringham and the city, and within minutes of one of her widowed sisters, who lived in a house grand enough to have suited even Granny Howard.

Buddie Marshall—who had always expressed great fondness for

both her parents—was perfectly willing to make a place for Brooke's mother in their life. Frequently she would join them for weekends in the country. At least one time Brooke found her a sublet in the city. There were men in Mabel's life, but she no longer seemed to consider them as serious suitors. The Belle of Peking seemed to have departed forever, to be replaced by a woman whose role had once been that of the High Commissioner's wife. "She was utterly unlike Brooke," a less than enchanted Louis Auchincloss would recall. "Brooke was catlike— she moved easily and was full of laughter. Mrs. Russell was stately. She was a person used to diplomatic life and full of formality."

No longer part of the diplomatic life, Brooke's once indomitable mother was a fish out of water—not really at ease in the life she was leading and, according to more than one concerned observer, sometimes critical of the daughter who had been charged with looking after her. The daughter herself never let on, at least in print, that there were moments when her patience was tried by this dominating woman who had become increasingly dependent on her. She simply did her best to honor her father's wishes.

Brooke always made sure to include Mabel in as many family occasions as she could manage—which was why in the fall of 1952 she and Buddie brought Mabel up with them to the country for Thanksgiving weekend. It was hunting season, which meant that Buddie was out with his rifle most of the day, while Brooke prepared Thanksgiving dinner for the three of them and also got some platters of canapes ready for a few friends who had been invited to drop by for cocktails.

In the morning, Buddie had been fresh and full of energy and had joined her and their dog, Maxl, in bed. By afternoon, though, he seemed to have caught a chill, heaping extra logs on the living room fire when, thanks to all the friends they had invited, the room was already too warm. That night, after their guests had all gone home and their Thanksgiving dinner had been eaten, Buddie went out toward the pantry to prepare for the next day's hunting and also to let the dog out. The sound of a cry alerted Brooke to the fact that something was wrong. She found Buddie on the floor, by the back door. All she could do was hold his head in her lap and pray that the man she had always thought of as her one great love would not be impaired in any way. By the time the doctor arrived, Buddie was dead. Indeed, according to the doctor, he had been dead all along.

Five

❦

VINCENT ASTOR,
1953–1959

When a woman marries a very rich man it is usual to say
that she married for money.

Suddenly, without warning, after twenty years of marriage, Brooke
Marshall had lost the man she would always portray as a thoroughly
desirable companion and a perfect husband. Before she had a chance
to fully take in what had happened to her, there would be other shocks
to come. For the moment, though, everything seemed to be in good
order. Buddie had left a sealed envelope at the apartment containing
all the papers he had gathered for just such an eventuality. In this
envelope could be found detailed instructions for a funeral service to
be held at St. James Church, a key to a safe-deposit box, and a last will
and testament. He had also left a second sealed envelope for his wife.

Buddie's will—"revoking any and all Wills and Codicils at any
time heretofore made"—had been written and signed three years earlier, in 1949, the year his senior partner, Arthur Butler, died. As wills
go, it was admirably straightforward. There were three bequests,
none of them to individuals: $3,000 to the endowment fund of the
Brook Club; $1,000 to the Seaman's Church Institute; and $1,000 to
the Home for Incurables of St. Barnabas Hospital, where for many
years he had served on the board of directors. The "residue and

remainder" of his "property and estate, both real and personal" was to go to his wife, Brooke Russell Marshall—who was designated as co-executor, with the Central Hanover Bank and Trust Company. No money was left directly to any child. But if his wife should predecease him—not a terribly likely eventuality, given the eleven-year difference in their ages—all of his assets were to be distributed "in equal parts" to his son, Charles Marshall Jr.; his daughter, Helen Marshall Schelling; and his stepson, Anthony Marshall.

In Charles Marshall's obituaries in *The New York Times* and *Herald Tribune*, which ran that Sunday, Tony was listed among his survivors. In these obituaries, where there were no legal ramifications, he was simply coupled with Peter as one of Charles Marshall's "two sons." Tony was also designated in the funeral instructions as a pallbearer. Among the papers found in the safe-deposit box was a letter written by Tony just before the battle of Iwo Jima, telling Buddie how much having him as a father had meant to him. It was a letter to touch the hardest of hearts. No matter that it was the letter of a soldier facing death—honest and sincere and full of feeling, but also charged with this soldier's understanding that these words might be the sole legacy he was leaving behind.

Charles Buddie Marshall's very natural response was to repay Tony in kind. To name his stepson in his will cost him nothing, since in all likelihood he would not be leaving him a cent. His own two children had already been well provided for by their grandfather's trust. Putting this stepson on the same footing with his son and daughter was a generous gesture. But, barring some unforeseen circumstance, it was no better than symbolic. Listing Tony as one of his two sons in the obituaries passed along to the *Times* and *Herald Tribune* was also symbolic, although it did contribute to some confusion—leading most members of the Marshall family to assume that he had been legally adopted.

Rather than relegate her husband to the care of a funeral home,

Buddie's widow chose to take his embalmed body home to their apartment and place his open casket in their drawing room, where friends could visit and she could be with him one last time. Her son, Tony, who had rushed up from Washington, went along with her wish that Buddie be allowed to wear his shoes in his casket and helped her choose a brown tweed suit for him to be buried in—again not customary but perfect with his tawny coloring and perfectly in keeping with the man he had always been. For her part, the new widow chose to adhere to tradition. She arrived for the service at St. James draped in black, with a black veil that was thick enough to conceal any redness and swelling from days of crying. Throughout the service and later at the grave, Buddie's sister, Evie, remained close by her side.

After the funeral, before the grieving widow had time to dry her tears and look to the future, it became apparent that, thanks to her husband's divorce agreement, one-third of his estate—valued at approximately $1 million before taxes—would go to fund a trust for his ex-wife, Alice. Safely invested and yielding a 5 percent return, the approximately $525,000 his widow would receive could support her for life—but not in the style she was accustomed to. Suddenly Brooke Russell Marshall found herself in the awkward position of being fifty years old and looking forward to living on a fixed income of about $26,000 a year. Neither of these facts was common knowledge. Her energy and gaiety made it easy for her to pass as someone a decade younger. And her late husband's standing in the community made it only natural to assume that he had left his widow comfortably fixed.

Brooke Astor would write in *Footprints* that there was nothing that could be done about the generation-skipping trust. But she also wrote that in a second letter in that sealed envelope Buddie had urged her to try to do something to break a "contract" obligating his estate to provide a fixed amount of money "to someone until that person died." She said he had thought it unfair that her own portion of his estate be so "small." The book's language here is guarded, but a trip to Surrogate's Court makes it all perfectly clear. Whether she was advised that she had little chance of breaking this agreement, or whether she simply hadn't the stomach for it, she chose to let it stand. Unfortunately, the moment Buddie Marshall died, the income he had been receiving from his father's trust ceased. Brooke's job at *House and Garden* could not begin to meet their current expenses. It was clear that the house in Tyringham would have to be sold.

Sadly, this time, she did not have her father to step in and salvage something from this unexpected turn of events. It never would have occurred to her to look for help from her mother. And there was no use approaching Tony: the CIA was very much like *House and Garden* in its assumption that its employees were all in possession of independent means.

For even the strongest of women her predicament would be paralyzing. All that Brooke Marshall could do was look to friends for company and sympathy while trying to address the immediate tasks stemming from Buddie's death. In the late afternoon—perhaps the worst time of day for her—a member of the Brook Club would stop by the apartment for a drink or simply for an hour's visit. In time it became apparent that these frequent visits were no accident. To talk about Buddie with men who had known and admired him was a comfort. At the same time, it was a comfort, for all that it required an effort, to try and respond to the fifteen hundred letters of condolence she had received, all of them letting her know just how much her husband had been loved.

In *Footprints*, Brooke Astor writes of how in those terrible winter months immediately following Buddie Marshall's death—when she could not muster sufficient energy to plan for the future or return to the job that was being kept open for her—her sister-in-law's children chipped in and presented her with the gift of a trip to France. In Paris she was able to stay with the Dunns, the family friends who had been at her second wedding. Also residing in Paris was a sister of Mabel's, who had been imprisoned in China by the Japanese at the outbreak of the war and was now living in greatly reduced circumstances, but who was still very much Roberta Howard's daughter, letting Brooke know that it was an insult to her late husband's memory to go around looking like a frump.

This stern lecture—nothing like the sort of advice her father might have given her—did not fall on deaf ears. She did a bit of shopping in Paris and then joined a friend for a drive down to the Riviera, where the sun was brighter, the climate was warmer, and she was free to make her peace with her new solitary state at leisure. If the trip to France did not leave her reconciled to her fate, it revived her spirits sufficiently for Brooke to consider returning to work after a decent interval had passed. But while she might once again be resorting to makeup and a weekly appointment at the hairdresser's, she was not yet ready to relinquish her widow's weeds entirely.

In late May, almost exactly six months after Buddie's death, when she ventured out for the first time in society—joining friends for a small dinner party at their apartment—she was still wearing black, albeit a recently purchased black dress with a becoming full skirt and fitted bodice, very much in the style of Dior's "New Look." At this dinner her hostess had seated her near Vincent Astor, whose wife, as was the custom, had been seated as far from her husband as her hostess could manage. Well over six feet tall, with a face that recalled a cigar-store Indian, frequently taciturn, and sometimes foul tempered, Vincent Astor was sixty-two years old. His great fortune alone should have made him attractive to many women. But over time he had acquired a reputation for being exactly the sort of man to induce panic in even the most stout-hearted dinner partner.

As it happened Brooke Marshall was seated directly across from Vincent at the dinner table. The whole time she was doing her best to be a good guest and devote the requisite amount of attention to keeping up her end of the conversation with each of her two dinner partners, she caught Vincent staring at her. Afterward, when the ladies adjourned for coffee, he followed her into the drawing room and immediately drew her aside. Vincent very much wanted to tell her how he regretted not writing her after Buddie's death. Before long, Vincent's wife, Minnie, joined them, and as the evening was drawing to a close Minnie and Vincent offered her a lift home.

The drive to her Sutton Place apartment was not a long one. Once the three of them were settled in the back of Vincent's large limousine, Minnie began insisting, with Vincent's strong concurrence, that she join them the following Saturday, for Memorial Day weekend, when they were having a few friends up to Ferncliff, their place in Rhinebeck. When she protested that Saturday was Tony's birthday, the two of them refused to take no for an answer. By the time they dropped her off, they had secured her reluctant consent. Saturday morning they sent a car for her. And, by the end of that weekend, Vincent Astor, with Minnie's strong encouragement, had proposed marriage.

According to Brooke Astor, Minnie wished to leave Vincent Astor, but she did not wish to leave until she was sure he was well settled, thereby helping to guarantee a generous divorce settlement. As Minnie saw it, this meant finding him a suitable replacement. By accepting Vincent's proposal, Brooke would be doing no harm. Indeed she would be helping Minnie escape a marriage that no longer suited her, while at the same time greatly improving her own prospects. Attractive though this proposition might be, she could not bring herself to agree to it immediately. It took months of persuasion on Vincent's part—well, at least two months, while he was traveling in Asia and writing her as many as five love letters a day. In September, Minnie secured a divorce. And that autumn, in the Bar Harbor home of friends, she and Vincent became man and wife.

In marrying Vincent Astor, Brooke Marshall was taking on more than a difficult, and not altogether attractive, enormously wealthy man. For five generations the Astor name had loomed large in New York, reaching its apogee during Caroline Astor's long reign as queen of New York Society. John Jacob Astor—the family's founder and Vincent's great-great-grandfather—was the son of a poor German butcher; he arrived in the city with nothing but the pack on his back, shortly after the British had vacated the premises, and died in 1848 the richest man in America. Having begun his life in his adopted country as an itinerant fur trader and then married the daughter of a widow who ran a boardinghouse, the family's founder had set about acquiring cheap Manhattan farmland and holding on to it long enough to see its value increase exponentially as the city expanded northward. Rather than build on the land he owned, he preferred to lease it, collecting rent from the owners of the buildings erected on his property.

During John Jacob's last years, it was said that his digestion was "so disordered that he fed only at the breast of a wet nurse," while he had to be tossed in a blanket in order to keep his blood circulating. At his death, he had left behind a fortune of some 20 million dollars, which William—his oldest mentally competent son and Vincent's great-grandfather—carefully tended, turning a blind eye to the increasingly squalid tenements that sat on Astor property stretching along the East River between Houston and Canal streets. William's oldest son, John Jacob III—Vincent's great-uncle and Caroline's brother-in-law—continued in this tradition, preferring to let others take the risks that came with constructing a building or dealing with tenants.

While the Astor business offices were always modest and the land they leased was rarely topped by imposing edifices, the Astors themselves could boast of private residences that numbered among the city's finest. But not until the late nineteenth century, when John

Jacob III's son, William Waldorf, ran for public office, did any of the Astors show themselves to be particularly civic minded. Nor did they number among the city's great cultural leaders. Given the family's origins, this failure hardly seems astonishing. When invited to dine at the home of a friend who had long been influential in state and national politics, a less than gallant and barely literate John Jacob I was said to have scooped up his peas with a knife and proceeded to wipe his mouth on the sleeve of the unfortunate lady who happened to be seated next to him.

Still, thanks to one of John Jacob I's few philanthropic gestures, the family name had long been associated with one of New York's great cultural institutions. In his old age this former pedlar who was neither a gentleman nor a scholar had been cajoled and flattered by his secretary and adviser and by his one literary connection, Washington Irving, into leaving $400,000 in his will to endow a research library. For this bequest he would be remembered as one of the founder's of the city's public library system. But even though the money he left was indeed sufficient to accumulate an impressive collection of books and erect a handsome building on Lafayette Street, it did not provide an adequate endowment, which meant that, despite periodic infusions of Astor money, access to this handsome building would remain limited.

The Astors, while not believing in wasting excessive amounts of money on charity when the money could better be used by members of the family, had always believed in adhering, whenever possible, to the English law of primogeniture, thereby fostering the consolidation of the family fortune. They also believed in marrying well. John Jacob Astor was not the only one in the family to find a wife better off than he was. William married Margaret Armstrong, a Livingston heiress, and then bought her father's lovely property overlooking the Hudson River. (In time this property would be given the name Rokeby and house the "Astor orphans," the sometimes unruly and frequently enterprising children of William's favorite granddaughter.) John Jacob III married Charlotte Augusta Gibbes, a well-born Southern girl who differed from most Astor wives in having a taste for serious books and an interest in the welfare of small children not necessarily her own. And of course John Jacob III's younger brother, William Backhouse, married the indomitable Caroline Schermerhorn—who went on to assume, as if by natural right, the role of "The Mrs. Astor." As such, Caroline took precedence over Augusta, her senior and far wealthier sister-in-law, who manifested no perceptible desire to take on this role and appeared to be more than happy to maintain cordial relations, sometimes standing at her side as Caroline received her guests at one of her celebrated balls. Until Augusta's death, the two Astor wives lived in harmony, in mansions that had been erected next door to each other, on two lots stretching along Fifth Avenue from Thirty-third to Thirty-fourth streets, the current site of the Empire State Building.

It was only when Augusta's son William Waldorf succeeded John Jacob III as nominal head of the Astor family that trouble began. William Waldorf felt that it was a great slight to his young wife for his Aunt Caroline to assume she had sole right to that title. How his wife felt is another matter. Unlike his immediate predecessors, William Waldorf harbored a desire to leave his mark on the city's body politic, leading him to stand for election—venturing into territory not necessarily congenial to a man of his upbringing, which, not surprisingly, resulted in his being roundly defeated. Feeling slighted on several fronts, William Waldorf eventually moved his family to England, where he believed his efforts might be better appreciated. There, while waiting to receive the titles that signified his adopted country's appreciation, he gradually went about putting down roots, by buying up two of England's great houses, Cliveden and Hever. However, he still found time to make his presence felt back home—exacting his revenge on his Aunt Caroline, by tearing down his parents' Fifth Avenue mansion to erect, immediately next door to her, a gigantic luxury hotel bearing the name "Waldorf," in the process turning a quiet residential block into a noisy construction site, with the promise that the noise would be little better once this hotel was open for business.

By then Caroline Astor had no husband to protect her, but she did have a loving son, John Jacob IV, whose response to his cousin's unprecedented real estate venture was twofold. First, he gave his mother more than 2 million dollars to build an even more magnificent mansion farther uptown on Fifth Avenue, covering the entire block between Sixty-fifth and Sixty-sixth streets—a mansion that he proposed to share with her, neatly dividing it in two in such a way that he and his wife would have their own private entrance and living quarters, while she would have not only have peace and quiet but also a suitable ballroom in which to receive her guests. Second, he set about demolishing his mother's old home and started work on a competing hotel to be built on the lot where it had once stood, forcing his cousin to see reason and agree to a merger, so that the two hotels were joined together to form the highly profitable Waldorf-Astoria.

John Jacob IV, that devoted and extravagant son of Caroline Astor, was Vincent's father. His privileged but not altogether happy life came to a premature and tragic end in April 1912, when—having taken care to usher his pregnant eighteen-year-old second wife, Madeleine Force, into a lifeboat and then lend a helping hand to the ladies who were hoping to join her there—he went down with the *Titanic*. For this "noble" gesture he would always be remembered as a gentleman. But until his death, more often than not, he had been regarded as a figure of fun. Sometimes called "Jack Ass-tor" by the press, he does not take a bad photograph, and in some appears to have been rather distinguished looking, but it would seem that in person he was sufficiently tall and ungainly to be universally regarded as a poor match for Ava Willing, the Philadelphia beauty he had married in 1891. Indeed the standing joke making the rounds of the various New York clubs was "Jack Ass-t'her and Ava's father was willing."

Ava—who was willing enough to give him a son and who later also gave birth to a daughter, Alice, who may or may not have been Jack's—made it painfully clear that she had little interest in her husband. But if she was not an especially good wife she was a good daughter-in-law and also a woman well aware of social conventions, even when she occasionally chose to flaunt them, waiting until thirteen months after Caroline Astor's death in 1908 to finally divorce Jack and move to England, where she made a brief marriage to a rather sour gentleman, an act that guaranteed her the lifetime use of the title of Lady Ribblesdale.

To John Jacob IV's last hours were attributed many fine actions. He was credited with releasing the dogs from the *Titanic*'s kennel, including his Airedale, Kitty. His last words to his frantic wife, quoted in the *The New York Times*, were "Good-bye, dearie, I'll see you later." He was credited with watching her departure while smoking a cigarette. He was reported as saying, "I asked for ice, but this is ridiculous," while leaning, in a manner both casual and debonaire, against the ship's bar—a remark that one Astor family historian would rule out as highly improbable, given that Jack was anything but a wit.

On the other hand, Jack Astor had already shown himself to be capable of personal sacrifice, if not outright heroism. In 1898, during the Spanish American War, he lent his yacht to the United States Navy, paid for a battery to be sent to fight in the Philippines, and rushed to serve with his cousin Theodore Roosevelt in Cuba, although he arrived barely in time to witness at a distance the charge up San Juan Hill, before contracting malaria—all of which had earned him the honorary title of "Colonel."

But it was the machinery that went into battle and not the actual bloodletting that interested Jack Astor. Indeed, modern inventions were his passion—particularly cars, of which he owned many. In the guise of a writer of privately published science fiction, he chose to look ahead to machinery that might be available in the future. A man less encumbered by wealth might have been called visionary. Or at the very least humored as harmlessly eccentric. As it was, grander pursuits were expected of the son of Caroline Astor. In 1911, Jack Astor married again. By choosing a girl young enough to be his daughter he had finally secured a wife who was not inclined to judge him and find him wanting. Unfortunately, the girl he married was judged in turn by those around him.

The feeling was that Madeleine Force's Brooklyn family was not fine enough, and she herself was not beautiful enough to compensate for her less than stellar pedigree, and he had once again made a fool of himself. Which was why John Jacob IV happened to be on the *Titanic* in the first place. Finding many doors closed to his new wife, he had carried her off to Europe, where Americans with deep pockets could count on being made welcome and where the two of them were more likely to find immediate acceptance as a couple. He had decided to return to New York only when he discovered that his young wife was pregnant, so that their baby would be born back home.

Jack Astor's body was found floating in its life jacket, his soot-encrusted face and body leading to the conclusion that he had been killed by the toppling of one of the *Titanic*'s giant smokestacks. Only the $2,500 in bills and gold watch found still ticking in his pockets served to identify him. His nineteen-year-old son Vincent—who had rushed to Halifax to identify the body and bring his father back to be buried at Ferncliff—would carry that gold watch with him always.

Six months after the sinking of the *Titanic*, John Jacob IV's young widow gave birth to a son, whom she quite naturally named for her late husband. She proceeded to rattle around in the big house on Fifth Avenue—which her late husband had only recently made over into a single-family dwelling and which was hers by right—until, having had her fill of the perquisites of being an Astor widow, she married a former sweetheart. By marrying again she forfeited the maintenance payments she had been receiving from her husband's estate but took with her a settlement of $1,695,000, which she had unwisely agreed to at the time of her first marriage, and also took with her little "Jackie," for whom she who would continue to receive financial support until he came into his inheritance.

In old age Brooke Astor would sometimes confide to close friends that the sinking of the *Titanic* had saved her. Or, rather, altered the course of her life. It was the belief of not a few people that as soon as John Jacob IV reached New York he would have written a new will taking into account the possibility that Madeleine was carrying a boy and splitting the bulk of his fortune, should this prove to be true, between Vincent and this second son. Madeleine Force Astor and her son, Jackie, would always profess to believe this. Madeleine—who would go on to find not one but two unsuitable husbands—would eventually come to a sad end, succumbing to an overdose of sleeping pills at the age of forty-six. Her son, Jackie, was left to make do with $5 million when he came of age, the same amount that Vincent's sister, Alice, had received in Jack's will—not a pittance by any means but nothing like what he might have stood to inherit if his father had lived. And nothing like the $87 million his half brother Vincent inherited at the time of their father's death.

In keeping with Astor tradition, Vincent, as his father's main heir, had also been responsible for running the family business. One year older than his father's widow, Vincent dropped out of Harvard and immediately took charge of the family's real estate holdings. In the early years of his tenure he took pleasure in acquiring and then adding to the value of some lots in Manhattan residential areas, with the construction of several handsome, well-designed buildings—including a great luxury apartment building at 120 East End Avenue, where he eventually made his home. At the same time he began divesting the family's portfolio of certain properties that no longer seemed viable, including the lot upon which Caroline Astor had built her great marble mansion, selling the front portion, facing Fifth Avenue, to the congregation of Temple Emanu-el for the construction of a great limestone synagogue. On a more ambitious scale, during the Depression, working in conjunction with Mayor Fiorello La Guardia's Tenement House Commission, Vincent sold most of his holdings on the Lower East Side for the bargain price of $189,000. This made it possible for the tenements to be razed and replaced with the city's first public housing.

If he was by no means a brilliant businessman, Vincent—at least during his early years—was a fairly enlightened one. At the same time, he managed to steer clear of potential disasters, while making relatively few unsound investments. By the Second World War, however, he seemed to have lost interest in further developing his existing properties. The assets he inherited at his father's death he managed competently, if not brilliantly. He survived the Depression relatively unscathed and then profited from the postwar boom, so that by the time Brooke Marshall met him he had increased the family's assets almost twofold.

From his father Vincent had inherited the St. Regis Hotel, built not long after the Astoria but free of all ties to the English Astors. He had also inherited Ferncliff, a vast property on the Hudson River just south of Rhinebeck, where his grandmother and grandfather had built an imposing marble mansion, to which his mother had added a "play house" designed by Stanford White. This play house boasted a gigantic reception room, a fully equipped kitchen, and a series of guest rooms, as well as an indoor tennis court and an enormous indoor swimming pool. Toward the end of his life, his father had begun acquiring neighboring properties, adding to Ferncliff's already large acreage and also adding land to a model dairy farm he had established. Vincent, who shared his father's enthusiasm for machinery as well as for farming, not only took an interest in improving Ferncliff's herd, but also in improving its barns and outbuildings, while treating himself to the pleasure of constructing a narrow-gauge railroad to traverse some scenic portions of this 3,500-acre property.

Vincent would always be fond of Ferncliff but his greatest passion—seemingly unaffected by his father's fate—was for sailing. During the First World War he had held the rank of lieutenant in the navy, at one point boarding and steering safely to port a captured German submarine whose sabotaged air supply permanently damaged his lungs. His first yacht, which was put to service against the Germans, was replaced in 1926 by the *Nourmahal*, more a liner than a yacht, which carried a crew of forty-two. On the *Nourmahal* Vincent made long voyages collecting sea creatures for the New York Zoological Society; he gave what were said to be wild parties; and he also entertained more sedately, cruising with his distant cousin and Hudson Valley neighbor Franklin Roosevelt, both before and after Roosevelt was elected president.

Although there was never an actual falling-out, Franklin ceased to be a guest on the *Nourmahal* after 1935, when he instituted tax reforms said to be designed to "soak the rich." Not long before this, Raymond Moley, one of Franklin's advisers, joined with Vincent to start a weekly newsmagazine, something along the lines of Henry Luce's *Time*, but more liberal in its views—a magazine that was eventually merged with another to become *Newsweek*. Along with the St. Regis—which he had sold off just before the stock market crash and then bought back in 1935 at a foreclosure sale—*Newsweek* was an Astor property that Vincent took a special interest in.

Although Vincent was too old to serve in the Second World War—and also, given the injury to his lungs on that German submarine, not an ideal candidate for active service—he did not let his differences with his cousin Franklin keep him from doing his part to help his country. Like Brooke Marshall, Vincent was an unabashed and firmly committed patriot. Once again he contributed a yacht to the war effort, selling the *Nourmahal* to the navy and parting with it forever. Before the United States entered the war and then after Pearl Harbor, he initiated and took part in secret meetings involving administration officials and covert agents who would help form the Office of Strategic Services, the forerunner of the CIA, in 1942. Not least of his contributions to America's counterespionage efforts was to offer the use of one floor of the St. Regis as a safe house. He also served as commodore of convoy, standing watch at night and commanding a ship load of men. For his contributions he received the rank of navy captain, a title comparable to John Jacob Astor IV's army colonel and one that he used proudly.

Unlike most of his forebears—and certainly unlike his father, who had left a tiny portion of his vast estate to charity—Vincent had a philanthropic bent. In 1948, he established the Vincent Astor Foundation, which had as its stated goal "the alleviation of human misery." As the Foundation's president, he immediately set about achieving this goal by making respectable annual contributions to such well-established charitable institutions as New York Hospital and the American Red Cross, as well as to an institution that he had helped found, the Astor Home for Children in Rhinebeck. Vincent's foundation at this point was primarily a funnel for his own charitable giving. On the board Vincent placed friends and business associates, his wife, and even his doctor, Connie Guion. For all that he took an interest in the Foundation's work, Vincent left its management in the hands of a paid director. Since the Foundation's work was limited, this director did not need to serve full-time, with the result that here Astor business and Astor philanthropy soon became intertwined. The first director was Charles Bomer. Serving as director from 1952 to 1958 was Hoyt Ammidon, who, like Bomer, also managed the Astor family holdings.

While Vincent did well enough in business, his success with

women had been mixed at best. As a child he had been awkward and ungainly, stumbling over his own extra-large feet. His mother, Ava— apparently liking him no better than she liked his father—was said to have had his nurse remove him from her drawing room because he was too ugly to spend time with her guests. She was also said to have locked him away in her dressing room and left him there for hours, having forgotten all about him. His grandmother, Caroline, however, appears to have taken pity on him. It is said that in delivering a lecture on how you can always tell a gentlemen by his feet, she caught a clearly miserable Vincent gazing down at his own oversized feet and immediately corrected herself, saying she meant *shoes*. A gentleman's shoes must be well polished.

In 1914, two years after his father's death, Vincent had married Helen Huntington, the taller, older, and plainer but infinitely more energetic sister of Buddie Marshall's first wife, Alice. Helen was long known to Vincent as the daughter of a Hudson Valley neighbor. In later years she would be known for her patrician good looks and for her love of music, which took the form of unstinting devotion to the interests and maintenance of the New York Philharmonic. But always she was selfless and kind and that rather boring word "gracious." If Vincent's marriage to Helen was not a great love match, it was a suitable match—one that on more fundamental levels also made sense, if only because she was everything Vincent's exciting and glamorous and utterly heartless mother had never been.

During the First World War, when Vincent enlisted in the navy, Helen went on to serve in the YMCA Canteen Service and was stationed in Bordeaux. She, like Vincent, had a special fondness for the Hudson Valley. Her interest in various charitable organizations may have had some influence on his later philanthropy, but generally the two of them went their separate ways. From the start, aside from the similarity of their histories, they'd had few common enthusiasms. If they'd had children, things might have been different. As it was, for months at a time Vincent would be off at sea on the *Nourmahal*—collecting marine specimens, like giant tortoises, in the Gálapagos for the New York Zoological Society, or merely enjoying a pleasure cruise in the company of close friends like William Rhinelander Stewart, or casual friends like Franklin Roosevelt, or special friends like Minnie Cushing. A second port for the *Nourmahal* was now Bermuda, where he had purchased another home. Frequently he could be found spending time there, also in the company of Minnie Cushing—a fact that the newspapers were not above pointing out.

Vincent's marriage to Helen Huntington, which after sixteen years remained childless, ended amicably in September 1940. Vincent had told Helen he wanted very much to marry this athletic younger woman who shared his love of maritime adventure. In a matter of days Helen, always prompt and efficient, had secured a divorce for "irreconcilable differences" in Wyoming, freeing Vincent to marry Minnie. In fairly short order she would go on to marry Lytle Hull, whose surname she would immediately assume, spending the next three decades as Helen Hull.

If Vincent's marriage to Helen Huntington had looked to be sensible, his second marriage to Minnie gave every indication of being a love match—at least to the not altogether discerning eyes of gossip columnists and reporters. But the newspapers were inclined to take an active interest in Minnie Cushing's romantic life in any case. The eldest daughter of the Boston surgeon Harvey Cushing, Minnie was one of three celebrated sisters who all had a knack for attracting highly eligible men. The middle sister, Betsy, would first marry one of FDR's sons and then go on to marry Jock Whitney; Babe, the youngest and most stylish, would eventually become Mrs. William Paley. Of the three sisters Minnie was the least good looking. She was skinny and gawky and, some said, bore a certain resemblance to a flamingo. But she was lively, witty, and *fun*.

It is one thing to be a difficult man's girlfriend. Quite another to be his wife. Minnie—who didn't have either her predecessor's stamina or nature—found that living with Vincent was harder than she'd anticipated. By 1946 she and Vincent would sometimes return by plane from Bermuda and part on the tarmac, heading in opposite directions, a fact not lost on gossip columnists.

During the war, though, when Minnie and Vincent Astor were newly married and often together, Vincent's niece Romana began to spend time with the two of them. Romana had been sent to New York from London, with her half sister and half brother, to escape the bombing. Vincent was fond of all four of Alice's children—even when he could not bring himself to forgive Alice for divorcing her first husband, Serge Obolensky, the father of the two oldest, Sylvia and Ivan. For the moment Ivan had been sent off to Vincent's old school, St. George's. Now Vincent tried to do right by the two girls, who were camping out during the week in a Manhattan hotel suite with only a governess to look after them while they attended school at Brearley. When he was at Ferncliff, Vincent had them for weekends and holidays.

Vincent liked children and he wanted them to like him. There was one time, however, when Romana was staying with Vincent and Minnie at a Los Angeles hotel after the war that she got a hint of what happened when you became someone Vincent didn't like. By then she was thirteen. "I put my foot in it," she recalled. "The concierge telephoned up and said, 'May I speak to Captain Astor.' He said Astor in a funny way. Like Ass-tor. I said to Uncle Vincent, 'Somebody wants to speak to Captain Ass-tor.' Uncle Vincent was furious. He thought I was making fun of him. I can't remember what he said, but he let me know I'd really got it wrong and he sent me to my room. I was in tears. Later, when he'd gone down to the pool, Minnie came in and told me what to do. She was absolutely wonderful. She said, 'Listen, darling, I know you didn't mean it, but when this kind of thing happens in life, the best thing to do is apologize.'"

In Minnie's life there may have been one apology too many. By

1953, it was no secret that Minnie wanted out of the marriage. Word had it that she was more than fond of the French actress Annabella. But rumors of this sort seemed to swirl around Vincent. In the early days of her marriage to Vincent, there had been talk of Helen Hull's friendship with a gallery owner named Betty Parsons. Then, there was the whole question of why there had never been children with either wife. It was believed that Vincent had contracted mumps at the time of his first wedding. Toward the end of her life, Helen Hull, chatting with Winthrop Aldrich, a younger Astor cousin now master of Rokeby, would say, "When there are no children, it's not *always* the wife's fault, you know." What she meant by that he wasn't quite sure. John Richardson would later say that during much of his marriage to Helen Hull, Vincent had a mistress, a real old-time WASP, who was tough and attractive and who predicted that the marriage to Minnie would never work because Minnie's wrists weren't strong enough. "Word had it that Vincent liked to have long nails raked down his back when he was having sex," Richardson would recall. "He was into S and M. A masochist. Of course what you get with this is that Vincent was also a sadist."

In marrying Vincent Astor, Brooke Marshall was marrying the heir to a great American fortune whose life had been brushed by tragedy. But she was also taking on a difficult and sometimes foul-tempered man who was set in his ways and not above using his money to get what he wanted. In short, Vincent Astor was no bargain. "Had Vincent been born Vincent Smith, nobody would have given him the time of day," Louis Auchincloss would later say. "Well, perhaps he would have developed qualities. As it was, Vincent tried to burn down the school when he was at St. George's, by setting a fire under his bed. It was a school legend." Thomas Hoving, too, did not mince words: "Vincent was a real shit. My father told me that at one of the clubs he belonged to Vincent had a special sitting all to himself. He was forced to dine at noon instead of one, because no one would dine with him."

In *Footprints*, and in interviews, Brooke Astor acknowledged that Vincent was not easy but she put a fine gloss on a marriage that had raised eyebrows as well as certain pointed questions. Always she was careful to say that she had turned Vincent down flat the first time he made his offer at Ferncliff. Just as she took care to point out that the Stanford White play house that Vincent and Minnie had turned into a full-fledged country home—having torn down the marble mansion during the war—was awkward and unattractive and not at all the sort of place where she herself would choose to live.

She told of having had very real cause for hesitation in the face of Vincent's proposal and Vincent's persistence; his agreeing to take a long trip to the Orient, to give her time to reach a decision, while bombarding her with those love letters; her finally relenting upon Vincent's return and their slipping away to Maine for a quiet wedding; their belated honeymoon in Europe, when at the Ritz Hotel she poisoned an already ailing Vincent by inadvertently administering a spoonful of tincture of benzoin meant to be used to soak cotton balls for his vaporizer; and their misbegotten cruise on a yacht rented from a friend of Vincent, which nearly resulted in her drowning and definitely resulted in Vincent's being depressed and disappointed by being confined to a vessel nothing like as grand as what he was accustomed to when he owned the *Nourmahal*.

In *Footprints* she had her chance to present her own version of what happened and have it stand for the truth. A much younger Society novelist has been known to tell of how her mother, reading this book on her deathbed, hurled it across the room and cried out, "It's all a tissue of lies." Deliberate lies? Perhaps. It seems more likely, though, that when the author diverges from the truth it is for her own comfort as much as it is from any concerted effort to deceive her readers. Lies can stem from the same impulse as stories we tell ourselves time and again until they have some of the cozy feel of those bedtime stories that put us to sleep. And of course sleep had never come easily to Brooke Astor. Not from the time she was a small child.

What *Footprints* does not go into at any length, but merely refers to obliquely, is the very real upset her marriage to Vincent caused in her late husband's family. "There was Brooke the grieving widow and then in no time at all she was going around with Vincent," Anna Glen Vietor would later recall. Buddie's sister, Evie, never forgave her. Elly Elliott, whose mother-in law had been close to both women, remembered how Evie put her mother-in-law on notice, telling her she would *never* come to dinner with Brooke: "You didn't cross Evie. Word went out to all of Evie's friends."

Even those members of the Marshall family who found Evie's response excessive felt Brooke should have waited at least a year before remarrying. There was some sense, however, that there was more to Evie's response than outrage at Brooke's undue haste. "Evie was going around saying, 'Poor little Brooke, what will poor little Brooke do,'" recalled Anna Glen Vietor. " It was a great shock to have poor little Brooke come up with Vincent Astor. Evie had money, but nothing like that."

For twenty years Brooke had been "the little sister of the rich." Now, in a matter of months, she had seen to it that she was richer than all of them. But that was not the way Brooke Astor saw it. In *Footprints* she writes of how she was left almost destitute by Buddie's death. Certainly she would be living on a fixed income, in relatively straightened circumstances. And until the estate was settled, money would be tight. Buddie's daughter, Peggy, would later say that there may have been a shortage of money, considering that her father was supporting two households, but she had not been aware of it: "If he had financial problems, he never let it show around our family."

And if there *had* been financial problems, Buddie's sister, Evie, believed she knew who was at fault. "After Brooke married Vincent, Evie made a great many caustic comments about how Brooke had gone through Buddie's money as fast as she could," said Anna Glen Vietor. "Renting that ridiculous Castello in Italy. Buying a much too expensive apartment on Gracie Square. Entertaining all those people who had no money."

The feeling among the Marshalls was that Brooke was exaggerating her financial predicament to justify marrying Vincent before the year was out. Louis Auchincloss would agree that she may have been exaggerating a little, but he also believed that there was a very real financial emergency: "I know there was one. I can remember around that time I was having lunch with Brooke and a friend of hers at the Colony Club and Brooke was laughing all the way through lunch. She was in high spirits, to say the least. The next day she announced she was marrying Vincent. She was tremendously relieved."

In *Footprints* Brooke Astor's response is more measured. She suggests to the reader that in agreeing to marry Vincent she was taking upon herself the task of making him happy, while doing her best to undue the damage caused by his mother's early mockery and neglect. In later years Brooke Astor would occasionally bring out a sheaf of love letters from Vincent and show them to friends like the editors Robert Giroux and Robert Silvers and ask if they thought these letters were worth bringing out in book form. This was a step no right-minded friend ever encouraged, although her fondness for the letters no doubt inspired the beautifully produced folio presented to Brooke and her guests at the celebration of her hundredth birthday. The feeling among both editors and less professional readers was that the letters were nothing special. Why, then, would Brooke Astor, a woman who knew good writing when she saw it, so value them?

First, she valued the letters because they showed that she hadn't been so desperate to get her hands on Vincent's money that she had jumped at his first offer. Second, she valued them because they reminded her that she had been touched by Vincent's feeling for her and hadn't merely married him for convenience—something even some of her most loyal friends at the time would always doubt. "Of course she married Vincent for the money," Louis Auchincloss would say. "I wouldn't respect her if she hadn't. Only a twisted person would have married him for love."

And, finally, she valued them because they showed that Vincent was really smitten with her—something she wished very much to believe, if for no other reason than it was common knowledge that at the time of the marriage there had been at least one other, more glamorous and altogether more eligible, candidate for the position of Mrs. Vincent Astor—Janet Rhinelander Stewart, the widow of Vincent's best friend and sailing companion, who was as beautiful as any movie star and had also received a marriage proposal from Vincent. Possibly the proposal had come the previous Christmas, when she was staying with her children up at Ferncliff. Possibly it came that Memorial Day, when Horace Kelland, one of the guests at the play house that weekend, would recall that Minnie had collected three possibilities for Vincent, including a third lady by the name of Andrea Cowdin. The weekend was never awkward. No harm was intended. And none of the ladies knew what Minnie was up to. One thing is certain: Janet Rhinelander Stewart was Vincent's first choice and she turned him down flat. The newspapers of the time were aware that she was in the running, if not of the fact that she chose to withdraw from the race. In the *New York Daily Mirror*, her photograph appeared with one of Brooke Marshall in an article that ran immediately after Minnie obtained her divorce. While the article indicated that Brooke Marshall was now considered the favorite, the photographs would seem to preclude any serious competition on the basis of looks.

Among the many reasons Janet Rhinelander Stewart had turned down Vincent Astor's offer of marriage was the fact that she had sufficient money of her own. Her daughter, Serena, would later have mixed feelings about this decision. Serena had spent many happy hours in the giant indoor pool at Ferncliff that Christmas and as a child had found "Uncle Vincent" a rather remote but perfectly congenial figure. To have all that money in the family might have been nice. But of course she would not have had to marry Vincent herself.

As an adult, Serena became aware that for many years an amusing tale had circulated in certain circles detailing exactly what had transpired when Vincent popped the question. The tale unfolded something like this: Vincent, when trying to persuade Janet Rhinelander Stewart to agree to marry him, finally informed her that his doctors had told him that he had only three years to live. Her mother's response was the stuff of legend: "But, Vincent, what if the doctors are wrong?"

As it turned out, the doctors *were* wrong. Vincent would go on to live at least another five years—drinking heavily and smoking, with his doctor's permission, while battling chronic emphysema and heart disease. In *Footprints* Brooke would question the judgment of Vincent's doctor. To be fair to Connie Guion, even though her recommendations may now seem cavalier, at the time it was a commonly held belief that the damage done by smoking was irreparable and a seriously compromised patient might as well be permitted his few pleasures. However, it's also worth noting that Connie Guion was one of the doctors who had prescribed heavy doses of narcotics for an ailing and soon seriously addicted Edna St. Vincent Millay.

In the end, Vincent Astor had apparently offered Brooke Marshall the same terms he offered Janet Rhinelander Stewart—a prenuptial agreement guaranteeing her $1 million outright and $5 million if the marriage survived more than one year—along with the spoken (unwritten) promise that one day she would have a chance to run the Vincent Astor Foundation. Serena Stewart would later say, with a laugh, that it was just as well that Brooke Astor had charge of the Foundation, since if her mother had been left the Foundation to manage, she would have probably given all the money to several ballet companies and the Black Panthers.

Brooke Marshall's third wedding was even quieter and more private than her second. Only Tony was invited to attend the ceremony. At the best of times Vincent was skittish with the press. But he certainly didn't want any kind of publicity for this particular wedding. All the attention devoted to Minnie's divorce had been more than enough for him. The preparations for the simple ceremony planned for the Pulitzers' home in Bar Harbor were not only secret but fraught—giving Vincent's bride some indication of the man she was marrying, although it was a young associate working with Roland Redmond, Vincent's lawyer at Carter, Ledyard, and Milburn, who bore the brunt of the work. It fell to him to arrange for top secret Wassermann tests for syphilis with two different New York Hospital doctors; to send the results up to Maine by special plane; to book a ticket for the bride on a commercial airline while Vincent went up in his own private plane; to see to it that no banns were posted; and to make sure that the Presbyterian minister in Bar Harbor was taking necessary precautions so that the press would not get the wind up. Then, when a drunk Joe Pulitzer—who had never liked Vincent Astor much in the first place—called the night before the happy couple was due to arrive and said things on the phone that Vincent declared to be "unforgivable," it fell to this associate to research the rules for filing for marriage in four nearby states for a last-minute change of venue. Whether it was Brooke or Joe Pulitzer's wife who talked a newly sober Joe Pulitzer around the next morning there's no knowing, but, like many another person in Vincent's life, Pulitzer called him and apologized.

That winter, there was a big dinner dance for 175 guests on the St. Regis Roof, the lovely ballroom atop the one piece of real estate Vincent owned that he took a special interest in. To that official celebration of her marriage Brooke Astor wore a beautiful Balmain gown she'd had made in Paris, having first seen to it that her old friend

Cecil Beaton made both formal and candid photographs of her wearing this glorious green ball gown before she and Vincent stepped forth from their apartment. After that, according to Brooke Astor, they never again gave a big party and went out about six times.

While this may have been a slight exaggeration, it wasn't far off the mark. There was nothing like the varied and relaxed but always full social life she had enjoyed with Buddie Marshall. Vincent went to the office every day. But when night came, Vincent was a virtual recluse, wanting nothing more than to enjoy his dinner and relax by the fire. At this point he was drinking heavily. And he also didn't feel well. "Vincent was very strange," recalled Anna Glen Vietor. "He may have been ill at the end, but he was also a terrific hypochondriac. He always had a thermometer in his mouth. And he had all those gloomy houses. Marrying Vincent, Brooke didn't get what she'd bargained on. She didn't get any fun."

Evie Clarkson, who had known Brooke as Mrs. Buddie Marshall in the Berkshires, was now married to Vincent's cousin Winthrop Emmet. She agreed that despite all the money it seemed a bad bargain: "One time I remember they came to a dinner at our place in the city. They walked in the door, but as I was greeting them, Vincent heard a lot of voices in the drawing room and told Brooke he wouldn't go in. 'Not with all those people.' He wouldn't look me in the eye and he was not in the least apologetic." Although Brooke finally managed to persuade Vincent to go in, his brief appearance at the party was not a success. Vincent did better when it was just the two couples at dinner at the Astors' apartment but things were never easy: "It was a strain. He didn't like people and he was selfish and charmless. But sometimes Brooke could joke him out of a bad mood. She could cajole him."

She did manage to cajole him into giving a dinner dance at their apartment for Louis Auchincloss and his new wife, Adele. "She wouldn't give up on it," Auchincloss would recall. And she did know how to handle him—better than Minnie ever had, according to

Romana McEwen: "If Vincent got grumpy or cross or gruff, Brooke had this brilliant tactic where she would roar with laughter. She would laugh and laugh and suddenly it was as if Vincent had been playing a role—playing the part of someone being the cross one in a Punch-and-Judy show. So it became a performance. And instead of being seriously angry, Vincent would play up to her and Brooke would shriek with laughter. She would defuse the real anger and make it all funny. I'm not sure Brooke didn't say to me at one point, 'The only thing to do is laugh.'"

The very thing that had gotten her into the marriage ensured that she would try to stick it out. Or so it seemed to Tom Hoving: "She had married Vincent for the name and the money, but it took some dedication." When asked how the marriage could have lasted as long as it did, Evie Clarkson would reply, without missing a beat, "Well, the money, my dear." This was the general consensus, even though Brooke would tell Evie Clarkson, just as she would tell readers of *Footprints*, that what kept her in the marriage was "something sort of sweet and defenseless about Vincent."

"You do become fond of someone you're doing something for," Louis Auchincloss would observe, while giving her credit for doing her best with a marriage that wasn't quite what she'd bargained on. "She was a sport about it. Jackie didn't take Ari on. Brooke took Vincent on and made him happy as a clam."

If her social life was not what it had once been, she was not exactly living the life of a recluse. Vincent enlisted her to oversee the redecorating of certain suites at the St. Regis and put her on the board of his foundation. She also joined the boards of the Bronx Zoo and the New York Public Library, but with Minnie Cushing on the board of the Metropolitan Museum of Art and Vincent's first wife, Helen, a key member of the board of the Philharmonic, two prestigious institutions were ruled out for her.

Having learned long ago to make the best of a bad bargain, she did her best to make their life at home as congenial as possible. Among other things, she engineered a rapprochement with Alice, Vincent's estranged sister, who had moved back to America from England, having divorced her third husband. At the same time, Brooke was careful to stay on the good side of Vincent's mother, Lady Ribblesdale, who also had returned to America. For Romana and her younger half sister, Emily, who had been born toward the end of the war, their grandmother would forever be a frightening figure, asking sharp questions, always wearing black, terribly old, and terribly hard to talk to. But for Brooke she would rise to the occasion and be the witty and amusing Edwardian lady Brooke believed her to be.

Only many years later, when she was well into her nineties, did Brooke Astor begin to let some of the strain of those years, or any flashes of resentment, show—saying, for instance, that Vincent's idea of a perfect evening was to dine at home, just the two of them, and then have her play the piano for him and sing. She also let it be known that Vincent wouldn't let her make or take phone calls when he was around. Of course, given her previous marital history, one might come to think of this precaution as not unreasonable.

Early on Brooke had taken Vincent up to see the house in Tyringham, which Vincent had briefly considered keeping and turning into a hunting lodge—until Gilly Palmer, Tony's boyhood friend, let him know that the village of Tyringham wasn't quite ready for a hunting lodge. Instead, they added a tennis court and sold the place to a man in the shoe business. Rhinebeck was too hot in the summer. Indeed, until Brooke protested, the play house at Ferncliff had no screens to keep out the flies. Vincent's house in Phoenix was fine in winter but was never going to be one of Brooke's favorite places. The long summer wedding trip to Europe had been a disaster. Rather than risk another trip like that, it was decided to get a summer house on the coast of Maine, an area she had first gotten to know back when she was Mrs. Dryden Kuser, which she had come to love over the years. One of Vincent's most lasting gifts to Brooke was the house they found during their search for the perfect summer place—a white frame house situated near the water at Northeast Harbor, with views of the water but no access to it, comfortable but not grand, and a little closer to town than was fashionable. The gift was something she had expressed a strong wish for, but Vincent didn't appear to give it much time or thought—having found this house said to be suitable, he sent her upstairs to check it out and purchased it on the spot. "Brooke said they saw the house and Vincent walked right in, sat down, and announced, 'This is the house we're going to buy,'" recalled Nancy Pierrepont, the wife of Jack Pierrepont, who had put his childhood "temper fits" behind him and was becoming one of Brooke's favorite younger friends. "Vincent simply didn't want to look any further. As it happens, it's a very nice house." It *was* a nice house, and she would make it even nicer, but Vincent's offer was pretty much "take it or leave it," Brooke Astor would recall in her old age.

As with much that came her way during those years, Brooke took the house and made the best of it. Summers she and Vincent spent in Maine at the house she called Cove End, where Vincent kept a motorboat. The way it worked out was Vincent loved the boating and she loved Maine. His niece Emily Harding would have happy memories of being on the big motorboat with Vincent and his young captain. Ordinarily she wasn't at ease with her uncle. "He was just very big and he barked. One of those people who think they're making jokes with a child and the child is terrified. He tried. He made little jokes. But going out on the powerboat with Uncle Vincent was fun."

With people he cared about, Vincent did make an effort. And evidently he cared about the Jack Pierreponts, recognizing that these younger friends of Brooke were dear to her, particularly Jack. Of Vincent, Nancy Pierrepont would have only happy memories—many of them from Maine. "My daughter used to row Vincent out to his boat when she was little," she would recall. "He would ask her, I assume, because he thought it would be nice for her. I liked Vincent. He made me laugh so. He was terribly funny. That's one of the things Brooke adored about him. I think they had a very happy life there in Maine—and of course in other places, too."

It was in Northeast Harbor that Emily Harding saw the lighter side of her Uncle Vincent: "He spoke of the ghost in the chimney. 'Chilly Willy,' he called him. It was a great joke. If you respected his foibles, he could be funny, but he definitely needed to be managed. Brooke was always bridging the gap. Making his bark into a joke."

Brooke could joke Vincent into most things, but she could never get him to change his mind about Tony. In *Footprints* she credits it to "jealousy" and says Vincent was also jealous of all her friendships from the Buddie Marshall years, perhaps hoping to take the sting out of it. This was a bad time in Tony's life, she writes, which didn't help matters. But while Vincent had no use for Tony, he adored Tony's twin sons, Philip and Alec, who had been born the same year he married their grandmother. He and Brooke would often have the boys stay with them. Vincent carted the twins around in a dog basket when they were infants and then, when they were older, played games with them and took them out on his boat. "He said that he thought we should adopt them as we 'had more sense than their parents,'" she wrote, adding that of course she never mentioned a word of this to the parents. Years later, Alice Perdue, Tony's longtime office manager, would say that Tony hated Vincent. One can see the feeling was mutual. What Tony did to set Vincent off it's hard to know. But it was typical of Vincent not to hold it against the children. And it was typical of Vincent at this point in his life to wish to adopt them.

Married to Vincent Astor, Brooke had a life that was punctuated by the regular change of seasons, as she and her husband moved from house to house, keeping New York City always as their base. Winters were spent at the modern house Vincent had in Phoenix, because he believed the climate was good for his pulmonary problems. Of all the places they spent time, this was her least favorite, although it got better once she managed to make friends of her own there. It was in Phoenix that she finally got to know Clare Booth Luce, who knew what it was to be married to a difficult man but who was, of course, not all that easy herself. Still, she was bright and interesting. And here she first met a young Nancy Reagan, daughter of her friends the Davises, who would remember Brooke as being the same then as she was thirty years later when invited to stay at the White House—attractive, gay, fun to be with, and a great flirt.

Ferncliff was for spring and fall. It was never as marvelous for Brooke as it had been for her predecessors or as it remained for Vincent. There were the flies, of course. And there was the sound of the trains down by the river, which woke her at night. But it was more than that. "Brooke asked Helen Hull for lunch one time when we were visiting," Nancy Pierrepont would recall. "I knew Helen Hull slightly, but not well. It sort of stultified the luncheon. Helen would say things like, 'Oh, this chair used to be over here' or 'Wasn't that table there?' Brooke was very patient with her. All these people from the old days were still up there, although I don't think Minnie was."

The Hudson Valley families lived in one another's pockets. Vincent's early attachment to Franklin Roosevelt had stemmed from this bond rather than any great sympathy with his politics. With rare exceptions, they were not the most stimulating neighbors. They felt no need to be. But when Vincent's sister, Alice, was in residence, things became livelier and a good deal less insular. Suddenly you were seeing Aldous Huxley or Gore Vidal for lunch or the Sitwells. And of course there were Alice's children. Vincent had always been fond of Ivan. And the girls were a delight.

In 1956, with Alice's death, things began to go sour. There were rumors of foul play or suicide, prompting a visibly shaken Vincent to order an autopsy to refute these claims. From the start, the press had a field day. Somehow her two lawyers had lost their copy of Alice's signed will. Compounding the embarrassment was Lady Ribblesdale's suddenly insisting that Alice's children return the jewels she had long ago lent Alice. At the time of Alice's death, Romana was in England with her father. But Emily, who had been living in New York with her mother was suddenly stranded with no real place in the city to live while she finished her education.

It was decided that the best place for Emily was boarding school. After she narrowed her choices to two schools, Brooke volunteered to go with her to check them out. "First Foxcroft, because I was mad about riding," she would recall. "Then Garrison Forest, outside Baltimore. After Foxcroft, when we were back at the hotel, Brooke said something like 'It was a bit intimidating, don't you think?' She saw to it that there was no pressure. At Garrison Forest there were two eccentric ladies, with large Airedales and smelly cocker spaniels. I felt much better immediately. What you had was eccentric ladies surrounded by eccentric dogs. Brooke said, 'I think this is more up our alley, don't you?'"

Vincent, much taken with Alice's youngest daughter and terribly upset by Alice's death at the age of fifty-four, began talking about adopting Emily. She would be company for Brooke and for him. Emily thanked Vincent but refused the offer, saying that she thought it best to go on to join Romana, who had a place for her in England. Her half brother, Ivan, would later say that Emily's sisters were making sure Emily didn't inherit the Astor fortune. That's not the way Emily would remember it, however. "I wanted to stay with my sisters very much," she explained. "Uncle Vincent was nice but somewhat forbidding. I was terrified by the idea. Uncle Vincent was *very* scary. My mother appeared to be scared of him. I wanted Romana to be my guardian. Romana was seven years older and about to get married and she was absolutely wonderful to me."

Not only had Vincent lost the sister he had grown closer to than ever before, but he was about to lose the girls. Business worries were also beginning to press on Vincent. Two assets he was proud of—the St. Regis Hotel and *Newsweek* magazine—he had every intention of holding on to. But his advisers had urged him to diversify his investments, something he had already begun to do. Next they suggested that he take a plunge in the real estate market, by building an imposing office tower that would cover an entire city block, stretching from Fifty-third to Fifty-fourth Street between Park and Lexington avenues.

From the outset there had been problems. One holdout made it impossible for a long time to put together the parcel. Then, when the land was ready, the banks refused Vincent a mortgage. Money was tight, interest rates were high, and the banks weren't about to loan millions to someone who was putting up his first office building, even if his name was Astor. The newspapers took great pleasure in reporting this story and not one of the articles was flattering. This embarrassing real estate setback weighed on Vincent, affecting his health and making him even more irritable than usual.

His wife blamed Vincent's advisers, particularly Hoyt Ammidon—whom it was said she helped push out as both Vincent's business manager and his foundation's director. In 1958, Ammidon was replaced by a man named Allan Betts. The fact was, Betts also felt it was a good idea for Vincent to diversify his investments. And it was his feeling, as it was the feeling of most of the people involved, that all Vincent had to do was stick it out and he'd be fine.

Eventually, with the help of Francis Cardinal Spellman, the block was sold off to First National City Bank at a loss. Half a century later Peter Paine, an admirer of Hoyt Ammidon and, like Cardinal Spellman, a member of the Astor Foundation board, would say that if Vincent had only had the courage to hold on to that parcel he would have made millions. Peter Paine had the benefit of hindsight. But Vincent didn't have the stomach for such a battle. In any case, he may well have had intimations that he wouldn't be around to reap those profits or to savor a victory over all the forces that were out to thwart him. Given the way things were going, he would do better to put his affairs in order.

In the late spring of 1958, Vincent's mother, Lady Ribblesdale, died. That summer he was admitted to New York Hospital, with vascular problems in one leg. By then Connie Guion had told him he had to stop smoking. During his stay at the hospital, he made a new will. That in itself was not remarkable—making new wills was an activity that he had always found pleasurable.

By the fall Vincent was well enough to set forth on a rare trip to Europe, sailing on the *United States* to England, where he met Brooke, who had been attending the coronation of Pope John XXIII in the company of Cardinal Spellman. In England they visited Bill Astor at Cliveden, whose mother, Nancy, had never been one of Vincent's favorites. At Cliveden, Vincent caught a cold, which, upon their return to London, seemed to worsen with time and the lack of central heating. He was well enough, though, to commission the design for a necklace to be made by Bulgari from a parcel of beautiful unset emeralds. By the end of their stay he was still feeling quite ill. Nonetheless, by the end of their voyage home on the *United States*, he was urging the ship's captain to race the *Queen Elizabeth* into New York harbor. But as fall turned to winter, his health seemed to worsen. On the stairs of a theater in Poughkeepsie, on his way to a screening of *A Night to Remember*, a movie about the sinking of the *Titanic*, where he was hoping to see his father release his Airedale, Kitty, from the kennels, Vincent complained of severe chest pains and seemed to suffer a heart attack.

On February 3, 1959, on the eve of their departure for Phoenix, Vincent sent Brooke off to a dinner party on her own. She returned to find him in bed, having severe difficulty breathing. The medication his doctor, Connie Guion, had prescribed seemed to do him no good.

Brooke had learned to take great care with Vincent's medicines. On their honeymoon to Europe, when Vincent had the coughing fit in their room at the Ritz and she snatched up what she believed to be his cough syrup only to realize too late that she had administered a teaspoon of tincture of benzoin, it had necessitated an emergency call for the hotel physician, who saved the day by administering an emetic and massive infusions of warm milk. Rather than continue to dose Vincent or call an ambulance, she called Connie Guion, who rushed over to the apartment at once. She and Connie Guion—a woman she had never much cared for—were both at Vincent's side when he died.

Six

VINCENT'S LEGACIES,
1959–1968

My mother used to say that I was like a bird, and I would
never lose my balance.

To have two husbands die at home, suddenly and unexpectedly within
the space of six years, had to be shocking. For Brooke Astor, this
shock was compounded by the fact that Vincent Astor, like Buddie
Marshall, died before her eyes. This time, at least, she had her husband's doctor to keep her company. For that, if nothing else, she
would always be grateful to Connie Guion. Given that Vincent's
doctor was responsible for medical decisions she believed had contributed to Vincent's death, there was some justice in his doctor's
being there to witness the consequences. Because Brooke and Connie
Guion had never been particularly friendly, or even shown much
sympathy for each other's opinions, there was little likelihood of some
troublemaker's hinting at collusion or foul play. And from the start of
the marriage, there had been troublemakers in abundance.

Both Vincent Astor's death and his big funeral three days later
received extensive press coverage. After all, whatever you thought of
the man, he was a major national figure. While the details of his
funeral were of some interest to readers, the main focus of all this coverage was the estate Vincent Astor was leaving behind. The initial

estimate was $134 million, with half—an estimated $67 million—going to the Vincent Astor Foundation.* For the most part, reporters got the numbers right (or as right as the numbers could be without a final accounting). The major surprise in Vincent's will—one that the press made much of—was Vincent's making no provision whatsoever for his half brother, John Jacob Astor VI, better known to tabloid readers as "Jackie" or "Jack." In case Vincent's half brother failed to take notice of this oversight, the press made sure to point out that this seemed not only surprising but also unprecedented and unjust. Jackie, after all, was an Astor by blood.

By the terms of Vincent's will, his widow, Brooke Russell Astor, was virtually his sole heir. In addition to the $2 million he left his wife outright, he also left her Ferncliff, the apartment at 120 East End Avenue, the houses in Maine and Phoenix, and virtually all of his personal possessions. Unlike Buddie Marshall, Vincent did not leave a will subverted by a prior agreement. And, unlike Buddie, he did leave a long list of personal bequests: including $25,000 to go to his first wife, Helen Hull, and $100,000, to establish a trust fund for his niece Emily Harding. Among Vincent's charitable bequests were two of some interest: $200,000, the largest, went to New York Hospital, where Connie Guion had made a reputation as both physician and fund-raiser. And $50,000 went to St. George's, the school he was said to have tried to burn down.

For all that it went on for twenty pages, Vincent's will was not complicated. The remaining portion of his property was to be divided into two equal parts. One part would go directly to the Vincent Astor Foundation. The other would go to establish a trust, whose net interest was to be paid to his wife, Brooke Russell Astor, during her lifetime and whose principal his wife would have the power "to convey and deliver" upon her death "to such person or persons, including her

---

*Vincent Astor's $134 million estate is the equivalent of $900 million in today's dollars.

estate, and in such estates, interests and proportions, as my said wife shall by her will appoint." In short, he was giving her "power of appointment." But if she chose not to exercise this power, then the principal would go directly to the Vincent Astor Foundation.

Luke Lockwood, the lawyer for Vincent's business office, and Allan Betts, Vincent's business manager, were named the will's co-executors, entitled to receive no more than $300,000 each for their services. In effect they were wearing two hats, entrusted with seeing Vincent's business through this period of transition and putting his affairs in order, while seeing to it that the will's provisions were carried out according to Vincent's wishes. Indeed, nine pages of the will were devoted to all the tasks they were empowered to perform. Not until Vincent's holdings were sold off would his two executors be able to fix the estate's final value. Of these holdings, the St. Regis and *Newsweek* were the two most significant. Already, though, it was clear that Vincent's widow would be receiving a healthy annual income from her half of the estate. And of course the executors themselves would both benefit nicely.

Once again Brooke Astor had to don full mourning. Like Buddie Marshall, Vincent Astor was buried out of St. James, with Reverend Arthur Kinsolving presiding. This time there were four hundred people in attendance, including Vincent's two former wives. While most of his pallbearers were not quite as grief stricken as Buddie Marshall's had been, they were every bit as distinguished. More important to Vincent than the men selected to carry his coffin, however, was the coffin's final destination. Vincent had chosen to be buried not in the Astor family plot at the Rhinebeck Cemetery but at Ferncliff. Along with the mourners who gathered to see Vincent laid to rest was a naval honor guard comprising eight sailors in uniform who, at the close of the brief service, fired three volleys over his grave. A bugler played taps and then the small group of mourners went back to the play house. Vincent had chosen as his final resting place the site of the old mansion his grandparents had built, high on a bluff overlooking the Hudson, where the only break in the quiet was the occasional sound of a train, just below, slowing down or giving a short whistle as it approached a nearby bend in the river.

In later years, as well as in *Footprints*, Brooke would always describe the period immediately after Vincent's death as one of emotional and physical exhaustion. His dying at home was one source of distress. Given that for months she had also been coping with Vincent's volatile moods and worsening health, she had good reason to collapse. The trouble was, she could not afford to. As Vincent's wife, her position was too public. In addition, there was a real possibility that she might have to do battle for the sizable legacy Vincent had left her. From the beginning—even before the press put its oar in—there had always been the question of what action Vincent's younger brother, Jack, would take. Had Vincent left him a token amount of money, the estate would have been on safer ground.

The fact was, Vincent left his brother nothing as a matter of principle. Whether this action was wise hadn't troubled him in the slightest. As far as he'd been concerned, from the time Jack came of age and into his inheritance he had given his brother sufficient opportunity to show he was a responsible if not a totally congenial Astor. Vincent had given Jack jobs in the Astor business office. He'd even left him money in earlier wills. What had finally convinced him that Jack was not worthy of being treated as an Astor was his behavior during the Second World War, when, as Vincent saw it, Jack had done everything possible to ensure that he would not have to serve his country. This when Vincent himself would have done anything to see active duty. To Vincent's way of thinking, Jack was no better than a draft dodger.

At the time of Vincent's death, Jack had run through three wives and countless girlfriends; he had also provided fodder for at least two generations of gossip columnists since first coming into his $5 million inheritance. He was now living in reduced circumstances in Miami.

His son from his first marriage was grown, but he had a daughter, Jackie, by his second wife to think of. He was not destitute by any means, but it was beginning to look as if there would not be all that much to leave her.

In March, Jack Astor's lawyers asked for a copy of Vincent's will so that a handwriting expert could examine it. They also brought in a typewriter expert—a man Alger Hiss had recently called on—to determine if one machine had been used throughout. Next, they asked for affidavits from all those present at the will's signing. Then, on June 26, when the tabloids began to suggest that it looked as if Jack Astor might not pursue this any further—and the will was about to make it out of probate—Jack Astor suddenly changed course. According to his daughter, Jackie, this decision was made on her behalf and her brother's. Not out of greed on his part or any such base motive. His two children had a right to share in Vincent's wealth, her father reasoned. If not immediately, then at his death. After all, they had Astor blood in their veins, while the same claim could hardly be made for Vincent's widow. Jack Astor, too, was acting on principle. Or so his daughter would always profess to believe.

Whatever the reason, Jack Astor hired a New York law firm no one had ever heard of and had his two lawyers subpoena all relevant documents and petition the court to have Vincent's will overturned. He also petitioned to have Vincent's two executors removed. Rumor had it that these lawyers were hired on a contingency basis. Because Vincent's legal residence was Ferncliff, a pretrial hearing was scheduled for the fall in Poughkeepsie, the Dutchess County seat. For this at least Vincent's widow had cause to be grateful. Here the Astors were regarded as local gentry. Here it would be easier to control the newspapers. And here they would be far from most New York City pressrooms and their toughest court reporters. In the meantime, the Poughkeepsie judge decided, after examining affidavits from various concerned parties, including Vincent's widow, it was fine to let the executors remain.

For years Vincent's personal legal business had been handled by Roland Redmond, a senior partner at Carter, Ledyard, and Milburn. Given that all Vincent's lawyers were from this firm—including Luke Lockwood, one of the will's co-executors—it made sense for Vincent's widow to look elsewhere for legal representation. At the highly regarded firm of Sullivan and Cromwell, she was directed to David Peck, a senior partner, who happened to be both an able litigator and a former judge, having recently retired from the bench of New York State Supreme Court.

In his motion to have Vincent's final will overturned, Jack Astor claimed that it was an established Astor custom to keep money in the family—which meant that he, not Vincent's widow, was the rightful heir and entitled to half the estate. He also claimed that in earlier wills he had been a beneficiary. Finally, he claimed that Vincent had not been of sound mind when he made his last will. Implicit in all this but rarely stated was that Vincent had treated his half brother shabbily. Certainly, had John Jacob IV lived, he would have given his younger son more than $5 million.

If Jack Astor could have Vincent's will thrown out, then he could claim that Vincent had died intestate—which would mean that half of Vincent's estate would go to his widow and half to any remaining siblings. By New York law, Jack was considered Vincent's full brother. Pretrial hearings began at the beginning of October. Although Jack Astor himself did not make an appearance in Poughkeepsie, his lawsuit was a source of endless fascination for the tabloids and a potential source of embarrassment for Vincent's widow—who found the lawsuit sufficiently threatening to feel it was necessary to show up for this first hearing. In *Footprints* she writes of how she came to trial buoyed by David Peck's words: "Never be afraid when you are speaking the truth. The truth will be recognized. You have nothing to fear from these people. Their lawyer has never met anyone like you."

Without question Jack's lawyer had never met a witness quite like

Brooke Astor. Having said she preferred to testify in a courtroom rather than in the privacy of the judge's chambers, she did her best to ensure that the press would see her as a helpless victim and Jack as someone deserving of no sympathy. For her appearances in Poughkeepsie she wore a loose-fitting black dress and an unbecoming hat with a thick veil attached. Even though it was almost nine months since her husband's death, she chose to arrive in the courtroom swathed in black.

But for all that she looked every bit the grieving widow, her actions were not exactly those of a woman too distraught to mount a carefully considered campaign. To represent her she not only hired an able trial lawyer but went to the expense of hiring a first-class public relations firm—which well ahead of time provided both the New York City and Poughkeepsie papers with copies of a printed brochure containing "Background Information for the Press." Once the hearings began, they made sure to hand any reporters hanging around the courtroom a daily press release keeping them up to speed.

Thanks to the efforts of this public relations firm, you could find Vincent's widow quoted in the papers as saying of Jack: "[Vincent] had nothing but contempt for him. He thought he was the most useless, worthless member of society, and he despised him because he was a slacker and draft evader. He also hated all the revolting and disgusting publicity that was constantly in the papers of Jack being married to two women at once." In fact, not one word of this had been uttered in the courtroom. What reporters were getting was a portion of her written affidavit of the previous summer. She was leaving nothing to chance. And when all else failed—when Vincent's lawyer queried her about Vincent's drinking at the time he was signing the will in the hospital—she broke down in tears, resulting in the headline "Widow Weeps over Drinking Query."

It soon began to look as if, once the case actually came to trial, a Poughkeepsie jury would inevitably decide in the widow's favor. Even without impugning Jack's character, she had two strong arguments on her side. First, in his previous wills Vincent had never left Jack more than $500,000; second, the last time Vincent had left Jack a penny had been in his will of 1939. What Vincent felt about Jack might be hearsay, but the wills and Jack's draft status could easily be checked by anyone with access to the documents. As for Jack's contention that Vincent had not been of sound mind when he made this last will, and had been coerced by his widow and his two executors, that was going to be very hard, if not impossible, to prove. Just in case, though, her lawyer had gotten Cardinal Spellman to say he had talked with Vincent the very day of the will's signing and Vincent had been fine. (Vincent was not a Catholic, but he believed that the Catholics understood how to run their charities, and so Spellman was a trustee of the Vincent Astor Foundation. And of course in a more worldly capacity, the cardinal had recently helped Vincent find a buyer for that worrisome Park Avenue property.)

Forever after, Brooke Astor would say that David Peck saved her. She would also say that she had defeated Jack Astor in court. But matters were not quite that simple. Jack Astor never showed up for these pretrial hearings. More to the point, there was never an actual trial. When his lawyers saw the way things were headed, they talked Jack into settling. According to Louis Auchincloss, who was working at the time as an associate at Sullivan and Cromwell, no one at the firm thought Brooke had ever been at serious risk. "Brooke was always saying 'Dave Peck saved my foundation.' A summer boarder in a law firm could have won the case," he would say.

Auchincloss believed that the suit had been brought in order to force Vincent's widow to buy Jack Astor off. As it turns out, that is exactly what David Peck and his associates did. They offered Vincent's brother a settlement of $250,000, half the amount that Vincent had long ago thought fit to leave him in trust. It was agreed that Vincent's estate would pay the taxes on the money, although Jack would be responsible for his legal fees. Because this payment was taken from the half of Vincent's estate reserved for the foundation rather than from Brooke's half, she could always say with perfect honesty that she had never given Jack Astor a cent.

What had most upset Vincent's widow during the hearings—at least if one is to trust the newspaper accounts—was the contention of Jack Astor's lawyer that Vincent was a senile alcoholic who had been drinking heavily during his stay at New York Hospital in June 1958, when his last will was drafted and signed. Vincent's mind was as sharp as ever, his widow contended, and she herself had not only brought the liquor to Vincent's room but mixed the cocktails and shared them with him.

Brooke Astor's impassioned and sometimes tearful defense of her late husband was carried by almost every New York and Poughkeepsie paper, sometimes with an accompanying photograph. What didn't make it into these papers was a rumor making the rounds that Vincent had been on the verge of divorcing his wife when he died. Vincent's friend and longtime lawyer Roland Redmond may have been the source of this story. Certainly it reached the ears of his wife, Lydia, and with the passage of time came to be regarded as accepted fact by Hudson Valley neighbors like Michael Iovenko and Winthrop Aldrich, the Rokeby Astor cousin. According to this rumor, Vincent had told his lawyer he was tired of the life he was having to lead and wanted him to draw up divorce papers. Vincent had taken his lawyer aside not long before he died, when the two of them were crossing the Atlantic on the same ship.

In life, timing is everything. Whatever transpired between Vincent Astor and his wife once he arrived in London, Vincent Astor apparently felt a need to present his wife with that gift of an emerald necklace—or, rather, as she later described it, to send for Mr. Bulgari from Rome and commission him to assemble the beautiful stones for such a necklace and then design it, along with a pair of matching earrings. Of course, for the moment all Vincent's wife had was the promise of an emerald necklace. When the two of them returned to New York, it would seem that there were no further conversations with any lawyer. And no divorce papers were drawn up. On land, as at sea, a change in course requires careful planning. And even straightforward planning calls for serious bouts of concentration. For months Vincent Astor had not seemed quite his old self. By the time he returned from England, he was not feeling at all well.

Later there would be rumors that it had been Brooke, not Vincent, who had been seriously thinking about divorce, having had her fill of the life *she* was having to lead. This seems somehow less likely. Without question, Vincent's death came at a point when life with him was becoming increasingly trying. On the other hand, Vincent's health was clearly worsening. If this rumor is indeed true, then here, too, timing was everything, and Vincent's unhappy wife was saved from sacrificing a great fortune when any action on her part was preempted by Vincent's heart attack. When she was in her nineties, Brooke Astor would confide to two younger friends, Susan Burden and Annette de la Renta, that the morning before Buddie Marshall died, when he joined her in bed, the two of them had made love. Whatever went on between the Vincent Astors in the bedroom, it is hard to imagine them ever "making love." Yes, Brooke was fond of him and sometimes felt sorry for him. But fond of him as she might be, some of her tears at his death must have been tears of relief.

Once the specter of a lengthy legal battle had been put to rest, Allan Betts and Luke Lockwood were free to get down to business. Without undue haste, but as quickly as was decently possible, Vincent's executors sold off the St. Regis and *Newsweek*, with Vincent's widow weighing in on the sale of the magazine—voting for Philip Graham, the publisher of *The Washington Post*.

Before many years had passed she herself had sold the house in Phoenix and then the East End Avenue apartment. Ferncliff, which she had never much cared for, she held on to longer—if only because it had been in the family for three generations and because Vincent was buried there. Also, it proved impossible to find anyone who liked the play house any better than she did. Finally, having found no buyer for the entire Ferncliff property, she sold off some of the parcels of land Vincent's father had acquired toward the end of his life and gave the land containing the play house, as well as a cluster of handsome stone barns and Vincent's grave site, to the Catholic Church.*

The grand East End Avenue establishment that had been Vincent's when she married him had been replaced with a terraced duplex apartment on Park Avenue, its main floor light and spacious and decorated with the help of Sister Parish and Albert Hadley so that it was comfortable as well as pleasing to the eye. Here any hint of formality was offset by fresh flowers and objects that were dear to her, as well as shelves crowded with the beautifully bound first editions she had inherited from Buddie. On the lower floor, there was ample space for offices and a separate apartment for her mother, whose eyes were failing and who had reached an age where she would do better not living on her own.

For weekends, once she had divested herself of the Ferncliff property, she bought a pretty rambling frame house in Briarcliff Manor, overlooking the Hudson, which she was able to make utterly her own. The house in Maine, which Vincent Astor had decided on in an instant, without so much as looking at it, was the one property from her marriage she had no wish to part with. But here, too, she was free to please herself—to landscape the grounds any way she wished and to make one corner of the property over into a giant cutting garden.

---

*When the Church later sold off the property, Vincent's widow had his coffin and headstone moved to Sleepy Hollow Cemetery, close by her new weekend home, where she planned to be buried beside him one day.

In his last will and testament, Vincent devoted ten pages to covering in some detail the tasks to be performed by the men he appointed as his co-executors. In this last will he had also devoted more than two pages to the trust that he was setting up for his wife. At the same time, he had devoted not quite ten lines to the Vincent Astor Foundation, "a New York corporation," which was to receive "[a]ll the rest, residue and remainder of my property and estate, real and personal, of whatever nature and wherever situated and whether acquired by me before or after the execution of this will." Nowhere did he mention who was to head the Vincent Astor Foundation once he was no longer there to serve as president. And nowhere did he suggest what effect, if any, this infusion of "all the rest, residue and remainder" of his assets should have on the Foundation's goals or its management.

Vincent Astor had established his foundation in 1948 with the proviso that it would contribute to "the alleviation of human misery"— fine-sounding words, to be sure, but ones that were open to interpretation. By leaving half his money to the Foundation, Vincent guaranteed that his estate would be spared a sizable inheritance tax. But no one who knew the man believed that this had been his sole, or even his major, concern. The Foundation would be his legacy, its board of directors charged with seeing to it that the income from its $67 million trust was used to promote goals in keeping with Vincent's original mandate. Because the way this was to be done was never explicitly stated on paper and because there was no hint of who might be best suited to take Vincent's place as president, this legacy was vexed. Two things were certain: First, with this enormous infusion of cash the Vincent Astor Foundation would cease to be a mere vehicle for consolidating a rich man's relatively modest charitable donations. Second, whoever controlled the Foundation would wield considerable power in the world.

At Vincent's death, Allan Betts, who was serving as the

Foundation's director, assumed that he would not only continue in this position but also take over as its president. This assumption was perhaps natural. So far as anyone could see, Vincent's widow had received scant preparation and manifested little appetite for this role. Immediately after her husband's death, she had been scrambling to fend off a lawsuit that threatened to be financially damaging and a source of public embarrassment. But, with the defeat of Jack Astor, she was free to turn her attention to the Foundation. As she told it, Vincent had assumed from the start that she would be replacing him as head of the Foundation. She quoted him as saying, "Pookie, you are going to have a hell of a lot of fun" running it. Unfortunately, although Vincent had made his wishes known to her, he never put these sentiments in writing.

In *Footprints* Brooke Astor writes that Vincent's oldest friend and former lawyer had reassured her on this point, saying that without question Vincent had expected her to take charge of the Foundation, telling her "[T]he will is drawn up so that you will have full control," and adding, "It is a great tribute to you." Well, perhaps. But it was going to take more than encouraging words for her to secure control of the organization she regarded as perhaps her husband's most important legacy.

In *Footprints* Brooke Astor does not name names but writes of how some men on the board—particularly one man who expected to be president—did their best to push her aside. She writes of how early on, she made it clear to these men that she had every intention of assuming her rightful place as the Foundation's head. And she writes of how the final showdown came at the Foundation's offices. She describes how she was seated behind Vincent's big partner's desk, when she let it be known that she was taking charge. "He was furious and never forgave me," she writes of the man who wanted this job. Unfortunately, the two of them were going to have to work together.

Charm can be misleading, especially in an attractive woman. At the start Vincent's widow may have looked like an easy mark.

Contributing to this impression was the state of her health. In *Footprints* she writes of how after successfully fighting off Jack Astor, she suffered a collapse, necessitating an extended stay at New York Hospital and leading her doctors to suspect that she might be suffering from a form of leukemia. Just the possibility of such a diagnosis was sufficient to get her to pack up her belongings, check out of the hospital, and head home.

To mollify her doctors she agreed to stay in the city and have her blood tested regularly—at least over the course of the next month. Soon, though, she was sufficiently recovered to reject any suggestion by the men in Vincent's business office that she leave everything to them and take herself off on a world cruise. While she had nothing against this idea in principle, she was not about to disappear for a year. Instead, she was soon asking friends to join her for a leisurely voyage down the coast of Yugoslavia and continuing to Monte Carlo. A cruise long enough to ensure that when she returned, tanned and rested, she would be ready to get down to business.

What the men who wanted to push her aside had apparently forgotten was that for many years Vincent's widow had held an impossibly demanding job at *House and Garden*—one that involved keeping a stable of high-strung writers, designers, and photographers on schedule, while keeping countless anxious and imperious celebrities and socialites happy. She knew how to get her way and she knew how to effectively wield power. But she was not about to burn bridges. At the same time, she was not about to let the Foundation, with its newly swollen coffers, meander along with a goal so amorphous, not to say ambiguous, as "the alleviation of human misery."

While the Foundation's new president still had much to learn, it didn't take her long to give her plans for the Foundation precise form. First off, she announced that since the original Astor fortune had been made in New York, the bulk of the Foundation's grants would henceforth be made within the city's five boroughs, always with the very specific goal of enhancing the lives of *all* its citizens. Second, she announced that, unlike the previous president, she would be taking an active part in the running of the Foundation. Here she was following the advice of John D. Rockefeller III, who had said to her, "The person who has control of the money should also be personally involved in the giving."

To her mind this shift in direction was only fitting. Just as it was only fitting that as president she take responsibility for putting this change into effect. Vincent, who had many business interests to tend to, had left the Foundation's day-to-day operation to its director. She had no such demands on her time. She was free not only to take an active part in the making of all substantive decisions but also to bring the Foundation's method of conducting business in line with her own personal style. As she set about this, she began taking John D. Rockefeller's advice one step further. One that played to her strengths.

It was Brooke Astor's deeply held conviction that no Foundation grant ought to be made without the director and the president actually visiting the organization in question. "We go and we see," she soon took to saying. "We never give to anything we don't see." All of this was to be accomplished without any increase in the Foundation's small staff, which at this point comprised the director's secretary and a full-time bookkeeper. And without any increase in its office space.

"God knows, she was full of hard common sense," Louis Auchincloss would say. Like her late husband, she was intent on getting good value for every penny that was spent. Of course she was coming at this from a very different direction. "[Brooke] had been a sharp observer with a front-row seat of the foibles and meannesses of the very rich," Louis Auchincloss would write, with an assurance that suggested some personal familiarity with this front-row perspective. "[N]othing trains the financial eye better than comparing one's own hard efforts with the incompetence of so many who are endowed with deeper pockets."

Brooke Russell Astor was a quick study, possessed of an excellent memory and a large reserve of practical experience, but, above all, she was good with people. Her position at *House and Garden* had owed much to the willingness of friends and acquaintances to open their homes for the first time to the magazine's writers and photographers. She knew how far to go. When to back off. How hard to press. Some of this was calculation. Some pure instinct. But she got on well with most people because her tendency was to regard them as being worth her attention.

This would serve her well in her work as president of the Foundation and would serve her well in her personal relations. With time the two aspects of her life would become increasingly entwined, so that it would be hard to see where one left off and the other began. Indeed, in turning for help to John D. Rockefeller III, she was establishing a precedent. With the Rockefellers she would early on begin to mix philanthropy with pleasure. Before long she would form close personal ties to Nelson and Laurance and eventually to their baby brother, David. Indeed Holly Hill, the new weekend home she bought in Briarcliff Manor, in 1964, would be conveniently situated only a short drive from the great Rockefeller estate at Pocantico Hills.

In the early years after Vincent's death, however, her work for the Foundation and her life as a rich widow remained, for the most part, separate. In *Footprints* she writes that when she returned from the cruise and was starting to turn the Foundation in a direction she found congenial, the design arrived for the emerald necklace Vincent had commissioned in London, along with a note from Vincent to Mr. Bulgari saying this was to be a birthday present. For a time, she writes, she was torn. To go ahead and order such an expensive necklace to be made up seemed a needless extravagance. In the end, on the advice of her banker, she concluded that if she liked the design, she should go ahead and order the necklace and accompanying earrings. "I felt that it was a sign of encouragement from Vincent," she writes. In some sense this necklace was Vincent's last legacy.

The necklace was terribly expensive and it was not anything she needed. But it did call to mind Vincent at his best, when he couldn't do enough for her. And that side of Vincent was not a figment of her imagination. "There is no question that Vincent loved Brooke," Louis Auchincloss would say. "I can remember his taking me aside and saying, 'The only thing I care about is being sure that my Brookie will be financially secure.' He was mad about her."

Brooke Astor's fondness for this extravagant necklace she went ahead and ordered was such that she once confided to her friend Mab Moltke that she planned to be buried in it. She was only half joking, Mab understood. But, then, she understood Brooke very well. The two women had become friends during Brooke's *House and Garden* years, when Mab was chief copywriter for *Vogue*. The friendship was based on many things—not least of them the fact that Mab could be trusted to keep a secret, her daughter Alexandra Isles later observed. Married to a Danish count and diplomat who had been a hero of the Resistance, Mab was short on money but long on style. She was also very smart. Even when Vincent had made it difficult to see old friends, Brooke had kept in touch. After Vincent's death, Brooke began to see more of Mab. Before long, she would have need of a trusted confidante.

Having enjoyed an active social life before her marriage to Vincent Astor, Brooke soon found herself once again in the thick of things—sought out for dinners and parties, if only for her new and much publicized wealth. As Mrs. Charles Marshall she had loved to entertain. Now she was free to celebrate the official opening of her new Park Avenue apartment, with a dinner dance for a visiting friend, Loelia, Duchess of Westminster, whom she had also gotten to know during her *House and Garden* days. Having married a rich man widely regarded as a monster, Loelia had ended up divorced and in possession of a tiny income.

"Brooke adored her," recalled John Richardson, who was first brought into Brooke's life, briefly but memorably, by Loelia. At the dinner dance there were a good many English guests and there was a three-piece band that played polkas and old-fashioned waltzes, and on a sash at her waist Brooke wore an enormous broach set with an emerald the size of a piece of soap. "Emeralds that size are never perfect, but they create an impression," Richardson would recall. "As we were dancing, there was a big bang. The thing had fallen to the floor. Everyone stopped. 'Oh, darlings,' Brooke said, 'It doesn't matter. We'll get it later—in the morning.'"

It was typical of her, at this point, to brush a fallen object aside rather than stop the music and have everyone scramble to find it. This cavalier attitude recalled the carefree abandon of the twenties, when she had first come to the city in search of a good time. It also reflected her natural inclination to value people over possessions. And when the emerald didn't turn up the following morning, there was always the insurance. But the fact was, she really loved to dance. In a 1938 profile by Cholly Knickerbocker in the *New York Journal American,* the interviewer noted that Mrs. Charles Marshall was taking dancing lessons with Arthur Murray. But while dancing lessons may have provided some diversion or improved her technique, she was a natural. Well into her nineties, still wearing high heels with her long dresses, she would be delighted to dance long into the night. And her partners, like Freddy Melhado, were only too happy to join her in this apparent folie à deux. "When I first knew her I was very young and she was almost sixty-five," Melhado would recall. "But she didn't seem like sixty-five. She was a beautiful dancer and I love to dance. And I remember having wonderful dances with her. When you dance with somebody, you know how they are from a physical point of view. *She was very strong.*"

After surviving three marriages Brooke Astor professed to have no wish for a fourth husband, but she was in need of escorts—preferably ones who could keep up with her as well as being free to accompany her. All of her husbands had been older than she was. Now many of the men in her life began to be younger. Not a few—although far from all—were homosexual, although she professed not to know this. Like most women of her generation, Brooke Astor saw what she wished to see. And, like them, she saw no reason to divulge exactly how old she was. Only her close friends had any reason to know that she was a grandmother. Her twin grandsons were rarely in evidence, if only because in the late fifties and early sixties her son, Tony, and his family were in Washington or Turkey, and then, not long after they returned to New York, Tony and their mother were divorced. After that, seeing the twins became more complicated, especially when their mother moved from the city.

Always Brooke Astor had looked younger than she was. Freddy Melhado was not the only young man she had fooled. Part of this was her natural vivacity. Part of this was the fact that, save for the period immediately after Vincent's death, she enjoyed what one might call "rude good health." From the time of her summers as a child in the Temple of One Hundred Courtyards in the Western Hills outside Peking, she had felt a special affinity with nature. And from the time of her first marriage she had taken pleasure in physical exercise. Now she quickly learned to conserve her strength by keeping to a schedule that kept her in the city only four days a week. Fridays she set off for long weekends at Holly Hill, with its indoor and outdoor pools for swimming, its extensive gardens and paths for long walks, and its quiet alcoves where one could escape with a book or a pencil and pad and begin to write.

But it was Maine that offered her a chance at a quiet private life. Maine could be said to be the one legacy she had received from Vincent when he was still alive. Only at his death, though, did Cove End become more than just another home she spent time in. Vincent had limited their stay in Maine to two months. But, once he was gone, she saw no reason to restrict herself in that fashion. During the summer, starting with a short visit for Memorial Day, she would retreat to Cove End, where she was now free not only to enlarge the gardens but also to put in a flagged terrace, turn a field into a lawn, and buy parcels of adjoining property when they became available, providing her with one large cottage with a view of the water and two small cabins for guests. Sundays she would attend church at St. Mary's-by-the-Sea, where the congregation of Episcopalians increased exponentially during the height of the summer season. On a good day she could feel like just another resident of Northeast Harbor and expect to be greeted as such when she wandered into a local store.

From the time of her marriage to Dryden Kuser she had loved the Maine coast. But she also felt at home with the people there. The writer Roxana Robinson, who would become one of Brooke's *much* younger friends and a Northeast Harbor summer resident, believed that although Brooke had not been raised in New England she had a natural affinity with her Northeast Harbor neighbors. "Brooke believed in hard work, discipline, good manners, thank you notes, living within your means, respect for the countryside, going to church on Sunday morning, walking to church, walking every day, not taking the car when it isn't necessary, knowing shopkeepers, being part of the community. Usually it takes three generations to be a true Northeast Harbor native. Until the summer of her hundredth birthday, Brooke took part in the Memorial Day parade."

Brooke's friends Charles Ryskamp and Ashton Hawkins would talk of how Vincent had helped to foster her attachment to the community, but only in a highly restricted fashion, by encouraging her during their summer stays to woo the old ladies of the Cranberry Club. The clubhouse, such as it was, was a small shack on Cranberry Island. If you brought guests there, you brought your own food and had a picnic. It was a group of bluestocking ladies, Ashton Hawkins would say, and Brooke made a concerted attempt to win some of them over, while avoiding others. For instance, she steered clear of old Mrs. Peabody, the writer Frances FitzGerald's grandmother—who could be fierce. "The chief Cranberry had a pet seagull," Charles Ryskamp would recall. "Brooke came to tea with a gift of chocolates. As they sat talking, she fed the seagull rich chocolate bits. The seagull was soon madly in love. The chief Cranberry wears a cranberry on a ribbon. For the Cranberry meetings the ladies bring bowls of things like potato salad, prepared by their cooks. They march to the shack to partake of the picnic lunch their servants have made. At the beginning these were old New England ladies. Brooke was the young one. The ladies went out to swim in the sea, in the ice-cold water. It seemed as if everyone was over ninety. You almost had to be over ninety."

Once Vincent was gone, she no longer had to swim with the Cranberries unless she chose to. She had money to buy a camp on the ocean, where she gave free rein to her imagination, creating a Chinese garden and a pavilion reminiscent of a Japanese teahouse, with the inspired addition of a saltwater moat for comfortable swimming. Even swimming naked if she chose. This exotic retreat, which she called "August Moon" and which was within easy reach by car but totally remote in feeling, was reserved for picnics and tête-à-têtes with intimate friends and guests. She might have no intention of remarrying, but she still reserved a place in her life for romance.

If at moments she seemed to be playing the merry widow, she took seriously the responsibilities that came with inherited wealth. Of course in New York, social position and philanthropy have long been intertwined. The Astors had been a rare exception, although Vincent Astor, during his lifetime, had begun to change all this. During the early years of her marriage to Vincent, Brooke had remained on the board of the Maternity Center Association. And with Vincent's encouragement, she had taken a place on the board of the New York Public Library and on the board of the New York Zoological Society, where, as the first woman to become a trustee, she had been asked to help form a Ladies Auxiliary. After Vincent's death, she remained on both.

To the Library she felt a dual connection, through Vincent but also through Buddie Marshall. Buddie was a descendant of James Lenox, whose collection, along with those of Samuel Tilden and John Jacob Astor, had served as a cornerstone of the New York Public Library when the collections were consolidated in 1895. Books had always meant a great deal to her. She felt it was important to continue to serve on the Library's board, which was composed almost exclusively of descendants of long established WASP families whose members seemed not to notice that the imposing Carrère and Hastings structure at Forty-second Street and Fifth Avenue where they met—and where the Library's justly celebrated collection of research material had long been housed—was rapidly deteriorating.

Her connection to the Bronx Zoo could also be seen as having been forged by not one but two of her marriages. Of course, it had begun early on, when as a young bride she had attended the Zoo's spring parties there with Colonel Kuser, who had underwritten William Beebe's expedition to India and his great monograph on pheasants. Then, Vincent had lent his yacht the *Nourmahal* for expeditions in the Gálapagos. But always her love of animals had been deep and abiding. From earliest childhood, she had looked to her dogs for affection as well as for company and with time had begun clapping her hands and calling out, "People," when she wanted her dogs to return to her side.

Conscientiously she helped organize receptions and dinner dances, trying to come up with ways to make the Library more appealing to New Yorkers with deep pockets. And conscientiously she continued to help with the Zoo's Ladies Auxiliary, volunteering occasionally to organize teas and luncheons, even though being relegated to a room full of women was hardly to her taste.

From the start, Vincent's widow was careful to keep her own private charitable contributions separate from the Foundation's—paying out of her own checking account for tables at benefits, making personal donations. Nonetheless, the Foundation provided her with access to deep pockets. A fact that was not lost on the heads of every important board in the city. After Vincent's death, it never occurred to his widow to join Helen Hull on the board of the Philharmonic. But she was delighted to accept an invitation to join the board of the Metropolitan Museum of Art—perhaps the most prestigious board in the city.

The invitation to join the board of the Met did not arrive immediately, however, if only because the second Mrs. Vincent Astor, now Minnie Fosburgh, continued to remain an active board member. Indeed it took four years before she was asked. In 1963, when an invitation was finally extended there was some trepidation, according to her friend Ashton Hawkins. But by then the need for the Astor name and the possibility of access to the Foundation's money had come to render moot any question of awkwardness. And by then the Met knew what they were getting. As a board member she could be counted on to pull her weight—asking the occasional pointed question, smoothing ruffled feathers, volunteering to call on friends for support.

As it turned out, there was never any friction between the second Mrs. Vincent Astor and Vincent's widow. All that worry had been over nothing. There were clashes at the Foundation, however, between Vincent's widow and Allan Betts—although, for the most part, they played out behind the scenes and not at board meetings and took a relatively civilized form. To the world at large the transition from a rich man's instrument for charitable giving to a private family foundation of some consequence appeared to be seamless. The face the Foundation presented to the world seemed both harmonious and placid, although it increasingly became associated with the real-life face of the Foundation's new president.

During Vincent Astor's time the Foundation had given away about $175,000 each year—a generous sum, but not an enormous one. The bulk of this annual disbursement had been divided between the American Red Cross, New York Hospital, and the Astor Home for Children in Rhinebeck, a place for troubled boys run by the Catholic Church and a favorite charity of Cardinal Spellman's. In Brooke Astor's first full year as president, 1960, the Foundation made grants adding up to over $3 million, which was more than it had given away during its first twelve years. However, most of this money—$2.5 million in fact—went to New York Hospital to construct a building that would bear Connie Guion's name, while the rest went to organizations that had received grants in the past. Not a few of these organizations had ties to board members. As a woman with some experience of the world, Vincent's widow could well understand this and, for the moment, did nothing to change it. After all, there might come a day when she would have her own favorite causes in need of special help.

In 1959, when the new president took over, the board of the Vincent Astor Foundation met four times a year—in October, November, March, and May. Tom Coolidge, a young associate at Carter, Ledyard, and Milburn who had recently taken on the job of board secretary, had a chance to observe the new president in action. He would be the only person, aside from the new president, to attend all board meetings for the next thirty-seven years (first as secretary and then as a trustee). "From day one, Brooke was in control," he would recall. "I think she prepared quite carefully. I don't think she ever just wandered into a meeting. She had everything organized in her mind. There was no lack of focus. She had tremendous executive skills. She was able to deal with strong characters. She never got into a situation where she had to say, 'No, we're not going to do that.' She never got herself cornered. From the beginning she very carefully avoided confrontation. Everything was done behind the scenes."

Allan Betts wanted her to make the Foundation more professional: to organize the files, hire a trained staff, begin to act like a serious philanthropic organization. Moreover, he wanted the Foundation to focus its attention on one particular area—to specialize in "youth services" (or, as the layman might call it, "juvenile delinquency"), which seemed to him a natural extension of Vincent's interest in the Astor Home for Children as well as being a particular interest of his own. He had no interest in giving large grants to institutions like the Metropolitan Museum of Art or the Morgan Library. Let their own board members support them. His plan was to carve out a niche as a funder of the city's settlement houses and youth organizations. Having had his way the three years he'd served as director, he saw no reason that he should be questioned now.

At *House and Garden* Brooke Astor had combined business with pleasure. It was only natural that, given the opportunity, she would do so again. On her nightly rounds, she began to meet people who had pet causes they felt were in need of immediate attention. Often she would pass their suggestions on to Allan Betts for further investigation. Sometimes she would make a commitment on the spot. How frequently this happened it's hard to know. As the Foundation's new president saw it, this was business as usual. As Allan Betts saw it, she was usurping his authority and bypassing the board.

"Behind the scenes there was a lot of head butting going on," Tom Coolidge would recall. "But Brooke didn't get into yelling and screaming matches." What Brooke did was to find a new area for the Foundation to focus on—one that she found appealing and that Allan Betts could not reasonably object to, if only because, at least tangentially, it touched on his own special interest. Having met Ira Robbins, a member of the New York City Housing Authority's board, through her friend Mayor Robert F. Wagner Jr., she became a passionate advocate of something she took to calling "outdoor living rooms."

"Outdoor living rooms" were in effect small parks that were to be placed within the confines of already existing housing projects, with the hope that these patches of green would miraculously foster a sense of community by making bleak clusters of high-rise buildings seem less institutional and sterile. The parks she envisioned would have attractive, well-maintained plantings and would provide the residents of these housing projects with such amenities as a band shell, an amphitheater, or a pergola. Ideally they would serve as playgrounds by day and meeting spaces at night. They would also offer a congenial place with comfortable benches for the projects' older residents to simply sit and enjoy the sun and fresh air. And, no less important, they would provide a clean, well-lighted space where the teenage residents could hang out. To Allan Betts she could always argue she was serving the youth of the area by keeping them off the streets.

"Outdoor living rooms" owed much to Jane Jacobs's 1961 book, *The Death and Life of Great American Cities*, where the author wrote of the destructive effect any dense concentration of tall buildings had on a neighborhood's social fabric. As such, the living rooms could be said to be influenced by current intellectual fashion. But they were also a natural outgrowth of ideas Brooke Astor had absorbed and made her own many years before when working for Dorothy Draper—ideas that she expressed most eloquently when she spoke at length to a reporter in St. Louis about the importance of providing low-income families with cheerful and comfortable surroundings.

To say that it was only natural for someone who had worked at *House and Garden* for many years to call these green places intended to foster a sense of community "outdoor living rooms" is not to disparage Brooke Astor's intention here, or her vision. As a philanthropist, she was finding her way. At the same time, she understood the importance of grounding any risky venture in her own personal experience. It made good sense to trust her instincts. It also made for a certain excitement. Several board members, including Tom Coolidge, responded to this proposal of hers with enthusiasm. As did the city. And eventually the general public, once they found out about it.

The two low-income housing projects the Vincent Astor

Foundation eventually chose to work with—the George Washington Carver Houses in East Harlem and the Jacob Riis Houses in the East Village—both had a high concentration of Hispanic residents, which may be why Brooke Astor envisioned these "outdoor living rooms" as serving much the same function she remembered the shaded public squares of Santo Domingo did when she was fifteen and staying with her parents there.

The first outdoor living room was completed in 1963 and opened with great fanfare. The second and more ambitious one was completed in 1966. Its opening attracted even greater attention, thanks in part to the presence not only of the city's new mayor, John Lindsay, but also of the nation's first lady, Mrs. Lyndon Johnson. Suddenly, with the apparent success of these two striking and ambitious departures from the Foundation's past ventures, Brooke Astor became the Foundation's public face. As such, she was invited later that year to join Lady Bird Johnson in bringing an "outdoor living room" to Washington, D.C.

By 1966, Brooke Astor had gotten the Foundation to give $300,000 to the Bronx Zoo, to help build its World of Darkness. She hadn't had to push terribly hard to get the Foundation to contribute $500,000 in 1962 toward the conversion of the Arnold Constable department store into the Mid-Manhattan Library, given the Astor family's long-standing Library connection; this building would house most of the circulating volumes of the Beaux-Arts Library across the street, allowing the latter to focus on research. Large donations were rare at this point to long established and high-profile city institutions she would later number among its "crown jewels." But by 1966 Allan Betts and Brooke Astor had finally found one new undertaking they could both approach with enthusiasm: the redevelopment of Bedford-Stuyvesant.

This once thriving but sadly deteriorated Brooklyn neighborhood not only housed the largest African-American community in the city but also boasted the lowest per capita income and highest crime rate.

Until 1964, when the damage caused by the rioting in its streets sur-passed that in Harlem, Bedford-Stuyvesant had remained tucked away, far behind the Brooklyn Navy Yard, well out of sight. Now it was a public embarrassment—or weeping sore, depending on how you looked at such things—impossible to explain away or ignore.

Allan Betts would tell his son Roland that he alone had been the original force behind the Foundation's involvement, persuading Brooke Astor and the board to go along with him. In *Footprints* Brooke Astor would tell her readers that she had been the one to approach Robert F. Kennedy, the man spearheading this project, but only after she had been considering doing something about Bedford-Stuyvesant for some time. From various sources she had been hearing about this community in distress, where even now one could find blocks of pleasant but rather dilapidated one-family houses. The problem was how best to give hope and encouragement to the people living in those houses.

In an unprecedented move, Robert Kennedy, New York's recently elected U.S. senator, had created within the course of a little more than a year a community-based initiative, which called on the advice and contacts of some of the city's most influential businessmen, but also gave final approval to members of the community. These two very disparate groups had eventually come together under the umbrella of an organization called the Bedford-Stuyvesant Restoration Corporation, headed by Frank Thomas, someone who had grown up in the community and gone on to get a law degree and become a prosecutor in the U.S. Attorney's office.

In 1967, the Vincent Astor Foundation gave $1 million for the planning and construction of two "superblocks"—closing off those blocks to traffic and turning the streets into a park of sorts. Then in 1969 it followed up this quite astonishing grant with $500,000 toward the construction of a community center. The Ford Foundation also provided money early on, but the two foundations were not in the same league. For the Vincent Astor foundation to provide seed money on this scale—particularly for a risky venture, unlike anything that had ever been attempted before in the city—was a major departure. Some might say a major gamble. But here Brooke Astor and Allan Betts were in agreement. It was Brooke Astor, though, whom Frank Thomas would remember. "She was just a force," he would say. "She was an incredibly generous person who had a growing curiosity and interest in what was then being described as community-based development—where the power to decide resides in the community and the institution that it creates. I think she had come to that really early. At least she was receptive to it. Whether she was convinced of it at that point based on experience, I can't say. But she got it."

That first summer of 1967, Frank Thomas and *his* board needed an initiative to engage the neighborhood's young men and women and also to demonstrate the advantages of what they were doing. To get things going, they decided to use locally trained young people to do the work and start renovating some of the housing stock that had always been seen as one of the neighborhood's strengths. Rather than go house by house, they chose to renovate entire blocks, an initiative that required the active cooperation of local block associations as well as individual home owners. Once two-thirds of a block agreed, the exterior renovations would begin—but only if the individual owners would sign a pledge to then follow up by spending on the house's interior an amount equal to the money they had saved on the exterior work.

It wasn't easy to get the home owners to agree. And it was here that Brooke Astor—a woman who cared how things looked and who was excited by the fact that Frank Thomas was going to do something demonstrable right away—decided to step in and help. "She came out to some of those meetings in the homes of people in the neighborhood," Frank Thomas would recall. "People were blown away by her. Well, even then you know she dressed the same wherever she happened to be going. It brought a style and level of quality that was very arresting and connected with the way that people dressed on Sundays when they went to church. The hat. The gloves. All of that. It connects. There was a resonance. She would sit in the living room of people and they would be talking about what was happening on their blocks. And she was very, very curious."

Meeting with the ladies of Bedford-Stuyvesant, Brooke Astor risked stumbling badly, but, instead, managed to strike just the right note. Not for an instant did she lose her balance. Whether the hat and gloves owed something to conscious models, like the Queen Mother visiting the East End of London during the Blitz or Nancy Astor walking through the ruins of a bombed-out Plymouth, they came across as a sign of respect and plain good manners.

Some gambles take a while to pay off. Or pay off in ways not necessarily anticipated. The restoration of Bedford-Stuyvesant would take much longer than anyone expected, but the approach used by the Bedford-Stuyvesant Restoration Corporation would begin almost immediately to serve as a model for hundreds and then thousands of such community-based initiatives. The Vincent Astor Foundation would never again commit so much money to a project of this kind, but Brooke Astor would make many such forays in the future.

Vincent's gift, which had come with one significant string attached, had turned out to be exactly what she needed. A perfect fit. She might no longer swim with the Cranberries, but many of the skills she had used in wooing them she had gradually brought to bear in winning over the board of Vincent's foundation. By 1967, she had begun to extend her reach. Before long she would be wooing an entire city, not with chocolates but with gifts its citizens sometimes didn't understand they needed until presented with them. To this new public life of hers she would bring discipline and imagination and also a sense of humor. She was no longer the little sister of the rich, but she would do her best to see to it that everyone had a good time.

Seven

A GREAT SMALL FOUNDATION, 1968–1976

In my mother's eyes a woman should know only what made her attractive to an intelligent man, and even then she considered that a woman should hide how much she really knew.

In June 1968, less than two weeks after Robert Kennedy's assassination and only two months after Martin Luther King Jr. had been killed—with the entire country polarized by the war in Vietnam and traumatized by the deaths of two men who seemed to hold out the promise of racial justice without violence—Brooke Astor sat for her first full-scale *New York Times* interview. For this interview she chose a small red sitting room in her large Park Avenue duplex. Sharing a sofa with two very active dachshunds and surrounded by some forty dog paintings, a "svelte, sixtyish" Brooke Astor managed, against considerable odds, not to come across as some out-of-touch Social Register do-gooder.

She managed this astonishing feat by bringing to the interview a heady blend of charm, genuine enthusiasm, and self-deprecating humor, as well as sufficient ammunition to mount one carefully placed preemptive strike. "I think I have to overcome quite a lot," she told the interviewer. "Being Mrs. Astor, a lot of social workers are against you. They think you're a silly Lady Bountiful who doesn't know a thing. When that happens I try to be as attractive as possible and win them over. I'm not there to show off."

Nor had she chosen to meet in the red sitting room just to show off. She had at least two causes she wished to promote and an entire city she wished to persuade of their importance. One cause she wished to promote· was the important work being done by the Vincent Astor Foundation. By her ninth year as the Foundation's president, she had definitely learned a thing or two. Rather than hide the luxury of her surroundings, she was prepared to make a virtue of them. Instead of pretending she had no interest in current fashion, she addressed the issue head-on. She knew what her visitor wanted from her and she was more than happy to comply.

The occasion for this interview was the culmination of one of the Foundation's most recent undertakings: the opening a few days earlier of a brand-new clubhouse on the Lower East Side for something called the Boys Brotherhood Republic. Within the confines of this spanking new clubhouse, "2,000 Negro and Puerto Rican youths" were going to have an opportunity to run a de facto city—a city where they would not only elect a mayor and city council but end up actually having their own police force and law court. The city's own mayor, John Lindsay, had attended the opening.

This ambitious undertaking, which would seem to fall under the general heading of youth services, wasn't really up Brooke Astor's alley—although the handsome new building would hold some appeal and elective politics happened to be a particular interest at the moment—but she made such a persuasive case for the Boys Brotherhood that the dazzled interviewer lost sight of the fact that it was Foundation money, not Mrs. Astor's, that had funded its expansion, writing, "[W]hile many of her contemporaries were having their daily massage or dawdling over lunch at a fancy French restaurant, Mrs. Astor dedicated the new $1,250,000 clubhouse she financed."

Seeing things this way, she or her editors titled the interview "The Goal of Brooke Astor: Easing Misery of Others." This confusion was not the sort of thing that would sit well with Tom Coolidge, the Foundation's secretary and lawyer, who was always telling the Foundation's president to be sure to make it clear that the Foundation was giving the money, if only to protect herself from hundreds of eager solicitors turning up at her door.

The interviewer *did* bring readers up to speed on the Foundation as well as the story of Vincent Astor and his legacy and her subject's own personal history—all of which was still necessary at this point. She then moved on to the "outdoor living rooms," which, she pointed out, "Mrs. Astor and her foundation have probably become best known for." To emphasize the importance of these "outdoor living rooms," she brought in one outside expert: Thomas Hoving, the former city parks commissioner and the brand-new director of the Metropolitan Museum of Art. At this point Hoving figured as a bright new star in the city's firmament. It did not hurt Brooke Astor any that she kept referring to him as "Tommy Hoving"—not when he chose to generously sprinkle some star dust in her direction. "Brooke Astor is the absolute leader of a whole new phase of recreation design," he declared. "She's a genius, it's as simple as that."

Finally, it was not really the philanthropist per se who interested the interviewer. It was the "swinging blonde grandmother with bright blue eyes" who was not merely aware that the world was in bad shape, but was actively trying to do something about it. Yes, Mrs. Astor had recently given "an interracial dinner in her apartment for members of the black and white establishments," but, more important, she had flown down to Atlanta with Governor Rockefeller for the funeral of Martin Luther King Jr. and then taken part in the long march to Morehouse College. Not only did she march, but she marched in good company—indeed company she was seeing a good deal of these days.

The second cause Mrs. Astor was trying to promote, while sitting and sipping a Coke in the company of her dogs, was Nelson Rockefeller's candidacy for president. Once Lyndon Johnson had declared that he was not seeking reelection, the field had become wide open—with Johnson's vice president, Hubert Humphrey, facing off against Eugene McCarthy and Robert Kennedy, and the Republicans suddenly scrambling to find a candidate ready to take advantage of this sudden disarray among their opponents' ranks. That candidate looked to be Nelson Rockefeller—at least to the eyes of many liberal Republicans. For her first foray into national politics, Brooke Astor had agreed to serve with John Hay Whitney as co-chairman of the national finance committee for Rockefeller's campaign. Just in case her interviewer suspected she was getting beyond herself, she pointed out that she had told the governor "that having a Whitney and an Astor on a finance committee for a Rockefeller seemed a bit much."

This interview would serve as a model for many to come, although before long Brooke Astor would put both the sitting room and her glasses of Coke (along with all caffeinated beverages) behind her. After a major renovation of the apartment's library by Albert Hadley, she found her new handsome red-lacquer library a more suitable venue for such encounters, and concluded, upon advice from various experts, that caffeine was not good for her. Although the interviewer makes no mention of sipping anything herself during their meeting, she, too, must have been offered a Coke or some beverage of her choice. At the very least a glass of water. That, after all, was only good manners.

This first big *Times* interview would draw to a close with Mrs. Astor revealing that while she didn't waste her time on fashion shows, she did like to shop. But then she went further and revealed that she did occasionally have her chauffeur pull over when she saw some dress she liked in a shop window. But by this point she had the interviewer totally on her side. When Mrs. Astor adds, "The life of the rich is *very* hard," she lets the reader know this is said with a wink, or rather, with Mrs. Astor "flashing her best you-know-I-don't-mean-it grin."

In the course of a couple of hours, Brooke Astor managed to have it both ways: on the one hand, to sound like a fundamentally serious philanthropist; on the other, to come across as a glamorous and amusing woman who never takes herself too seriously. This was true, according to Louis Auchincloss.

In those days, when she chose, she could come across as a bit daring. But only to a point. In fact this "swinging blonde grandmother" was not going to be found hanging out with Andy Warhol or frequenting discotheques. Unlike such fashion icons as the Duchess of Windsor, she would never don a miniskirt. At night she might go out dancing in a gown that bore a Paris label, but during the day you could count on her for good pearls, a neatly tailored suit, and sometimes even a hat. At a time when sexual adventures were regarded as anyone's business, she continued to favor discretion. At a time when fashion was undergoing a "revolution," she held on to her own style. For many years she could be found in the company of two Rockefeller brothers—first Nelson and then Laurance—but she saw to it that nothing untoward was made of this. At the moment one of her favorite designers might be Valentino, but her style in dress and her discretion were basically those of a Park Avenue lady blessed with "old money."

Brooke Astor did indeed have "a lot to smile about" back in the spring of 1968. Here the interviewer was not wrong. But her life was not all that it appeared to be. Within the recesses of this glamorous duplex, for instance, was a small separate apartment for the mother of this engaging and confident grandmother. With friends, Brooke Astor carried the presence of her aging mother off with brio, but it couldn't have been easy. Mabel Russell had thoroughly approved of her marriage to Vincent Astor, and no doubt encouraged it, but that didn't mean that she approved of everything this daughter of hers did. As was her custom, she did not hold her tongue.

Rather than hide her mother away from her friends, Brooke introduced her, giving her friends a chance to form their own impressions. It was what she had done during her marriage to Buddie Marshall. And when Mabel's eyes began to fail badly, Brooke, ever the good daughter, made sure that there were handsome young men to come read to her. One of these young men was Nelson W. Aldrich Jr., who would go on to become a well-known writer and editor, with a special interest in "old money"—something he knew about first hand. For a few weeks one summer Aldrich filled in for a friend, reading Shakespeare aloud to Mabel and having his pronunciation corrected.

By 1968, Mabel Russell's days of flirting were long behind her but, as her days began to seem numbered, she had formed one serious new attachment—to the Roman Catholic Church, which her father had joined in middle age and which she had first gotten to know as a boarder at a Sacred Heart school outside Philadelphia. Here, too, Brooke saw to her needs. And here, too, the relationship with Cardinal Spellman she had inherited from Vincent stood Brooke in good stead. Friends noted that on the stairs between the two levels of the Park Avenue duplex one could find not only handsome young priests but princes of the Church.

As a young person Brooke had been drawn to older people. Now, as she herself was getting older, she found herself increasingly drawn to the young. Tom Hoving, whom she'd known since he was thirteen, was one of several attractive sons and daughters of friends that she had been adding to her circle. Not a few of the young people she had taken to seeing she'd met at Sunday lunches given by the theater critic John Mason Brown and his wife. At one of these lunches she'd first encountered a young law student named Ashton Hawkins, who shared an apartment on the west side with the Browns' son Preston. Ashton would go on to become a special friend and frequent escort, joining her for cruises on the various yachts she would rent or borrow. Then, once Ashton joined the Metropolitan Museum as its general counsel, he would provide her with a second set of ears and eyes.

And of course one young friend begat another. It was inevitable. Through Ashton Hawkins she met Renata Adler, the *New Yorker* writer, who would view her as part mother, part older sister, and part patron. The two friends would spend more than one Christmas Eve watching *Miracle on Thirty-fourth Street* in tandem, each in her own home, and then phone afterward to discuss a movie they both loved. And when Renata was writing her novel *Pitch Dark*, Brooke happily offered Renata the use of one of her Maine cabins for the summer.

Through Charles Wrightsman, a fellow board member at the Met, she first encountered a young Everett Fahey, just down from school in Boston and about to join the museum's Department of European Painting—a department he would eventually head. Many years she would join Everett to mark their almost identical birthdays with a quiet dinner at his apartment, where she would have a chance to partake of such long forgotten delicacies as a potato roasted in the embers of his fireplace.

Through Jane Engelhard, another museum board member, she got to know Jane's daughter Annette, who was married at the time to Samuel Reed.* She would absorb much over the years from observing Jane Engelhard, who was already a master of the art of giving money wisely. "Brooke used to say, 'Jane's the power. I walk in her wake,'" her friend George Trescher would recall. If the two women were never intimate, they had a liking and respect for each other—indeed at one point Jane Engelhard commissioned a small portrait of Brooke as a special gift—but it was Annette who would have her heart, becoming in many ways the daughter she never had.

But at this point there were several friends' daughters in her life. Through Mab Moltke she first got to know Alexandra Isles, who as a

---

*In 1989, Annette would go on to marry Oscar de la Renta.

little girl had helped pass hors d'oeuvres at Mab's parties. She would go on to see Alexandra through her first marriage and her subsequent love affairs and then keep her close by her side during one terrible scandal. On the eve of that first marriage, she had sent Alexandra on her way by telling her to remember that the secret to a happy married life was for the wife to have a love affair on the side. It was advice she would give to more than one young woman, with an authority that appeared to come of experience.

She had always liked young people and she had always been open to novelty, even if she didn't necessarily choose to embrace the latest person or idea that came her way. Still, she was prepared to be amused and entertained, so long as you had something to say for yourself. She had immediately welcomed the new Lindsay administration, with its bright young men bringing new vision to the city. Indeed, she had taken a hand, as a relatively new but nonetheless active member of the Met's executive board, in getting Tom Hoving his job as director. This took persuading on both sides—something she was more than up to. As far as most board members were concerned, Hoving was a little young and perhaps a little wild, although he had handed in a sound performance as head of the Cloisters before he dropped everything to rush off and work for Lindsay. Hoving, on the other hand, seemed to be enjoying his sudden celebrity as an innovative head of the Parks Department, who had made a languishing Central Park suddenly available for concerts and gatherings, leading a disaffected middle class to start regarding it as an attractive and reasonably safe place to spend time.

Her method was simple when she set about persuading Tom Hoving to relinquish what looked like the perfect job for one that was rumored to have helped cause the death of James Rorimer, the last occupant. On the drive from the memorial service for the recently deceased Rorimer, she broached the subject. "She was the one delegated to speak to me about taking the job of director," Hoving recalled. "The two of us were in the back of a limousine. She said, 'I hear from inside sources that Lindsay is beginning to hate you. You're ebullient and he thinks you're a publicity hound. Tommy, I think you ought to make a move.' That was Brooke at her best. Straightforward. Good common sense."

When it came to the arts, she had always had a special sympathy. Especially for writers. Of course her own writing had always been important to her, from the time she began keeping a journal as a girl. As an editor at *House and Garden*, she had turned in her fair share of serviceable but graceful copy. Then, in 1962 she had published her first book—*Patchwork Child*, a memoir brought out by Harper and Row, which concentrated on her years in China and took her to the brink of her first marriage. And while the memoir had been far from a best seller, it had received respectful and even admiring attention from reviewers, inspiring her to go on to write *The Bluebird Is at Home*, the novel that presented an idealized version of her miserably unhappy first marriage. With time, most people became aware that, among other things, she was a published writer.

What most people didn't know was that she was a founding backer of *The New York Review of Books*, after it first set up shop in the winter of 1963 in response to a long newspaper strike. Robert Silvers, one of the founding editors, would recall that a mutual friend had brought Brooke Astor to the *Review*. Or, rather, brought the review to her attention and then brought Robert Silvers over to her apartment to talk to her about it. All they needed to raise was $125,000—a reasonable enough sum, until you had to actually get hold of it. With Brooke Astor there was no dithering or drawing out this awkward business. She immediately came up with $50,000 of her own money. For them it was key. Some time after 1968, when the *New York Review* was beginning to turn a profit, she let the editors buy her out.

Jason Epstein, another founding editor, would say that by then Brooke and the *Review* had parted ways over the Vietnam war. The articles they were running were much too radical for her taste, particularly one, on the front page, that provided a blueprint for making your own bomb. Whatever the reason, her timing was perfect. And it didn't make for any break in her friendships with Bob Silvers or Jason Epstein. During the course of the sixties Bob Silvers began to receive invitations to dinner, but the friendship would only deepen later on, during the late eighties and nineties. From the start Jason was a close friend, flirting with her and visiting with her at Ferncliff and then later at Holly Hill and Cove End.

Both men admired the woman but they also admired the writing. And of course part of what they responded to in both the writing and the woman was that she was direct and honest. Jason Epstein, though he granted her much, did see certain limitations—limitations that stemmed from her very nature and her heritage. She was a little too much of a WASP, he felt, to be a truly great writer.

Brooke Astor was not one to dabble with the Black Panthers or take pleasure in the prospect of even hypothetical violence. Her politics were moderate. She was a Rockefeller Republican, but that hadn't kept her from breaking one of her own cardinal rules for the Foundation, which was to restrict the Foundation's giving within the boundaries of the city of New York. She had joined forces with Lady Bird Johnson, the wife of a Democratic president, to create a park for young people in the city of Washington. In 1966 she had received a good deal of newspaper coverage for this in both New York and Washington. Less attention was paid to the fact that she was joining Jock Whitney as co-treasurer of Nelson Rockefeller's campaign for president. For all that she took pride in the unexpected role she was playing, she was prepared to make light of it, the way she did in that interview in the *Times*.

She believed Nelson, whom she first got to know well when they both served on the board of the Metropolitan Museum, was a terrific governor. When she told the interviewer at the *Times*, "He has wisdom and maturity and he's a man of decision," she wasn't exaggerating. And, like many women, she was not immune to Nelson's charm. But she was also close to, and fond of, his wife, Happy. Everyone would make note of that. Still, she was more than willing to support him in any undertaking at the museum—making up the difference later when he defaulted on some of the payment he had promised for a new wing for primitive art to be named for his son Michael, a specialist in this art, who had died in New Guinea under mysterious circumstances.

To Thomas Hoving, Nelson Rockefeller was a "grifter," who bankrupted the State of New York with all the new universities he built. To Brooke Astor, Nelson Rockefeller would always be a heroic figure; his photograph would rest on a table at Holly Hill with photographs of men who had been important in her life. She was delighted to help with his campaign, if only by lending her name, and to take time off from her summer in Northeast Harbor to fly down to Miami, for the 1968 Republican National Convention. Here things did not go quite as she had hoped they would. There was some embarrassment in the press about choosing a segregated club for one of their gatherings. But that was not the worst of it. In 1964 Rockefeller had been booed by delegates on the convention floor. This time, there was no public ruckus but it was soon apparent that he had started his campaign too late. After two crushing electoral defeats, the presidency in 1960 and the California governorship in 1962, Richard Nixon had devoted himself to cultivating and winning over the party heads who had the delegates at their command. While Nelson had been making headlines back in New York, Nixon had been doing his homework.

Nelson's performance in Miami was a bitter disappointment. But it did afford her the opportunity to get to know Nelson's youngest brother, David, who was now at the helm of the Chase Manhattan Bank but who at one point had done some writing himself, serving while still in college as Fiorello La Guardia's press secretary. Quiet and reserved and utterly unlike the outgoing Nelson, David actually had many interests in common with his brother's friend. In time that would become apparent to both of them. And while she took Nelson's defeat hard, it didn't keep her from contributing to the Republican Party or from accepting a White House invitation from Richard Nixon, who then went on to appoint her son, Tony, as ambassador to Kenya.

Brooke Astor might never choose to run for office, but she definitely understood politics. And nowhere did she show this more clearly than at the Metropolitan Museum of Art, where in a few short years she made herself a force to be reckoned with—or at the very least consulted. She did not have the kind of money available to her of a Charles Wrightsman (or his wife, Jayne, who would soon be replacing him on the board), nor did she possess an important collection of art. Such donations as she made amounted to little more than some small and not particularly valuable paintings by well-known artists, the occasional fine decorative object, and several custom-made designer gowns she thought might be of interest to the Costume Institute. As someone in a highly visible position she could not wear the same outfit too many times. Such gowns as she did not pass on to the Costume Institute she passed on to her friend Kitty Carlisle Hart, who put them to immediate use in her role as a regular panelist on the television game show *To Tell the Truth*. In those days TV shows did not provide performers with lavish wardrobes and the newly widowed Kitty Carlisle Hart did not have much money to spend.

From the start Brooke Astor was an active member of the Acquisitions Committee, once she was invited to join it, but she was never regarded as a great connoisseur. One museum curator, who happened to be extremely fond of her, noted that Brooke bought with her ears and not her eyes. She listened to others. And if what they said made sense, she went along with what they suggested, contributing the necessary money out of her own pockets for the most part, to help out—whether it was to purchase some new work of art necessary to fill a gap in the museum's collection, or, as sometimes happened, to purchase a work of art that had been on loan to the museum for decades, but which had to be ransomed at the collector's death from heirs eager to sell off what looked to be a valuable asset.

As a collector, Brooke Astor's most valuable asset was a splendid Childe Hassam painting, *Flags, Fifth Avenue*, which she bought in 1970. Aside from that, she inherited from Vincent a handsome group portrait of the William Astor family painted by Lucius Rossi, and she possessed some very good drawings on paper—one of which, "The Flight into Egypt," by G. P. Tiepolo, was purchased with the advice of Jacob Bean, the Met's distinguished curator of drawings. But while she did not bring deep pockets or any great connoisseurship to the Met, she brought something every bit as valuable. And in the end perhaps more so.

In 1969 the Metropolitan Museum celebrated its centenary, with eighteen months of festivities. Brooke Astor, who had been instrumental in acquiring the museum's new director, had already begun, with his enthusiastic support, to set about acquiring new museum donors. Soon she was not only giving cocktail parties in her lovely duplex apartment but giving weekly dinners to woo likely supporters from sectors of the city's population hitherto ignored or given the cold shoulder by the museum and its board.

It was here that Tom Hoving was first struck by the fact that his old friend had the skills of a consummate politician—effortlessly recalling the names of every new guest invited and then knowing exactly the right words to say to them before drawing them over to introduce them to some people she thought they would enjoy meeting. Not only was she adept at working the room during the cocktail hour, but she saw to it that the seating at her dinners was never awkward and was at times inspired. If one didn't know better, one would believe that these dinners came together with no effort. Within the confines of her apartment, intent on promoting the interests of an institution she saw as being in need of her help, she proved to be a born matchmaker. But Hoving saw these skills as being easily translatable to a much larger venue. As he saw it, she could have been New York's first woman senator.

It was during the preparations for the Met's centennial celebration that Brooke Astor met her own perfect match in George Trescher, a good-looking bachelor in his forties who had come to the museum from *Sports Illustrated*, where he had served on the business end and developed an increasingly valuable expertise in public relations. Decades later, George Trescher would still be amused by their first encounter: "When we first talked, Brooke said, 'I gather we need to find new checkbooks. I think it's a wonderful idea—there are too many people who have been around too long.' She then said, 'I discover new people all the time in *Women's Wear Daily*. You *do* see *Women's Wear Daily*, don't you? I'll send you a gift subscription for a month or two.' Brooke was right. We did find new young people with checkbooks and a lot of them came from *Women's Wear*'s pages."

Just who was taking the lead here is hard to say. With some justice, Ward McAllister, full-time man about town and sometime columnist, can be credited with serving as the perfect henchman for the first Mrs. Astor in her climb to the pinnacle of New York Society. Although George Trescher has sometimes been seen as serving the same function for Brooke Astor, he never saw himself in that light. Soon after the Met's centennial, he left the museum. For the next three decades, as the head of his own public relations firm, he would help Brooke Astor plan benefits and formal parties and would consult with her on her guest lists, but she was only one of his many clients. He always took care to stay in the background and give credit where it was due.

At most, he took credit for teaching her how to keep the upper hand in her dealings with the press. That it was better not to talk to a reporter if there was some question she didn't want to answer. That it was best to sometimes say nothing. Certainly he kept a more modest profile than McAllister. No newspaper column ran under his byline. There was no pretension of being a social arbiter. And there were no public feuds. Of course, he and Brooke Astor were living in an age where exclusivity was hardly at a premium. So long as you had the money to pay, you could achieve a certain level of acceptance. It helped if you were attractive, but it wasn't a requirement. Although there would always be hurt feelings, there were fewer occasions for anger and disappointment.

Both George Trescher and Brooke Astor had the advantage of having arrived from elsewhere. If nothing else it gave them perspective. At its best theirs was a symbiotic relationship—two people seeing eye to eye on how things should be done, one a full-time professional and one a highly gifted amateur. Whereas the first Mrs. Astor had no illusions as to the end she wished to achieve, this Mrs. Astor could always tell herself that, first and foremost, she was attracting attention to the causes she was trying to promote. If there was any personal gain to be had, it was surely only secondary. She was not getting beyond herself—something her mother was always warning her against.

One could argue that Brooke Astor had little need of anyone to handle her public relations. She had come a long way from the battle with Jack Astor. She knew from her days at *House and Garden* how to get her message across and she knew exactly what her interviewer wanted. Just look at her *Times* interview of 1968. After all, she had worked on the other side for many years. But it was more than that, George Trescher would argue. Some things cannot be taught.

By the late sixties New York, along with the rest of America, was beginning to see the rise of a celebrity culture. Ready to lend her name and presence to causes she considered worthy, Brooke made a willing and charming celebrity. And from the start she was a natural.

Reporters liked her. They liked what she stood for. But, no less important, they appreciated the way she always seemed willing to talk to them. She did not have a press office. She took all phone calls herself. That, after all, was good manners. In interviews she was direct and that was disarming. And of course she was amusing. She also had an ability to put what she had to say in one sound bite. But, unlike most celebrities of the time, she was prepared to back up her support for any worthy cause she championed with hard cash—frequently the Vincent Astor Foundation's but sometimes her own.

At the same time, philanthropy was coming to be regarded by the government as a serious business, worth keeping a tight rein on. After serious investigation by a congressional committee into the abuses of family charities, the government changed its tax laws. No longer could a family foundation be used as an easy means of funneling money to family members—men and women who might serve as its well-paid officers or have the exclusive use of yachts, planes, or imposing residences deemed necessary for the foundation's day-to-day operations. Suddenly nonprofit organizations had to prove that no one was personally benefiting from any money received or generated.

Nonprofit organizations, which were being funded by these private foundations, also had to prove there were no secret ties to their benefactors. Books had to be open to inspection. Careful accounting had to be done, no matter how small the sums involved. To earn the right to qualify for nonprofit status, they had to register with the IRS. But that was not the end of it. For both the recipient and the benefactor this involved a good deal of paperwork. An immediate result of this fairly draconian measure would be that many small foundations ceased to make small grants to up-and-coming or unconventional nonprofit groups. Here the Vincent Astor Foundation gradually took up some of the slack.

Philanthropy is not immune to changes in fashion. During the late sixties there also began to be an increasing emphasis on the personal when giving money—a growing sense that people were as important as things. At the same time, it began to be taken as a given that environment can make an enormous difference. This was something Brooke had always believed. Here she had been on the cutting edge with her "outdoor living rooms." For her, social gatherings would never be frivolous. They promoted a sense of community and well-being. If all of this sounds impossibly idealistic, it seemed to make a certain sense at the time.

Brooke would never be seen at a "love-in" and she was hardly a "flower child" but she was susceptible to ideas floating in the zeitgeist. In this she was not alone. With many better established and better funded foundations, you were seeing a shift in direction. Urban planners, sociologists, and paid professionals of every persuasion were embarking on projects that would have been unthinkable a decade earlier. For her, a natural extension of her "outdoor living rooms" was Wild Asia, an enormous plain created from undeveloped land to the south of the Bronx Zoo. As she saw it, this venture, which would greatly benefit many of the Zoo's inhabitants, would also improve life in the surrounding neighborhood, creating a park where there had been a wasteland and attracting hundreds of additional visitors to the area.

When it looked as if the city might put up some uninspired housing or end up leaving the land vacant, in 1969 the Foundation came up with a grant of $5 million to acquire this land and develop it for the Zoo, with the promise that the city would come up with a matching sum to put this plan into effect. What was envisioned was a great plain which would come as close as possible to approximating the natural habitat of certain of the Zoo's elephant and antelopes and tigers—animals who until now had lived out their days within the confines of traditional zoo cages. A monorail would make it possible for visitors to see the animals who ranged there, separated only by barely perceptible natural barriers protecting prey from their natural predators.

18. The new Mrs. Vincent Astor

19. Philip and Alec Marshall at Ferncliff

20. John Jacob Astor VI with his third bride, the former Dolores Margaret Fullman

21. Brooke Astor and dogs, 1962

22. Thomas Hoving and Douglas Dillon

23. Brooke with
Jack Pierrepont

24. Brendan Gill in his *New Yorker* office

25. Nelson
Rockefeller, 1964

26. Laurance Rockefeller, 1969

27. Linda Gillies during an
on-site visit, 1974

28. Annette and
Brooke, 1977

29. Charles Ryskamp

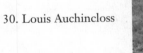

31. Brooke Astor with her favorite president

The Zoo had always been one of Brooke Astor's own personal philanthropies. A plan that freed captive animals from narrow barred cages could only appeal to her, although the idea wasn't exactly revolutionary. The San Diego Zoo had long done something similar. (When the city failed to come up with the matching money it had promised, the Foundation came forward with another $1.5 million, and by the time Wild Asia opened in 1977 the Foundation had given $7.6 million, all told.)

While this Asian plain eventually proved to be everything the Foundation's president had hoped for, it may have well proved to be the straw that broke the Foundation director's back. A project Allan Betts had never cared for had become ever more costly, taking money away from what he believed to be more pressing work with young people in the city's slums. Yes, the Bronx was in bad disarray. And the Zoo there was suffering because of the deterioration of the surrounding neighborhood. But he did not see that refurbishing the Zoo was going to help mend that. He was interested in doing something more along the lines of what had been done in Bedford-Stuyvesant.

Brooke Astor was a pragmatist. Unfortunately, by the early seventies it was clear that the redevelopment of Bedford-Stuyvesant—particularly without the presence of Robert Kennedy—was going to go more slowly than anticipated. In addition, it was apparent that ambitious undertakings like this tended to produce controversy. "Youth services" might be less controversial, but the rehabilitation of delinquent adolescent boys, while worthy, came with a high incidence of recidivism. And by now the Foundation's president had her own list of pet projects.

In the late sixties, when Waldemar Nielsen was researching *The Big Foundations*, his influential study of philanthropy in America, the Vincent Astor Foundation looked sufficiently successful for him to cite it as a model for what a well-managed and enlightened small foundation could accomplish. Compared with the generously appointed and amply staffed Ford and Carnegie foundations, the Astor Foundation was a shoestring operation, with a staff consisting of one bookkeeper, one program officer, and one director. Its offices might be on Park Avenue but they occupied only one small corner of the seventeenth floor of a nondescript office building. Here there was little wastage or fat. By contrast, in 1968 the Ford Foundation possessed more than $3.5 billion in assets, operating out of headquarters near the United Nations that featured an indoor garden. Of course the Vincent Astor Foundation's importance could not be measured in mere dollars. A grant often provided critical seed money for an up-and-coming nonprofit, like the South Street Seaport Museum, or underwrote the cost of producing a potentially controversial documentary on drug abuse for public television.

Nielsen singled out the Astor Foundation's president for special praise—not merely for her vision but for her willingness to take on work that other philanthropists left to their staff. He liked her spontaneous approach to philanthropy. And he rather admired her for resisting attempts to professionalize her foundation. While he was clearly charmed by the president, he took note of the fact that she and the Foundation's director were not always in agreement. Of course, by then their underlying differences may have been all too apparent. At the end of his section on the Vincent Astor Foundation, he wrote, "Mrs. Astor herself prefers to avoid projects that are controversial, fearing entanglement in power struggles and factional confrontations, but Betts and some other trustees feel the foundation should undertake 'gut projects' in the ghettos, eliminating conventional grants, such as its $5 million pledge in [1969] to the Bronx Zoo." He then went on to say that the Foundation's future didn't look all that certain. "It may become a more professionalized institution," he wrote, "but it is equally likely that it may dissolve itself and distribute its assets to institutions in the New York City area."

When *The Big Foundations* came out in 1972, the Astor

Foundation had not dissolved itself. But by then Allan Betts, seeing the direction in which the Foundation was headed, had already called it quits. "Brooke didn't confront Allan Betts," Tom Coolidge would later say. "She got even. She made it clear that he had outlived his usefulness in that position." To take his place, Brooke Astor had hired Bob Bickford, an affable young lawyer—who had gone to school with Tom Coolidge—with the understanding that he would be helping move the Foundation out of youth services.

Bob Bickford, who had no training in Foundation work and never pretended to be an expert in this field, may have been younger and more malleable than his predecessor, but it soon became clear to both parties that he and Brooke Astor were not an ideal match. Part of this was owing to the fact that Allan Betts had given him strict instructions on how to proceed in professionalizing the Foundation, something that was bound to produce conflict.

Unlike Allan Betts, Bob Bickford didn't mind the president's wanting him to escort her to the occasional dinner or benefit. He did mind her making verbal commitments to people she met at these dinners. This was because the whole business seemed so haphazard, not because it undermined his authority. After all, she was only committing the Foundation to looking into this project. Increasingly, though, she was having her own way with the board, as well as with the staff. As it happened, this pleased neither of them. Before two years had passed, Bob Bickford was ready to admit defeat and Brooke Astor was remembering some advice she had received from Waldemar Nielsen: that she might do better working with another woman.

It was while Bob Bickford was still serving as director that Linda Gillies first came to the attention of Brooke Astor. To help Nelson Rockefeller with a big conference said to address "The Future of America," Brooke Astor was putting together a special daylong panel of young people to be called "Forty Under Forty." To do all the groundwork needed to get this panel up and running, George

Trescher recommended Linda, the attractive mother of two small children, whom he had first met when she was the assistant to the Met's curator of drawings, and whom he regarded as a friend. George Trescher's recommendation was backed by one from Ashton Hawkins, who had known Linda from the time they were teenagers.

Her first day on the job, Linda Gillies set up a card table in one corner of the Foundation's offices and, after getting through a rough patch at the beginning, she discovered that she and Brooke Astor worked well together. In addition, the panel was a great success. As Linda was wrapping up her work, Mrs. Astor suddenly asked if she'd like to try working as the Foundation's director. When it came to the director's salary, Mrs. Astor was equally direct. What did Linda think might be a reasonable figure? When, after consulting with her husband, Linda suggested perhaps twenty to thirty thousand—with the lower figure higher than anything she'd ever earned before—Mrs. Astor offered her a salary of thirty thousand dollars per year.

In hiring Linda Gillies, Brooke Astor was getting a woman whose husband was working as head of the Whitney Foundation, funded by Jock Whitney, who had joined with Brooke to head Nelson Rockefeller's finance committee. Linda and her husband, Arch, had actually met and fallen in love while working on that ill-fated campaign. Linda came from a long-established East Coast family. Both of them had attended good schools, from which they had gone on to jobs that could never be counted on to pay much money. Linda needed to work full-time. But she also needed a job that provided sufficient flexibility so she would be available when her children needed her. Although she herself had never been a working mother with small children, Brooke Astor had sufficient experience in the workplace to understand this.

Both women were venturing into unknown territory and for both women there was the promise of a fresh start. It was immediately apparent that Waldemar Nielsen had been right. Linda, who had no experience working in philanthropy, had no preconceived idea of how things *must* be done. For the most part, she tended to see things the way Mrs. Astor did. In addition, she was well organized. Without making a point of "professionalizing" the way the Foundation was run, she quietly took steps to accomplish this. Her job, as she saw it, was to screen all grant applications—creating folders, making follow-up calls, sending out forms, and sometimes doing a bit of extra research, before pulling together a pile of applications that seemed promising, to be discussed with Mrs. Astor.

In the spring and fall, almost every week the president would set out with her new director and her car and driver to visit and inspect the handful of community centers, shelters, libraries, museums, parks, drug rehabilitation programs, or neighborhood groups whose grant applications had passed muster. Linda would usually pick her up before or after lunch. At each stop they made, she and Linda met with personnel, asked questions, and sometimes paused for a cup of tea, while, discreetly and politely, giving the facility the once-over. Not all of these were first time visits. Sometimes they were there to check out how an earlier grant had been spent. With Allan Betts and Bob Bickford, Brooke Astor had done more or less the same thing. But suddenly the on-site visits were fun.

Linda's arrival coincided almost exactly with an important change in the Foundation's status. By the early seventies, thanks to several shrewd investments, the Foundation had $100 million in its coffers—money the board had decided to spend down. Suddenly the Foundation went from giving away an average of $3.2 million most years to giving away anywhere from $4.6 million to $12.2 million in one year. Not only could more grants be made but the grants could be considerably larger. Inevitably this would give the Foundation a higher profile.

By this point, the Astor Foundation had grown a bit, its staff of five working in the rooms in the southwest corner of the seven-

teenth floor at 405 Park Avenue. There were now a program officer, a secretary, a bookkeeper, and a clerk to support the director.
There was no major renovation, but the offices were freshened up.
Walls were painted. Chairs were recovered and when necessary
reupholstered. A photograph of Vincent's beloved *Nourmahal*
remained in the waiting room and his portrait hung over the president's desk. At the same time, his sailing prints were replaced with
an ever growing number of press clippings, plaques, citations, and
on-site photographs.

These changes, which struck the eye immediately, signaled a sea
change in the way the Foundation operated. Brooke Astor and Linda
Gillies were both practical energetic women who also liked to have a
good time. Occasionally, files and folders were examined a block
from the Foundation's offices, at Kenneth's, while Mrs. Astor was
having her hair colored. Sometimes Mrs. Astor would stop by the
office before joining a friend for lunch at the Four Seasons or the
Knickerbocker, where she enjoyed special privileges as the widow of
a member. Although she had a membership at the Colony Club, she
was not inclined to seek out the company of women for lunch. Those
days when Mrs. Astor was having her hair colored it was possible to
get a good hour of work done. Once a month or so, they would have
a working lunch at the office, with Linda ordering in what came to
be Mrs. Astor's favorite meal—a fruit and Jell-o salad from a local
delicatessen.

On occasion a day of on-site visits would end with a shopping
expedition at Bergdorf's. If the Foundation's president was treating
herself to a scarf, she would make sure that the director received one
as well. She was generous, but she also wanted her director to be
happy. One Monday morning she couldn't help noticing that Linda
looked exhausted. It turned out that to save money, Linda and Arch
had spent the weekend painting their apartment themselves. Upon
hearing this, Mrs. Astor immediately insisted on paying for Linda to

go out and hire a professional painter to do the work. And when Linda presented her with a bill of $5,000, she did not blink an eye.

Attractive bound reports were prepared for the board meetings held four (and later, with everyone's agreement, three) times a year in the president's corner office. After Linda's arrival the meeting continued to be held at four in the afternoon and the board members continued to sit on the one sofa or in armchairs, with the president facing them from behind Vincent's old partner's desk. As always, the director, who came prepared with a stack of grant folders to be considered, sat to one side of the desk. With the arrival of Linda Gillies, however, one significant change was made. Any late afternoon drowsiness during the hourlong deliberations was offset by a cup of tea, accompanied by cookies and little sandwiches ordered from William Poll.

As directors like Cardinal Spellman and then Connie Guion died or retired, Mrs. Astor replaced them with friends or allies. In 1975 she asked Jack Pierrepont, whom she had known as a small boy, to join the board. Board members did not receive payment for the work they did. Instead, they were given $10,000 of Foundation money to direct to their favorite cause. Since Mrs. Astor could not be everywhere, the board ideally provided additional eyes and ears.

The unanticipated but welcome growth in the Foundation's endowment coincided not only with the arrival of an ideal director but also with a moment when the city was most in need of private support. John Lindsay had taken office as mayor in January 1966 brimming with ideas and confidence, only to be confronted with a devastating transit strike. Sadly, the fresh ideas of Lindsay and his young associates, along with their serious attempt to deal with the city's racial problems, had not merely come to very little but occasionally seemed to make matters worse. Some of this was owing to inexperience. Some to concessions the mayor had been forced to make to the city's unions, run by men who had no use for someone who came across like an old-time member of the establishment. Ventures that had sounded highly promising on paper didn't always turn out as expected—such as his agreeing, in the face of parental protest in many quarters, to decentralize the city's schools, and even his bringing New Yorkers back to Central Park, during those early heady years when Tom Hoving was serving as his parks commissioner.

In 1974, when Abe Beame, a longtime Democratic party stalwart and the city's controller, was elected mayor, he was faced with an almost impossible task. The city's parks, its streets, its schools, and its branch libraries were rapidly deteriorating; its museums, which had come to rely on city funding to help meet rapidly escalating operating costs, were finding themselves suddenly cut off. At the same time, most of the country was reeling from an economic recession and runaway inflation—the toll of waging a losing war in Vietnam exacerbated by an oil crisis brought on by a cut off of oil from the Middle East on the heels of the Yom Kippur war.

By the beginning of 1975, the municipal government was swimming in debt—it owed $1,800 for each of its 7 million citizens (by comparison, Chicago carried only $425 of per capita debt). When credit markets denied the city access to any more loans in April, Mayor Beame and Hugh Carey, New York's governor, appealed to the federal government for help. But Gerald Ford, a Midwesterner and fiscal conservative, seemed to regard the nation's largest city with even less sympathy than his predecessor, Richard Nixon, who had mistrusted the epicenter of the Eastern establishment as a hotbed of antiwar agitation. The *Daily News* famously summarized the president's reaction: "Ford to City: Drop Dead."

New York was eventually saved from bankruptcy when Felix Rohaytn, a partner at Lazard Frères and the newly appointed head of the Municipal Assistance Corporation, set up by the state to help the city avoid defaulting on its payroll and other obligations, was able to get both the banks and the unions to agree to key concessions, making it possible to attract buyers for an emergency issue of bonds. Among the major buyers were the unions' own pension funds. Eventually he sold $10 billion worth. Although by 1976 it began to look as if the city's finances would recover, there were immediate crises and near defaults until the end of the decade. The way things looked at this point, New York's museums and libraries and even its parks would never again be able to count on the city for the kind of support they had always taken for granted.

It was during this period that the small Vincent Astor Foundation began to make its presence felt, by stepping in to take up the slack. One way was to provide grants to keep branch libraries open so that children with working parents or homes that were overcrowded would have some place safe to go when school let out, and, if all went well, some place that made it possible for them to do their homework.

In 1975, in conjunction with a matching grant from the Fairchild Foundation, the Vincent Astor Foundation made an emergency grant of $150,000, to keep the Metropolitan Museum open on Tuesday nights—a popular but costly program inaugurated by Tom Hoving, specifically intended to attract working people who were not free during the museum's regular weekday hours, but soon embraced with enthusiasm by all New Yorkers..

In 1975, the Foundation also began providing money to help save a rapidly deteriorating Central Park, where benches were broken, paths pitted and cracked, lawns studded with bare patches, and trees were in desperate need of attention. Decades of neglect had taken a toll on the park's infrastructure. But matters weren't helped any by the fact that long entrenched park workers were not being held accountable. Faced with an almost impossible task, even a reasonably dedicated worker was inclined to give up if no one cared whether or not he put in a full day.

During the early Lindsay years, Tom Hoving had gotten New Yorkers to return to Central Park by making them think of it as a safe and exciting place to gather. Unfortunately, the very things that had brought people to the park—the Happenings of the sixties and the well-attended concerts that had become a regular summer feature— had only exacerbated matters, by tearing up what remained of the grass at the Sheep Meadow and on the Great Lawn. In fact the threadbare lawns were simply a strikingly visible manifestation of a pervasive deterioration. Belvedere Castle, a faux-medieval folly over- looking the Great Lawn and Shakespeare in the Park, was crumbling— the weather station there had become outmoded and moved out; the loggia was gone; and kids, with nothing better to do, were knocking off the coping. The lovely old Dairy, first designed by Frederick Law Olmsted as a place where poor children on a Sunday outing could get wholesome milk, was now a storage depot for tools.

With its paths and benches and buildings in a shambles, Central Park was looking increasingly unappealing. "It felt unmanaged," Betsy Barlow Rogers, the first head of the Central Park Conservancy, would later say.* "The graffiti, the lack of grass, and the broken lights and benches made people feel unsafe." The Parks Department offices were housed in the Arsenal, a redbrick building at the entrance to the Central Park Zoo, built in 1848 as a munition supply depot. Hoving's successors had lacked his energy and had been thwarted by the park's entrenched bureaucracy. "There was manpower available, but the workforce was unionized and we were dealing with a broken-down system. People did the least possible," Rogers would explain.

Walking her dogs herself at least once a day, Brooke Astor was one of the park's regular users. She understood at first hand what an important resource it was and she could see with her own eyes how it

---

*Elizabeth Barlow Rogers, who became the first Central Park administrator in 1980, was the founding president of the Central Park Conservancy, serving until 1995.

was badly in need of repair. She first became involved through Louis Auchincloss's wife, Adele, who as deputy parks commissioner established the Central Park Task Force. Adele was seeking funding to draw up plans for a renovation of Belvedere Castle and also the Dairy, which would eventually be turned into an information center.

Betsy Barlow Rogers—who had been trained in landscaping and park development and thought of herself as a writer—came to the park through her former Tulane professor, who was brought in to help design the two renovations based on old photographs and plans. Although she knew Linda and Arch Gillies, she met Mrs. Astor through Adele Auchincloss. "That was one historic meeting in my life," she would later say. In 1975, Adele Auchincloss got a federal grant for a summer youth program and asked Betsy Barlow Rogers to take charge of sixty young people who would work in the park. After that Rogers was hooked. With no more federal grants in sight, she went to Linda Gillies, saying she not only wanted to work with the kids but also wanted to work on the plans for the park's restoration. "From then on the funding for my tiny salary came from the Astor Foundation," she would say.

Beginning in 1975, the Astor Foundation gave $65,000 annually for three years. Out of that Betsy Barlow Rogers paid for herself, a secretary, and an educator. After Adele left city government, it wasn't easy. Finally there was a showdown. "The parks commissioner was a retired sanitation commissioner. Someone told him I was getting money from Mrs. Astor. Suddenly time sheets had to be filled out and presented to the commissioner, who then refused to sign my time sheets for six months. Finally I went to Linda, with the result that one day Mrs. Astor marched into the Arsenal with her gloves, her hat, and her pearls to meet with the commissioner. I remember the commissioner's saying, 'You mean you want *her* to manage the grant?' Mrs. Astor said, 'Yes, Commissioner, that is what I mean.' That was that."

Out of the showdown that Betsy Rogers remembers so vividly eventually came the Central Park Conservancy, a cooperative venture between the city government and the private sector which guaranteed that Central Park would never again have to depend solely on city patronage. Not until a new parks commissioner came in with the new Koch administration in 1979 would major work begin on the restoration of the park. And not until Gordon Davis, this new commissioner, insisted Betsy take direct charge of the park as the first Central Park administrator, with an office of her own in the Arsenal where she'd had the showdown, would the Central Park Conservancy—a partnership between New York City and the private sector—begin to take shape.

Betsy Rogers, who knew nothing about managing an organization, would end up running Central Park for fifteen years. In the process, she would get better at fund-raising and begin to seek money elsewhere, but it was the Astor Foundation that came through with crucial money when she needed it. And Astor money that contributed to the renovation of the Dairy and Belvedere Castle. "Many rich people are strange—always worrying about people sticking their hands in their pockets," Betsy Barlow Rogers would say. "Brooke Astor wasn't like that. She trusted people."

With Betsy Rogers, Brooke Astor relied on the judgment of Adele Auchincloss, an old friend, but she was also willing to take a risk on people she'd just met. She trusted her intuition, even though sometimes she was later disappointed. For instance, she would soon be one of the board members active in easing her former protégé Tom Hoving out of his post at the Met. Over the course of ten years there had been a series of public embarrassments: a cracked Greek crater, whose provenance raised serious questions and whose purchase price seemed to be excessive to the average reader of *The New York Times*; a quiet but extensive deaccessioning of works of art donated to the museum in order to provide funds for expensive new purchases; a threatened incursion by the museum into surrounding land belonging to Central Park.

Of course one could say that Hoving was also facing a very different city from the one he and Brooke Astor had been living in back in 1968, when she sat for that first interview with the *Times*. Already it was becoming apparent that, without adequate city funding to help maintain them, the "outdoor living rooms" were subject to much the same sort of deterioration as Central Park. If anything, it was more rapid. Eventually the George Washington Carver Houses would become a co-op, which would have a positive effect on its "living room." And in the eighties the Astor Foundation would give a grant to help clean up and refurbish the "outdoor living room" at the Jacob Riis Houses, which for a time had become the preserve of neighborhood drug dealers.

Not all projects turned out the way they were envisioned. But Brooke Astor remained more than willing to have the Foundation back any fledgling organization that struck her as having possibilities for improving the quality of life of New York's citizens, particularly when she found its director to be articulate or energetic. Immediately she had taken a liking to Jay Iselin, the young head of WNET, New York's public television station, while checking the station out for a grant. One of the things the station needed was a block of studio space. But she didn't stop at that, going on to fund two pilot programs written by John Russell with Rosamond Bernier talking about modern art and eventually becoming one of the early funders of Charlie Rose's program of interviews. Over a lunch with Jay Iselin and her friend Jane Engelhard, Brooke Astor gave Iselin a chance to witness firsthand her well-honed fund-raising technique. Lunch was under way, with the conversation touching on various subjects, including the station's programming, when Brooke turned to Jane Engelhard and suddenly said, "Jane, I'm giving five hundred thousand. How much are *you* going to give?"

What perhaps pleased her best was when she found a new organization that was trying to honor or bring back to life part of the city's heritage, particularly when it touched on the Marshall or Astor family's early histories, when the first Charles Marshall was founding the Black Ball Line or John Jacob Astor was making his fortune in fur trading and shipping. In 1971 Peter Stanford, the president of the

South Street Seaport Museum, approached the foundation for money to help underwrite the restoration of the dilapidated South Street waterfront. Under the Lindsay administration a parcel of land had been promised by the city if the South Street Museum could raise $5 million for development. Stanford was hoping for an organic development, with many individuals involved in creating a marketplace that looked as if it had grown naturally and haphazardly.

Brooke Astor liked the idea and the Astor Foundation initially gave a grant of $150,000 for seed money to help restore some of the buildings and expand the museum. Over the next three years, individual buildings were renovated and two great sailing ships, *Wavertree* and *Peking*, were moored at the docks. Pleased by the way things were going, the Foundation then gave $1 million to help underwrite a comprehensive plan for development of the area, with the proviso that professional management would also be put in place. But times were hard, the rest of the money wasn't coming in, and city planners in the Beame administration began to seek a single developer for the project.

"Thanks to Mrs. Astor's advocacy and support, South Street had become a honeypot with bees clustered around it," Peter Stanford would later say. The bee that finally walked away with the contract was the Rouse Corporation, which had already created a marketplace in Boston's Faneuil Hall and done another waterfront restoration in Baltimore. In April 1976, when he saw the way things were headed, Peter Stanford resigned and packed up his museum and eventually moved to Peekskill, where he established the National Maritime Historical Society.

By 1976, the Vincent Astor Foundation had been making available to its citizens far larger sums than it had in the past. In 1975, it gave grants totaling $6,463,735, which included $50,000 to help start up the Citizens Committee for New York, an organization intended to encourage volunteer self-help at a grassroots level, within neighborhoods, at a time when city services were badly compromised. In 1976 it gave $5,439,429. But Brooke Astor was also giving away her own money. At charity benefits for her favorite causes you could almost always count on her to take a table or two. And when it happened that the board of the Foundation really didn't want to go along with some grant she was proposing, she would simply back off and say, "I may be committed to this one. I may do something myself."

Every week her picture would be in the newspapers—not only in the society pages but in articles about programs she wanted to bring to the public's attention. Always she was dressed up, the way she had been when she had visited those homes in Bedford-Stuyvesant. And in these pictures she looked as if she was happy to meet the people she was visiting. The city was not exactly bombed out, although parts of the South Bronx had been leveled by fire. But the effect of these pictures truly was akin to that of seeing a photograph of the Queen Mother during the Blitz. How much good Brooke Astor ultimately did, there is no telling. A drop in the bucket is a drop nonetheless.

"Her presence was important symbolically," Felix Rohatyn would say. "The effect she had in terms of her commitment was clearly very important. As was the similar symbolic commitment of Paul Moore, who was preaching from the pulpit of the Cathedral of St. John the Divine about businesses leaving the city." But what impressed Rohatyn wasn't merely her symbolic presence. "I remember I invited her to lunch at La Grenouille. It was quite a few years ago. This was a spring day and she was late. When she finally arrived, she had on white gloves that were all soiled. Practically black. I said, Brooke, what happened to your gloves? She said there was a guy who was trying to open a fire hydrant on Fifth Avenue and she decided to help him—to hold the tools while he was wrestling with the hydrant. That was Brooke."

In 1976 Brooke Astor was seventy-four years old, one year younger than Caroline Astor was when she gave her last ball and retired from society, only to be seen now and then driving in her carriage in Central Park, with an attendant at her side, nodding to greet friends she imagined were passing in their carriages—friends who had long since died. Word had it that Caroline Astor—who would never have risked soiling her gloves by holding tools for anyone—would start her day by making long lists for parties she was planning and would even have printed invitations made up, which her staff would quietly toss out. On occasion she could be spotted shopping with her attendant in some of the city's finest stores, ordering fabulously expensive items, which would be carefully wrapped and delivered, only to be returned later the same day.

Approaching an age when her famous predecessor's life had narrowed to the point where it had become a travesty of the life she had been leading, Brooke Astor found herself busier than ever. With the help of her foundation's new director, she felt as if she finally was free to make a difference. At the same time, she was having fun. Through her work with the Zoo she had gotten to know Laurance Rockefeller better. On the spur of the moment she had brought him down to South Street Seaport, to meet Peter Stanford, and had teased and coaxed him into giving some money. At the Met she was working closely with Douglas Dillon, the new chairman of the board, to help create a first-rate Asian wing. Indeed for that wing she was having plans drawn up for a replica of a scholars' garden that would be very like the ones she remembered so happily from her childhood years in China. If all went as planned, thanks to Nixon's opening up China, she would be going there herself, to visit that garden and take one last look at the Legation Quarter in Peking.

Brooke Astor was a hands-on philanthropist. And by 1976 she was a fairly experienced one. If she was distressed by what was happening at South Street Seaport, she was also not a woman who fought losing battles. Certainly she didn't let it keep her from continuing to support, or take an active part, in the Beame administration's plans for marking the completion of the nation's second century—a bicentennial celebration that called for a flotilla of tall ships from around the world and a visit from Queen Elizabeth II. As an inveterate American patriot and a long-standing Anglophile, she would have found it hard to resist.

Her plan for the Bicentennial was to come down from Holly Hill for the day with George Trescher and another friend, and then join Charles Ryskamp, with whom they'd watch the tall ships and have something to eat at Fraunces Tavern. Then all four of them would get a quick nap at rooms she had reserved at the Seaman's Church Institute, an organization the Foundation funded, before going on to a celebration down at the Battery, at Castle Clinton, where there was going to be a large crowd gathered. As far as the three friends knew, it was just a celebration, nothing more. But, when they arrived and were ushered to a patch of grass close to the speakers' platform, it turned out to be quite a lot more than that. Brendan Gill had ordered a medal struck to honor Brooke Astor for her work with the Municipal Art Society. So there was a presentation. But that wasn't all. Writing in *Footprints* the medal's proud recipient would describe what happened next as Brendan's asking the crowd to "give a cheer for 'Brooke'"—which they were more than happy to do. What George Trescher remembered was the crowd's spontaneously starting to cheer and call her name and realizing that, without his ever noticing it, his good friend Brooke Astor had become famous.

Eight

BROOKE,
1977–1996

Giving away money should be exhilarating.

In 1980, Brooke Astor's second nonfiction book, *Footprints*, was published. On its dust jacket *Footprints* was billed as an autobiography. The dictionary definition of autobiography is "a biography written by the subject," but true biography pretends to objectivity, relying on specific dates and verifiable events to create the illusion of authenticity. Of course in *Footprints* Brooke Astor was really giving readers a highly personal memoir. What gives this second memoir of Brooke Astor's its special flavor is an awareness on the writer's part that she is shaping the story of her life as she approaches the end of it. At times the tone seems almost elegiac, conveying a sense that she is looking back over what has happened, taking stock of past battles, of failures and successes, and trying to make sense of it all. Given that the writer was approaching eighty, this tone is hardly surprising. She had every reason to believe that the most important part of her life was behind her. As it turned out, nothing could be further from the truth.

Actually, the writer of this memoir had one thing she was very much looking forward to: the completion of the scholars' garden, which was to be her major contribution to the Metropolitan Museum of Art—the culmination of her collaboration over the past few years with Douglas Dillon, a very dear friend, in his push to see to it that the museum had a Far Eastern department fitting for a world-class institution. Upon assuming the chair of the museum board in 1970, Dillon had noted immediately that the Far Eastern Art Department consisted of little more than some enormous statues donated by John D. Rockefeller Jr. and a number of late Ch'ing Dynasty porcelains. With Dillon's urging, Tom Hoving had enlisted the aid of Wen C. Fong, a classmate from Princeton, to serve as part-time consultant and de facto head of the department, and together the three of them had quickly set about correcting this embarrassing inadequacy.

Wen Fong, who was given the title of "consultative chairman," managed in short order to come up with a very good group of twenty-five ancient paintings the collector C. C. Wang was thinking of selling. To pay for the paintings the museum sold a group of rare and valuable coins, and Dillon himself provided the other half of the purchase money. Immediately other owners of Asian art began to approach the museum. "Until then the museum had a very bad reputation among collectors because it hadn't shown any interest," Dillon would recall. "We doubled our holdings overnight."

Dillon, who had served in Washington as secretary of the treasury and undersecretary of state, was a man who weighed his options and took no unnecessary risks, but, like Brooke Astor, he was blessed with infinite curiosity. The two of them first got to know each other in the late sixties, when Brooke joined the Acquisitions Committee, where the curators came to make their case for any purchase they wished to make. "The Acquisitions Committee is the most fun," he would later say, "because it's educational. A lot of people on the board are not hard workers, but Brooke was quite different. She took an interest and she had good instincts."

Once Douglas Dillon's project got under way, Brooke Astor— whose interest in China he recognized as being both deep and long-standing—was more than happy to do what she could to help out.

When a collection of fine Ming period furniture owned by the collector Bob Ellsworth became available, Dillon purchased the collection for the museum. Then when plans were discussed to house the furniture in a space that would be created to resemble a scholar's room of that time, she offered to build a Ming period garden court as a setting for that room—one that would resemble courtyards she remembered from her childhood.

By 1980, thanks to the efforts of Douglas Dillon, the museum was well on its way to becoming a serious player in the field of Asian art. And, by then, he and Brooke Astor had become good friends. "She just stood out, she charmed you utterly," he would say. "She took an interest. In a restaurant she would stop to ask a waiter about his son. She was interested in what you were doing and saying—not interested in holding forth about herself—so she would draw you out and make you think you were wonderful. It's a great gift. Pamela Harriman had it too, but let's put it this way, Brooke was a flirt. Pamela was a femme fatale. She'd end up on your lap."

In 1983, when Gordon Davis, the city's excellent parks commissioner, gave a speech honoring Brooke Astor, he sounded more than half in love with her. In this respect he was hardly unique. Early on she had seen that flirtation and philanthropy were not incompatible and could, on occasion, be highly productive. Sometimes the flirtation would take a more serious turn. It was no coincidence that, when she insisted that the Foundation give the $5 million dollar grant for the Asian plain at the Bronx Zoo, Laurance Rockefeller happened to be chairman of the New York Zoological Society's board. In return he joined her for a lunch with Peter Stanford down at South Street Seaport. Laurance Rockefeller was also on the board of Memorial Sloan-Kettering, the city's great cancer hospital. In 1963 the Vincent Astor Foundation had given Sloan-Kettering a grant of $200,000 toward construction of a research laboratory, but not until the departure of Allan Betts would any more Foundation grants be forthcoming. But there was more money given during this period—money provided by Brooke Astor out of her own pocket. Learning of this years later, Laurance Rockefeller's eyes would well with tears. "But Brooke didn't have much money," he would say. And, in a sense, he was right. Compared with a Rockefeller—or to many of the men and women she was keeping company with—she really didn't.

During the months when Brooke Astor had been finishing *Footprints*, China had been very much on her mind. The previous summer she had gone to China, bringing along her French maid, Raymonde Tissot-Bellin. "She explained to me that she told the authorities that Raymonde was her secretary," Rosamond Bernier would recall, "because she thought that in Communist China if she said Raymonde was her ladies' maid it would make the wrong impression."

She and Raymonde and her real secretary, Daphne Riley, made the visit in the company of Wen Fong and his wife, Connie. The ostensible purpose of the journey was to see with her own eyes the garden court at Su-chou that was to provide a model for the court-yard to be created in space set aside in a quiet corner of the museum's new Asian art wing. Already portions of this courtyard were being crafted by Chinese artisans familiar with the old traditions and materials. Once these pieces had been assembled, they would be shipped to the New York, accompanied by a crew of specially trained work-men who would then fit them together permanently.

But for Brooke Astor, the highlight of this trip was a visit to the old Legation Quarter—a visit that proved to be bittersweet. "In a way that dreary-looking Marine barracks house, now abandoned, with a coal heap in front of it, is the only concrete thing that remains from my childhood," she wrote in the prologue to *Footprints*. "Here is the only solid evidence that a family called Russell really existed. But, of course, no one knows that but me."

George Trescher, her good friend, would later say, "Remember the most important quote in all the books she was writing is in the first page of *Footprints*. She talks about her family and says something like I learned early on that life is a lonely game to be played out alone. She believed that. For all the charm and froth, she was perfectly aware that at the end of the day you cry alone."

At this point in her life Brooke Astor was seeing to it that there was little time spent alone. In interviews she liked to say that she looked forward always to retreating to Holly Hill or Maine, where she would have large blocks of time to write on yellow tablets of paper in long-hand—conjuring up images of Edith Wharton writing in her bed at Lenox of a morning, tossing papers on the floor to be gathered up by her secretary later to be typed. While she may have been using yellow tablets of paper, her writing recently had been mostly scribbling on airplanes, she had confided to her editor, Betty Prashker.

That she loved to write, there is no question. "She loved the process—seeing the words come out. That was one of the things that was distinctive about her," Betty Prashker would say. But even at Maine and Holly Hill she rarely had time for long periods of concentration. Her months in Maine, for instance, were crowded with visitors. When the visitors were writers, she could count on their understanding her need for moments of privacy. But of course she could also count on their observing everything that transpired with a sharp eye. Rosamond Bernier, who, with her husband John Russell, was a frequent Maine visitor at this point, would remember fondly the lack of formality and the simple pleasures to be had at Brooke's camp, August Moon, where they would go for picnics and Brooke would take care to swim her thousand strokes, but she would also recall what it was like to first arrive: "Brooke would say, 'Well of course there's nobody—we're not doing anything.' And then it turned out there were twenty people coming to dinner that night. And then we were going out to lunch the next day. We were going out here, we were going out there."

During quiet times in the morning, when Brooke Astor would

remain in her room, free to pick up pen and paper, the phone would start ringing at about ten. "The main house is really a small house," Bernier would recall, "and when I would be staying in the next room to Brooke's, it would be chat chat chat. There was only one line at that point and after ten there was no question of getting a call in to anyone. Brooke was on the phone."

The camp, on the other hand, was pure heaven, with a picnic lunch of fresh lobster, and no servants in attendance. "For the picnic we all set the table. Afterward, she meticulously cleaned up. No trash left behind. A dramatic moment came when we were on our way back from the camp one day and she discovered that one of the dogs was missing. All hell broke loose. Back we drove. Frantically she was calling the little dog. It wasn't in the pavilion. She was worried that it had wandered off too far."

Fortunately, the dog was recovered and peace was restored. Dogs were part of her daily life everywhere, but especially so in Maine, where she would often meet her friend Nancy Pyne at around four and they would take their dogs for a long walk—sometimes around a nearby lake and sometimes along a path by the golf course.

"I had four dogs and Brooke had two and we were some sight, let me tell you," Nancy Pyne would recall. "We would go up mountains and down mountains. Mine were Norwich terriers and one would go after some squirrel and Brooke would whistle and whistle. Brooke had a wonderful whistle, something like what you'd use for a cab in New York. These were easy trails, but as her dogs got older, Brooke had to carry them down the mountains. I had a dog called Sappho who was crazy about Brooke. One time we were sitting on the ground with our knees up, the way you do, resting. Sappho sat herself down under Brooke's legs and growled at Brooke's dogs when they tried to come close. My husband and I had a portrait painted of Sappho and had a copy made for Brooke, with an inscription on the back: 'All I want is to be Mrs. Astor's dog.'"

"She loves those dogs of hers," Laurance Rockefeller would say. "And she loves the company of people. If she can't have people, she talks to the dogs as though they were people. She does." For Brooke, dogs were in a way her family. Certainly they were her most reliable companions. During her many years of philanthropy Brooke Astor tended to respond to the people involved with the institutions she was committed to—either the people who were running the institutions or the people who were being served by them. This was especially true for the Animal Medical Center, where back in 1975 she and Linda Gillies had first put together Seniors' Animal Veterinary Endowment (SAVE), a program to serve elderly people with pets.

During her own visits to the center, she had observed that elderly people tended to have elderly pets and very little money to care for them. The fund that the Foundation helped set up would help cover these costs. Before long she had also made friends with the staff—not only with William Kaye, the director, whom she liked to drop by and visit, but with a young veterinarian by the name of Philip Fox, whom she first met on a hot July day, not long after he'd arrived from Ohio, when she was sitting in the waiting room, waiting her turn. "At that time it looked like the waiting room at the Port Authority Terminal," Fox would recall. "I remember she was wearing a white dress with black polka dots, a black hat with a little black veil, and white gloves. She was sitting there with a little schnauzer on her lap. I pulled up the record and called Brooke Astor, but I had no clue who she was. She followed me into a small examining room and put the dog on the examining table and then in a second she reached out her right hand and said, 'Hi, call me Brooke.'"

From then on, Philip Fox would take care of all her dogs. And until her late nineties, she would bring them in to see him herself, waiting her turn and paying for the visit in full. Their first exchange, which left him laughing, was typical of many that would follow. "I remember she said, 'This is Jennie, named after Jennie Churchill—

with permission of course. I have another dog named Winston. He's named after Winston Churchill—also with permission. And then I have Freddy. He's named for Frederick the Great.' She then said, 'But of course he's long dead'—implying there was no need to ask *him* for permission."

It wasn't only dogs that she saw as being special. After Wild Asia, the enormous plain at the Bronx Zoo, officially opened in 1977, she would sometimes stop by at twilight to see the deer being called in for the night. The Zoo was understandably grateful for the more than $7 million the Foundation had spent to make Wild Asia possible. In 1979, when one of their Asian elephants suddenly became pregnant—a rare happening, attributable the keepers believed, at least in part, to this wonderful new environment—a decision was made to name the baby "Brooke" if it was a girl and "Astor" if it was a boy. When the elephant was finally born, after twenty-two months of gestation, it *was* a boy and an instant media star. "Astor the elephant had three mothers—Mrs. Astor and me and his real mother," his keeper, Penny Kalk, would recall. "After Astor was born, she would go right in there with him. Baby elephants are very personable, sociable, playful, smart, and inquisitive. They want to connect. We all felt Astor was the most enchanting baby that ever was. Mrs. Astor was really proud and really thrilled and she should have been."

When Astor died eighteen months later—having suddenly begun to fail for no apparent reason—it was heartbreaking for everyone. Rather than have her read it in the newspaper, Brooke Astor called Linda Gillies at home, to break the news to her. " I remember she called and said, 'Astor died. Just like that,'" Linda Gillies would recall. "No beating around the bush. She taught me to be direct and come out with it when something terrible happens." Brooke Astor was a realist and by then had lived through many terrible deaths. Nonetheless, she was ready to reach out and comfort someone she understood was in distress. "Mrs. Astor and I exchanged notes. He was such a powerful spirit. It was the most painful loss I've ever experienced," Penny Kalk would say.

When it came to animals, Brooke Astor tried always to be fair, just as she did when dealing with people. Certainly she tried to give them the benefit of the doubt. During the summer of 1988, seeking to break up a fight among her dogs, she would reach in to separate them, and the third finger of her right hand would be badly banged up. In the end she would lose the tip. There was some debate about having the dog who had done this destroyed. But she held off. "It was a Norfolk terrier," William Kaye, the head of the Animal Medical Center, would recall. "The way she was stepping in to break up the fight was typical. Hands on. Not with a bucket of water. Friends of hers were concerned for her. Bites are traumatic and they hurt. Some friends wanted to have the dog killed and she asked me my opinion. I said it was an accident. For someone who had lost a finger, she was remarkable. She was as concerned about the dog as she was about herself." In the end she did not have the dog destroyed, but she didn't keep him, either. Instead, she saw to it that he went to a "good family."

She was fair, and she was always ready to give someone a chance. When Henry Kissinger, whom she'd met through Nelson Rockefeller, and knew a bit from when he was secretary of state, first arrived in New York in 1977, she gave a number of dinners to introduce him to her New York friends. Kissinger was definitely a controversial figure. And he was no longer in power. But she had made up her mind. It was a quality he valued perhaps the most in her. "She doesn't look for approval, although she is happy to have it," he would say. "She is prepared to walk alone. She likes to be appreciated, but she does not act in order to seek appreciation. She likes to know important people but she doesn't cater to them. And she is very loyal to her friends."

She was loyal to her friends and happy to share in their good fortune. In December 1980, she created a far greater stir than she had earlier that same year with the publication of *Footprints* when she quickly pulled together a dinner to honor a newly elected Ronald Reagan, whose wife, Nancy, she had met more than twenty years before, during her stays in Phoenix with Vincent Astor. Just as she had taken care to introduce Henry Kissinger to New Yorkers she liked and admired in positions of power, she was more than happy to do the same for Nancy and her husband, the country's next president. She didn't consult with the Reagans about the guest list, but, instead, invited to a sit-down dinner at her apartment seventy people she believed had one thing in common: their concern for New York.

Here, the woman with a natural gift for politics may have been doing a little matchmaking or "consciousness raising"—since Ronald Reagan's immediate predecessors had shown no particular interest in the city. But she couldn't very well say that. Instead, Brooke Astor told the reporter from *The New York Times*, one of many journalists who were treating this hastily thrown together gathering as groundbreaking news, "I have always been a Republican and I've done nothing for the Republicans for a long time." The list of people who she believed shared her concern for the city was quite diverse, ranging from political figures and foundation heads to media moguls and star television reporters. Henry Kissinger and his wife were among the seventy people seated at round tables of ten set up in the apartment. As were the William F. Buckleys, the Douglas Dillons, the Felix Rohatyns, the Oscar de la Rentas, the Arthur Sulzbergers, the Samuel Reeds, the Mike Wallaces, and Frank Thomas, now head of the Ford Foundation. In addition, you could find Charles Ryskamp, Jane Engelhard, Vernon Jordan, Marietta Tree, Bill Blass, Happy Rockefeller, and Aileen Mehle, who as "Suzy" covered the goings-on of New York Society for the *Daily News*.

Aileen Mehle, who enjoyed the good fortune of being among those favored, returned the favor in kind, by comparing Brooke Astor with the first Mrs. Astor: "Today, as any social arbiter will tell you, times have changed," she wrote. "But we still have a Mrs. Astor, *The* Mrs. Astor, a slender, attractive philanthropist who administers the Astor Foundation, writes books and charms all with her wit and verve. She doesn't try squeezing the 400 into her ballroom—she doesn't even have a ballroom—but she does give spendid dinners at her beautiful duplex apartment on Park Avenue, to which invitations are coveted."

The dinner served was nothing like any meal the first Mrs. Astor would have given her guests, although it bore some resemblance to the dinners Sean Driscoll's Glorious Food had been catering for Brooke Astor for some time. This Mrs. Astor liked "homey food," her favorite menus being chicken or quail or pheasant pies.

There was no chicken pie that night, but the dinner relied, as all her dinners did, on good quality straightforward food that was bound to please men. After a first course of pasta, the guests got to feast on cold ham and spinach and salads and cheese. The dessert was a chocolate cake. Sean Driscoll would later say, "Mrs. Astor was old-fashioned in that she was of the school that believed the way to a man's heart was always to end the meal with chocolate."

If that was her intention, she succeeded. Indeed when one of her pearl-and-diamond earrings fell off during dinner, the President-elect, who was seated on her right, joined in the search—first shaking out his trouser leg and then crouching on the floor with her, beneath the table, and then, when nothing came of this, suggesting (with a prescience that seemed to bode well for the future) that she might try shaking out the bodice of her knee-length black Chanel lace dress. The earring was retrieved and a close presidential friendship was forged.

In New York, the same night of the Reagan dinner, the James Van Alens—who claimed a close relation to Caroline Schermerhorn Astor—were giving their annual performance of *A Visit from St. Nicholas*, to which *they* were expecting four hundred people. James

Van Alen, whose wife, Candy, cut quite a swathe in Newport and Palm Beach, was in fact the grandson of Caroline Astor's eldest daughter, Emily. No one had seen fit to mention the connection in the brief article in the *New York Post*, where the performance was mentioned as providing a potential conflict for some guests. And Brooke Astor saw no reason to include the Van Alens in her original guest list. But the slight may have rankled.

Certainly the Van Alens were not pleased by the talk Brooke Astor gave a year later at the Knickerbocker Club, an evening organized by Ashton Hawkins, to which several Astor relations had apparently been added by the club at the last minute—perhaps with the hope of filling empty seats. The other Astors attending the talk were Jack Astor's daughter, Jackie; and Winthrop Aldrich, the Astor descendant currently residing with his family at Rokeby. It was a talk that Ashton Hawkins would remember as a great success, and one that Winthrop Aldrich would remember as ill prepared and given without any notes.

The talk delivered at the Knickerboker was a variation on one that Brooke Astor had given before and it would eventually be printed, in a more polished form, in a South Street Seaport bulletin. The tone was characteristic—light, amused, and gently self-deprecating. Brooke Astor was pleased to be part of the Astor family when it served her purposes—or suited the purposes of the organizations she was helping—but she refused to take either the family or herself all that seriously. At one point, Winthrop Aldrich would recall, she spoke of the first John Jacob Astor's marrying Sarah Todd and then added, "Vincent always told me that old John Jacob married above his station. And I guess I did, too."

It was the conclusion of the talk, however—when she went on to say that now that Vincent was dead she guessed she was the last of the Astors, although there were some Astors in England—that provoked Candace Van Alen to rise up and shout, "'How dare you say there are no Astors left," pointing out that not only her husband but also Winthrop Aldrich and Jackie were in the room.

It would seem that the room emptied quickly, but, owing to a heavy downpour outside, there was no getting away quickly from the club. Winthrop Aldrich would recall waiting in a long line for a cab, standing next to a visibly upset Happy Rockefeller, who—turning at one point and seeing the two women going at it on the landing behind them—said, "One doesn't know what to do. After all, it's a family matter."

It *was* a family matter and Brooke Astor had long since given up on the American branch of her family. Among the English Astors she had always been welcome, and she happened to prefer the English Astors anyway. Since childhood she'd had a special fondness for England and all things English. Unlike her mother, she did not have much use for Continental novelists—Dickens and Trollope were more to her taste. Having her purse snatched when she had visited London on her way back from Peking had done nothing to sour her feelings toward the city. Her honeymoon visit to Buddie's mother had been idyllic and with Vincent she had stayed with Lord Astor and his family at Cliveden. The fact that Vincent had sickened there several months before his death didn't diminish this fondness.

At least once a year she would make a trip to London and stay at the Hotel Connaught, where she had them store her linens in antici-pation of her arrival and where she would give a lavish luncheon for all her London friends before going on to visit with friends in the countryside—preferably friends with many dogs. In the country she might stay at Hatfield with Molly Salisbury. Or with Molly's son Lord Cranbourne and his wife. Or she might stay with William Astor and his wife and family. In London she tried to see Vincent's niece Romana McEwen and visit with her own good friend Nin Ryan, who made England her home half the year, and with Nin's daughter, now Countess Airlie, lady-in-waiting to the Queen.

These trips to England were pure pleasure, steeped in the romance of history—burnished further with her reading of Henry James and Edith Wharton—and unencumbered by any bad feeling from people with long memories who regarded themselves as her social equals or superiors. Even in her eighties she was making new friends among the English aristocracy—most notably, the Duchess of Devonshire, the youngest sister of Nancy Mitford. The literary connection surely pleased her, but she couldn't help admiring the way the duchess, a handsome but hardworking entrepreneur, and her husband, Andrew, had turned Chatsworth, one of the great houses of England, into both a beautiful museum and a flourishing business.

It had taken her longer to warm to William, Lord Astor, who had gone on to marry the granddaughter of the writer Enid Bagnold and become a successful businessman and even, for a time, a member of Margaret Thatcher's government. She had first gotten to know him when he came to New York as a young journalist back in 1970, with the long hair and style of dress characteristic of young men of his generation. "I don't mean this as a kind of criticism," he would later say, "but the first six months I was in New York, I remember Brooke not being disappointed exactly but feeling not as cozy as I had felt with Brooke when I was a boy. Suddenly Brooke decided that even though I might look long-haired I was an adult. Once she made that decision, it was all fine."

In England, being the wealthy widow of Vincent Astor did her no harm and actually carried some weight. The same could be said for most circles in New York. Certainly the name Astor as well as the money she had inherited with it made her welcome on almost every important board in the city. She was not only the first woman to take a place on the board of the New York Zoological Society but the first woman to be asked to join the board of Rockefeller University, where she early on let the gentlemen there know that she would greatly appreciate it if they would forgo their cigars at future meetings. While the Astor name may have helped get her onto boards, like that of the Morgan Library, it was her performance that continued to make her welcome. She asked good questions. And when called on to contribute to a discussion, she always offered an opinion that was lucid and concise and, above all, showed good common sense.

The Astor name was one that frankly added luster to the Foundation she ran, just as her presence added glamour. Some might call it "branding." If so, then it was a very high-quality brand. Coupled with the fact that she and Linda Gillies ran a foundation whose judgment over the years was shown to be sound and almost unfailingly reliable, by the early eighties a grant from the Vincent Astor Foundation was tantamount to a Good Housekeeping Seal of Approval. Knowing the organization in question had been carefully vetted, other foundations felt comfortable following in their wake. Viewed in a certain light, the Vincent Astor Foundation could be seen as venture capitalists. Even a grant as small as $1,000 was potential seed money, capable of producing, with time, substantial returns.

In the spring of 1981, the scholars' garden, now known as the Astor Court, opened with great fanfare, having cost the Foundation a total of $9.6 million. This was a considerable sum—among the very largest that the Foundation had seen fit to dispense. During the course of the past two years Brooke Astor had had the pleasure of welcoming a crew of twenty-seven skilled Chinese workmen, whom she had happily put up in a hotel for the six months of their stay. In her effort to see that they felt at home in the city, she had a chef brought along to prepare the regional dishes they were accustomed to eating. In addition, she made sure that they were not neglected on weekends— going so far as to arrange a trip for them to Washington to see the gardens at Dumbarton Oaks. All of this had made good copy for the newspapers. And all of this had given her great pleasure. Whatever you thought of the finished structure, the process of building it had been extraordinary. The opening had to be in some ways anticlimactic, if only because it was fundamentally like all museum openings. After the initial excitement, visitors to the Astor Court began to taper off, in part at least because this island of serenity was tucked away at the rear of all the new Asian galleries and difficult to find. Given all this, a letdown was probably inevitable.

Then, in 1982, within a year of the Astor Court's opening, Brooke Astor was asked to retire from the museum's board. She was way past the official age for retirement, which was set at seventy-two, with a little leeway to allow a board member to serve out his or her seven-year term. (Of course, at this point her age was still a matter of conjecture.) Ashton Hawkins, who had been delegated to deliver the news, would later say that she seemed to take it gracefully. No one likes to be asked to step down, he noted, but with time they become resigned to serving the museum in an emeritus capacity. Contrary to what he might believe, she did not take this gracefully. And she did not become resigned to it. Why exactly, it's hard to say.

Partly it may have been because she thought Douglas Dillon could have intervened on her behalf, but chose not to. Partly it may have been because she believed she might have done something to cause this. Certainly her relations with the board's president were not what they had once been. Earlier in 1982, Douglas Dillon's wife, who had been ill for some time, had died. During the period of his wife's illness, the two of them had become closer than ever. "Douglas Dillon was very keen on Brooke," Nancy Pierrepont would recall. "I remember her staying with Jackie and me in the country and she'd gone upstairs and he came over. Our two places were on either side of the road. We hadn't asked him or anything. He ran into the house and then right upstairs—Jackie was astonished." After his wife's death, he became even more keen on Brooke, it would seem. "There is a whole chapter to be written about *their* relationship," Ashton Hawkins would later say. "He certainly—for reasons nobody could completely understand—not only became deeply fond of her but even wanted to marry her."

The trouble was, she didn't want to marry Douglas Dillon. "I don't want to end up having to take care of that old man," one of her friends would recall her saying, although that old man was actually eight years younger than she was. "He was younger," Nancy Pierrepont would say, "but he didn't have as much go as she did. Nobody did."

The fact was, she was fond of Douglas Dillon and would no doubt have been happy for things to continue as they had. Seeing the way things were headed, she chose, instead, to exercise some control and set about finding him a wife—taking credit for coming up with the widow of both DeWitt Sage and Jack Buchanan, the English Fred Astaire. Then, having found Douglas Dillon a suitable wife, she came to feel that this wife was treating her badly. By then, though, she herself had taken action on another front, which might well have been upsetting to Douglas Dillon.

In 1983, not long after she had been asked to officially retire as a full board member and remain in an emeritus capacity, she announced that she was resigning from all boards in the city in order to devote herself exclusively to the New York Public Library. Her decision, which was announced with no prior notice, received major play in the newspapers. Possibly she meant exactly what she said. After all, she would also be retiring from the boards of the New York Zoological Society (now known as the Wildlife Conservation Society), the Morgan Library, and Rockefeller University. Possibly the timing of this announcement was a coincidence. Possibly, having seen that the museum was in better shape than it had been in decades—and having recognized that the mission she had embarked on with Douglas Dillon had been accomplished—she concluded that it made sense to move on to an institution that needed her more.

Whatever the motive behind this decision, the announcement caused great consternation within the museum, prompting its director, Philippe de Montebello to write her, asking her to please reconsider her decision. She had no idea how much she meant to the museum, he told her in no uncertain terms. It was a letter few readers would be able to ignore. If she was feeling wounded, it could have provided more than sufficient balm for those wounds. In time she did relent—albeit quietly—not only serving on the board, the Acquisitions Committee, and as head of the Asian Traveling Fellows Committee but also providing a generous endowment to maintain the Astor Court and endowing a chair for James Watt, who joined the department the year before it was renamed the Department of Asian Art, in 1986, and became its first full-time head and eventually, in 2000, the Brooke Russell Astor Chairman.

Seen from the museum's perspective, Brooke Astor's announcement had been damaging. Seen from the perspective of the New York Public Library, it had been a very public vote of confidence from a very public figure. From the time of her marriage to Vincent, Brooke Astor had been sitting on the board of the New York Public Library, more out of a sense of duty than out of any passionate commitment to the Research Library. Always she had been happy to fund the branches, providing money to keep them open for children after school and also to purchase books. Of course, books had always been a key part of her life. And of course she herself was a writer. From the start she had seen to it that Vincent's foundation provided support for the Library.

Early on the Foundation had helped underwrite the conversion of the Arnold Constable building across the street from the imposing Beaux-Arts structure. And here at least the newly renovated building appeared to be in reasonable shape. But the Main Research Library—which could rightly be regarded as belonging among the city's "crown jewels"—was in grave disrepair. The branch libraries were basically supported by city funding, but the beautiful Hastings and Carrère building on Fifth Avenue, world famous for its enormous reading room, relied on private donations for 75 percent of its budget. Most New Yorkers were not aware of this—although they were aware of the fact that the Library was not a place they wished to visit, unless they had to. For most New Yorkers, the Library had long ceased to be a destination of choice. Behind the Library you had Bryant Park, a resort of drug dealers and junkies. Within the building itself you had poorly lit corridors, crumbling walls, peeling ceilings, a staff that tried its best but was desperately underpaid and overworked, as well as a total lack of security. It was no exaggeration to say that you could be mugged in those dark halls. Stepping into the recesses of this library you were taking your life in your hands. No less important, the books that you were holding in those hands were rapidly crumbling because of deteriorating conditions. Everyone involved, from the librarians to the board members, was aware that matters were desperate. But no one knew quite what to do about it, or even where to start.

Pleading in ads for money seemed not to help. If anything those ads seemed to put people off. Contributions to the Main Library were dwindling, and the board seemed, for the most part, to be sleepwalking. Bryant Park, though it looked to be part of the Library property, fell within the domain of the city's park's commissioner—which was part of the problem, since funding was difficult to come by and oversight was virtually impossible. Gordon Davis, walking into the office of the Library's president one day to discuss what, if anything, could be done about Bryant Park, discovered the Library's president sitting reading a novel. Given the insurmountable problems this president was facing, Davis couldn't really blame him. In his place, too, he might have done the same.

The Library had been hemorrhaging money. City financial support had been cut way back and there were worse cuts coming. The Library was closed on Wednesday and closed early Friday and also closed every other weekend. While she held out little hope for things getting better,

Brooke Astor, as a committed board member, had continued to help fund the ongoing operations of the Library with grants from the Vincent Astor Foundation. Sometimes they amounted to nothing more than $10,000 or $20,000, although in 1975, the Foundation gave a $1 million grant to help the Library's endowment. But in 1977, seeing the situation at the Library only worsening and seeing no help forthcoming from either private funders or the city government, she decided to give the Library an unprecedented grant of $5 million. By then, however, she was an experienced philanthropist. She had no intention of watching that money go down a bottomless black hole. At the same time, she was concerned by the fact that Richard Couper, the Library's president, had also been elected as the board's chairman, in large part because no one on the board wanted the job. She knew this was a terrible idea and was even thinking of resigning.

There are several quite articulate and conflicting versions of what happened next. What is clear is that Brooke Astor, Richard Salomon, Andrew Heiskell, Gregory Long, Marshall Rose, and Vartan Gregorian took upon themselves the task of making things better. Together they managed to transform this disaster area into one of the city's premier cultural institutions, not just a viable destination but also a place where one would want very much to be seen.

What was accomplished was heroic, and unquestionably there were real heroes. But for a sense of what was going on behind the scenes, even before many of the real heroes became involved, it is helpful to rely on William Dietel, who would always regard himself as someone who was there to bear the hero's shield. At this point Dietel was director of the Rockefeller Brothers Fund. The turnaround began in 1977, he would say, with Brooke Astor's approaching Laurance Rockefeller, then chairman of the fund, and asking him to help her make sure that the Foundation's $5 million dollar grant would not go to waste. A study had already been done showing what was needed. The problem was how to go about putting it into effect.

William Dietel was called in to meet with the two of them. The first necessary step, it was decided, was to make some changes in the Library's board. The trouble was, no one of any stature wanted to take on the job of chairman. First, fine sounding as the title was, the position made great demands on one's time. Second, to accept the position was to accept a poisoned chalice, if only because things at the Library seemed bound to get worse, no matter how hard you worked. Dietel's task was to find someone who would agree to be chairman, despite all these evident drawbacks. That's when luck came in, he would recall. Not long after that meeting he had the good fortune to run into a young man working for the fund whose father had retired as president of the cosmetics company Charles of the Ritz and was now retiring from its board. That young man's father was Richard Salomon, who turned out to have spent a lot of time at his neighborhood library as a boy growing up in New York. After the two men talked, Salomon consulted with Ben Sonnenberg, the great public relations man, whose judgment he respected. Sonnenberg advised him to meet with Brooke Astor before making any decision. That was all it took. "Dick met Brooke and was swept off his feet," William Dietel would recall.

Not long after Richard Salomon was elected to the Library's board as chairman, William Dietel joined him there. "Dick had a capacity to think ahead. In today's jargon 'to think strategically,'" Dietel would say. First, though, Richard Salomon had to tell the board how bad things really were. Second, he needed to find another strong board member, who had the time to devote to turning things around and who could replace him in five years when he ran up against the Library's age limit for chairmen. In 1978, he and Dietel turned to Andrew Heiskell, who was about to retire as head of Time, Inc., but had tremendous energy and excellent connections, as well as an office and full-time secretary. They persuaded Heiskell to join by promising him he could resign after a year if he didn't like it.

All they had to do now was ease the novel-reading president of the

Library out of his comfortable office. The fact was, he was a gentle and perfectly likable man who, faced with rapidly worsening conditions, had long ago given up hope. To ease him out, Richard Salomon came up with a face-saving strategy, telling him the Library was ready for new leadership all round. To soften the blow Salomon stepped down as chairman of the board. A search committee was immediately formed to find a new president; Richard Salomon stayed on the board; and Andrew Heiskell took over as the board's chairman.

William Dietel was the head of the presidential search committee and Vartan Gregorian proved to be the most impressive candidate. He was still serving as provost at the University of Pennsylvania but actively seeking a job elsewhere, having been rejected, for reasons that didn't make much sense in hindsight, as the university's next president. "I interviewed Vartan Gregorian and immediately knew he was what we were looking for," recalled Dietel. "When I sent him on to Andrew, their first conversation was supposed to last for half an hour and went on for two hours instead. Afterward, Andrew came running into my office, crying, 'Bill, he's it.' The third person to interview Vartan was Dick Salomon. And the fourth was Brooke. Brooke thought Vartan had what it took."

Brooke gave a dinner to welcome Vartan Gregorian and his wife, Clare, to New York almost exactly a year after her dinner to welcome the Reagans, using virtually the same guest list she had used before— if not the same menu. The dinner was a good idea, but the choice of Vartan Gregorian was inspired. "Vartan was made for New York," William Dietel would recall. "I don't know who said it first, but it was true." Instead of crying poor, Vartan Gregorian made it known to the press that the Library was now getting contributions from donors who had faith in it. Gordon Davis saw an immediate change. When someone stole the Christmas wreaths from Patience and Fortitude, the two lions who flank the imposing entrance to the Main Research Library, he called up saying that the Parks Department would be happy to provide new wreaths and a guard to protect them. "Vartan said, 'I'll tell you what. I'll raise the money to replace the wreaths and you provide the security.' I thought, Well, it looks like we may have a new era here. Then all of a sudden the Library took off."

The arrival of Gregory Long from the Bronx Zoo as vice president in charge of development was instrumental in making this possible. Long was a master of public relations. "But he was doing much more than that," William Dietel would say. "He was the one who kept the program going—who reminded us of the next steps to take." One of the first steps, it was decided, was to attract donors with deep pockets. The trouble was, those were not the people who tended to use the Library. A way had to be found to get them in the door. And the best way to accomplish this was to make the Library building look well cared for and safe.

In addition to its vast collection of books, the New York Public Library, including its branch libraries, owned some very impressive real estate—all of it in need of immediate repair. A few months after Vartan Gregorian's arrival, a young but well-regarded real estate lawyer named Marshall Rose was brought in to head a newly formed building committee. Instead of buying books with a $4 million grant the Library had received from the Ford Foundation, the board decided to start fixing the buildings these books were housed in, starting with the Main Library on Fifth Avenue. Andrew Heiskell saw to raising the money and Marshall Rose saw to it that they had the best architects and contractors available—cleaning the façade, restoring the main hall, and tearing apart a rabbit's warren of office cubicles on the main floor to reveal a glorious old exhibition space rechristened Gottesman Hall.

When it came to attracting private donors, Brooke Astor proved invaluable, not only by serving as a highly visible Library patron, whose last name was used to christen the newly cleaned main hall, but to join with George Trescher and Richard Salomon in organizing events that would make the Library chic. Between them, Trescher and Salomon came up with the idea of the Literary Lions dinner. One of the first writers to be invited was Robert Caro, who had been living for a year in Texas, cut off from news of Gregorian's arrival. Caro had written *The Power Broker*, his study of Robert Moses, in the Library's Allen Room. When he received a phone call from a friend in Gregorian's office, asking him to come speak, he demurred, having had disappointing experiences at Library dinners in the past. When he hesitated, he was told, "This guy does everything right." Caro and his wife were flown up from Texas and a car came to collect them from their apartment. When they arrived at the Library there was a red carpet. An attendant in a red hunting coat stepped forward and slipped a wide ribbon with a gold medallion over Caro's head. Upstairs, on the third floor, he recalled, "I turned the corner and was surprised to see the whole right world of New York." How, he wondered more than two decades later, did Vartan Gregorian and Brooke Astor manage to pull this off?

The way Brooke did it was to work hard, according to Gregory Long, who had worked with her during his time at the Zoo. Once again she was happy to invite potential donors to dinners at her apartment. Happy to write special notes. Sometimes he would send her a draft and she would recast what he sent her, using her own voice. This sort of thing was not typical of most board members. "She was a real workhorse," he would recall. In effect, she was once again doing what she had done years before for Tom Hoving. Now, however, she brought to her efforts a visibility she hadn't enjoyed back then.

It was the Astor name in part. And that part worked quite well down at City Hall. Although three-quarters of the Library's funding came from private donations, it was important to keep the city's mayors aware that municipal contributions were also very much needed. When budget cuts were threatened, Brooke Astor was happy to join Vartan and Andrew Heiskell to visit the mayor. Every city mayor was in awe of her. And people with deep pockets wanted to be with her. But it was more than that. "What makes Brooke special is the totality of herself," Andrew Heiskell would say. "The way she goes about doing things. Her ability to talk up projects. And then her particular charm. There are so many sides to her. What makes her less than perfect is she is also very human. In her humanity she reveals all sorts of aspects that do not make her perfect, but make her fun."

The Library board was notoriously stodgy. Marshall Rose would recall the impression he had at the first meeting he attended of a room full of WASPs. Old money was not going to turn the Library around. And it was Brooke Astor's great achievement, in conjunction with Vartan Gregorian and Andrew Heiskell, to lure new money onto the Library board. Between them they got Dorothy Cullman, Liz Rohatyn, and Carter Burden to join the board, persuading them that they, too, would have fun.

In 1985, when the Library was undertaking a major capital campaign to raise more than $300 million, Brooke Astor kicked it off by having the Vincent Astor Foundation contribute $10 million, the largest single grant that it had ever made. Gregory Long saw to it that word got to all the papers, just as he had seen to it that the papers were notified when Brooke announced two years earlier that the Library was getting the benefit of her full attention. This donation spurred David Rockefeller to contribute $2.5 million to create a Brooke Russell Astor Rare Books and Manuscripts Reading Room. Next Dorothy Cullman came up with $10 million to create the Brooke Russell Astor Scholars and Writers Center. After that, major contributions poured in.

The Library might be the focus of Brooke Astor's attention, but she still continued to devote most of her hours to Foundation work. The grant of $10 million to the Library marked the end of an era. In 1986, having given away more than $85 million in ten years, the Foundation found itself with assets sufficient for only $1.5 million worth of grants a year. No one in New York seemed to notice the difference. If anything, the Foundation had never been more visible. Although many of its grants now came to no more than $2,500, its annual list of grants were almost triple what it had been in the sixties.

The fact was, with Mrs. Astor's presence and the Foundation's backing, a grant was every bit as valuable as it had always been. The reputation of the Foundation was such that a grant continued to be regarded as a seal of approval, making it possible to solicit money from better funded sources. And the presence of the Foundation's president had become an instant guarantee of free publicity, attracting as she invariably did reporters and photographers.

In 1986, on the heels of the publication of her second novel, *The Last Blossom on the Plum Tree*—a novel that went into seven (modest) printings and inspired Michiko Kakutani of *The New York Times* to invoke the ghost of Jane Austen—Brooke Astor was honored by the American Academy of Arts and Letters. This time she was being honored for what she had done for the arts instead of for her more civic-minded philanthropy. In the early days she had relied on long prepared speeches or a stack of index cards when she spoke but she now had enough stock phrases to fall back on so that she could safely ad-lib. On this occasion, she used a printed text that came to less than a page. If nothing else, she had learned to keep her speeches brief. But sometimes she liked to push the envelope, perhaps to let her audience know she was not just another sweet little old lady.

Standing before a gathering of several hundred writers and visual artists at their big May meeting, she thanked the academy for the honor it had bestowed upon her. She then said that from the very start of her foundation work she had kept in mind one simple idea. Taking care to make mention of a long dead and totally respectable academy member, she proceeded to share with them this nugget of wisdom: "I remembered that Thornton Wilder said, that money was like manure and that it should be spread around. So what we have done is to spread around this manure, and I have been raking it."

Diligently she continued raking it. But she never lost her appetite for mischief, or her taste for drama and adventure. In that area at least Brendan Gill had always been able to satisfy her, perhaps because he, too, liked to wring as much excitement as possible from any occasion. In 1978 Brendan Gill had enlisted her support to save the Villard Houses from being torn down by the Helmsleys, real estate developers who had bought the property from the Catholic Church and who planned to raze three adjoining nineteenth-century mansions fronting Madison Avenue across from St. Patrick's Cathedral, in order to build a great luxury hotel. By getting all parties to meet in the Foundation's offices, Brooke Astor and Linda Gillies helped not only to get the Helmsleys to revise their plans and preserve the existing buildings but also to get them to permit the Municipal Art Society to purchase the decrepit north wing, to use as its headquarters. The Foundation then provided money to help purchase the north wing, which for many years had been the headquarters of Bennett Cerf's Random House. Space was set aside on the ground floor for a highly specialized architecture bookstore, which the Kaplan Foundation was prepared to underwrite. Making this all the more satisfying was having had the adventure of climbing the unlit broken staircase of the north wing on a rainy winter morning, with Brendan Gill leading the way, holding a flashlight and treating the band of intrepid adventurers to a piercing rendition of "Danny Boy."

Unfortunately, most undertakings weren't quite that much fun. Over the years Brendan Gill had impressed upon her the importance of historic preservation—something she had mixed feelings about, understanding that its ramifications could be complicated. Nonetheless she had joined with Jacqueline Onassis and other concerned citizens to prevent St. Bartholomew's Church from selling its air rights to a developer. She'd also joined the fight to keep the developer Peter Kalikow from razing City and Suburban Homes, a large block of yellow brick six-story walkups, with good ventilation and decent lighting, stretching from Seventy-eighth to Seventy-ninth streets, and from York Avenue to the FDR Drive. City and Suburban was the first public housing project of its kind, financed at the turn of the twentieth century by a group of millionaires, including John Jacob Astor IV, who hoped to do good while turning a profit.

The fight with Kalikow would drag on for almost a decade. But you could find Brooke Astor all dressed up, sometimes alone and sometimes with Linda Gillies, sitting in on community meetings; writing letters to *The New York Times*; offering support through a dispiriting series of legal setbacks as the Coalition to Save City and Suburban Housing tried to attain landmark status for the entire square block; and finally providing a grant of $25,000 to cover the cost of a well-researched report to prove that in its present form, once important repairs were made, this historic complex could become commercially viable.

Like Brendan Gill, Vartan Gregorian could be counted on to provide excitement wherever he happened to be. On the surface, he and Brooke Astor couldn't have been more different. He was an Armenian immigrant who at first seemed to be nothing more than that—a big hugger, cheerful and enthusiastic—but he was also a scholar and a man of great energy and curiosity. Like Brooke Astor, he, too, was full of common sense. Before long, his social life was even more active than Brooke Astor's, with sometimes as many as two or three breakfast meetings and lunches per day as well as the various dinners he had to attend every night.

They had been reared in different cultures and belonged to different generations, but Brooke Astor and Vartan Gregorian saw the world in similar ways. Gregorian, who had spent his early years in Iran, had an acute awareness that there was much to be learned from the natural world and much to be learned from other cultures. What he admired in Brooke Astor, among many things, was the fact that she was not parochial in her outlook. He had arrived at the Library feeling unappreciated, but he was not one to let personal disappointment stop him in his tracks. After 1982, a mutual if mostly unacknowledged sense of aggrievement may have reinforced the special bond between them.

Douglas Dillon and Laurance Rockefeller were both eight years younger than Brooke Astor, while Vartan Gregorian was young enough to be her son. Indeed he was *younger* than her son. In addition, his wife, Clare, was a friend. She enjoyed the Gregorians as a couple. Most of their extracurricular time was spent as a threesome. This was not a romance in any traditional sense. But, without her quite realizing it, Vartan Gregorian—who by no stretch of the imagination could be seen as an old man—had become the most important man in her life.

For this, she could only be grateful. But it also made her fearful. All those meals and long hours were taking a toll on Vartan Gregorian's health. In 1987, when it looked as if Vartan might take a job elsewhere, she wrote him a note saying how relieved she was that he had decided against it: "Every day I pray to God that you will have the strength to stay on at the library. If you left, it would be as though an earthquake, a tornado, and a thousand bulldozers had touched the library. I don't think we could ever recover from it."

Unfortunately, it was only a matter of time. Vartan Gregorian, who was no fool, understood that his opening act was going to be impossible to follow. Furthermore, he simply couldn't keep up this pace. In 1989, having done more than his part to see that the Library was not only safe but actually thriving, he took a job as president of Brown University. Brooke tried to be understanding about his return to academia. Indeed, when he was sworn in as president she was there on the dais delivering a short impromptu speech in which she said, "I knew from his eyes that he was missing you—sooner or later he would come back to you." But that didn't stop her from missing Vartan. She liked and admired his successor at the New York Public Library, the

Jesuit priest Timothy Healey, and was grief stricken when after two years as president he suddenly died of a heart attack. And she would like Healey's successor, Paul LeClerc, whom she would urge from practically his first day at the Library to make sure that he was doing things there that were fun. But on September 30, 1992, she added a handwritten postscript to a typed note she was sending Vartan, saying, "I think of you so often, and miss you. I am rather depressed."

"There's a term for a racehorse of known quality," her old friend Freddy Melhado would say. "The sort of horse you know you can bet on: 'Does not disappoint.'" Brooke Astor had always been someone you could rely on. Someone who kept her word. Who showed up at events. Who did her part. 1992 had not been an easy year for her. Like it or not, that March, she had been forced to admit to the world that she was ninety years old. For years she had been fudging her age, even though she enjoyed celebrating her birthdays, responding one year with quiet but perceptible horror when Henry Kissinger made the mistake of raising his glass for the first toast and saying, "Here we are at Brooke's eightieth birthday." Later, he would say that he was afraid she would never forgive him. She did forgive him, and did her best to carry this off with her customary light touch. She called Charles Ryskamp as early as was decently possible the following morning to say: "Wasn't Henry in the most *extravagant* mood last night."

She had made the mistake, however, of admitting publicly that she was the same age as her good friend Nin Ryan. When Nin Ryan celebrated her ninetieth birthday, Brooke Astor had no choice but to follow suit. Making the best of what looked to her to be a bad bargain, she agreed to celebrate this birthday publicly with a mammoth gathering of 2,000 New Yorkers, 1,300 of whom would pay to sit down for dinner. The party, which was held at the Seventh Regiment Armory three weeks before her actual birthday, was to benefit the Citizens Committee for New York. The Citizens Committee had first gotten under way thanks to the Vincent Astor Foundation. And she had known its head, Osborn Elliott, since he was practically a child.

Macy's, the same store responsible for the Thanksgiving Day Parade, was brought in to make the cavernous and deteriorating armory look like a glittering bower, with a seventeen-foot-high rose trimmed-gazebo, giant trees confected of hammered metal, and thirty-one huge chandeliers borrowed from the Metropolitan and City operas as well as the Shubert Organization. Brendan Gill was commissioned to write the text for the attractive gray book each dinner guest received, celebrating the guest of honor.

A short film was also produced for the occasion, showing Mrs. Astor making her rounds one winter day with Linda Gillies—starting with a visit to the Eldridge Street Synagogue, a deteriorating but still functioning house of worship, stranded in a neighborhood that was now part of Chinatown, which the Foundation was helping to bring back to something approaching its former glory; a visit to a former tuberculosis hospital overlooking the FDR Drive that had long been an empty shell and was now being converted to subsidized housing; a visit to Furnish a Future, where families who had been given city housing could come to find furniture for their apartments' bare rooms; and a visit to a residence for the mentally ill run by two Franciscan brothers, where she was shown deep in conversation with "Nancy," a fine-boned woman of indeterminate age, living in a neat small room, its walls taped with mementoes and clippings dating back to the time she was attending classes at Juilliard. Afterward in the car, as she tries to talk to Linda about this visit, a visibly shaken Brooke cannot keep back her tears.

This film did not show her on a happier, though no less moving occasion, having tea in the impeccably neat front parlor of a three-story brick house in Harlem, whose crumbling wooden porch the Vincent Astor Foundation was about to help restore. This brick house—part of Astor Row, a group of identical houses, on the south side of 130th Street, running between Lenox and Fifth avenues—had been built in the 1880s on land belonging to Vincent Astor's grand-father. On her first visit, the year before, she had made the acquain-tance of the owner, an eighty-one-year-old African-American woman by the name of Eloise Calloway, who had books in every room and lace curtains on her windows and who had welcomed her like an old friend. It was a house probably no smaller than the one she had lived in with her mother in Washington. And it was far grander than the little cabin where she had chatted up those elderly Cranberry ladies in her efforts to court them. There was no need to court Eloise Calloway, who understood what it was to dress for an occasion, to live among books, and to enjoy a quiet moment on a winter afternoon.

At the armory, there was a Marine Corps band to play, as well as Peter Duchin and his band. The guest of honor's silver gown was by Arnold Scaasi—who, one reporter noted, was known for designing the gowns of First Ladies. Mayor David Dinkins, it was reported, had declared her actual birthday, March 30, as Brooke Astor Day.

And naturally, in at least one article, the first Mrs. Astor was invoked. Having outdone the first Mrs. Astor in exclusivity with her guest list of 70 for the Reagan dinner, she was now outdoing her by cramming 2,000 guests into a gigantic ballroom, which for that one night, if you didn't peer too closely, looked quite magical.

At the party itself she appeared to be in the best of spirits, chatting with friends who stopped by to congratulate her and then, when din-ner was over, dancing in a pair of satin high heels with all her favorite men, until two in the morning. Among those men who danced with her was Freddy Melhado. The first dance, however, went to her din-ner partner, Mayor Dinkins. All of her close friends attended the party, as well as friends who were not so close, among them the direc-tors of organizations the Foundation had funded over the years.

This big birthday was also the occasion for dozens of interviews. As was her custom, she was amazingly forthright. At times even confiding. Her eyesight was terrific and she'd just gotten a new driver's license, she said, but her hearing was getting so bad she had to wear a hearing aid—something she didn't care for at all. She spoke of how she didn't feel old. "I feel liberated by my age," she told one reporter. "I can do anything as long as it's not unpleasant." "A nasty old person is awful," she then added. One pull quote, however, captured completely her attitude in the face of this big milestone: "I never imagined ninety. I used to think people at forty were old."

Nine

A COURAGEOUS ACT,
1996–2001

"Don't die guessing," cautioned Mother, and I hear-
kened to her words. I am not guessing. I have lived a full
life.

In September 1996, when she was honored by the New York
Landmarks Conservancy as one of the city's great "living monu-
ments," Brooke Astor made it clear that this designation was the last
thing she wanted. Slowly and surely, however, a living monument was
what she had become. Sometimes the role suited her; sometimes it
did not. But it was a role that she began to find increasingly difficult
to live up to. As she settled into her nineties, her energy, though
prodigious, was not what it had once been. More important, it was
noted by those close to her that under pressure she herself was not
always what she had once been. Whereas before she had managed
almost invariably to keep her sense of humor, now at a sudden setback
she might express irritation or even anger. While in the past she could
be counted on to be delighted when presented with a knotty problem,
she often seemed disinclined to make the effort. And while she had
always been known for seeking out suggestions from all quarters, she
now seemed less disposed to take those suggestions into account.

More important, her responses were no longer easy to predict.

On public occasions she could still be marvelous. Indeed, the previous June, celebrating the renovation of St. Peter's Episcopal Church on East 140 Street, in the South Bronx, she had dazzled onlookers with her sangfroid. The Vincent Astor Foundation had recently contributed $35,000 toward the $63,000 renovation of this hundred-year-old church, which had for decades served as the spiritual anchor of a devastated neighborhood where David Rockefeller's New York City Housing Partnership had recently renovated thirty-three homes. Housing Partnership Director Kathryn Wylde accompanied David Rockefeller that day and so had a chance to observe Mrs. Astor firsthand. Already, in their conversations, she had noticed that Mrs. Astor, like Mr. Rockefeller, understood how important it was to include the neighborhood in any plans that were made. Both also seemed to share an unwavering faith that "New York would bounce back." On the other hand, they brought to their philanthropy two very different approaches—perhaps because of temperamental differences between men and women or simply because they'd had different life experiences. Mrs. Astor was more "bottom up" or "grassroots," Wylde observed, crediting this to the fact that for decades, starting back in Bedford-Stuyvesant, Mrs. Astor had been "working in the vineyards."

Mrs. Astor had made the journey in her own car and was accompanied by her two dachshunds. Because the weather was warm and sunny, it seemed only natural to mark that day's celebration with a walking tour of the renovated block by the church. A crowd had gathered, Wylde would recall. Things started off well, with the two old friends walking arm in arm, until a "very crazy lady" who lived in one of the apartment buildings threw a lamp from her window and then followed it with a roast pig. The pig landed directly in front of them. "It was very close, but they did not miss a beat," Wylde recalled. "They simply smiled and stayed on the tour. They had such confidence in the neighborhood, in the people, that one crazy person was not going to shake them." Unfortunately, that wasn't the last disruption to threaten their neighborhood stroll. "A large black guy who was kind of a neighborhood character came running up and gave Mrs. Astor a kiss on the cheek. She was fine with that. Then he said to Mrs. Astor, 'Sweetheart, you don't look a day over fifty.' Mrs. Astor beamed and said, 'Why thank you.'"

But in private, Brooke Astor wasn't always so ready to be amused. She might suddenly take against someone who said something perfectly innocuous. Or argue with a statement that was consistent with all her prior thinking. More often than not, these sudden bursts of contrariness appeared to stem from some misunderstanding on her part, perhaps owing to the fact that her hearing was becoming increasingly unreliable. Although she had access to state-of-the-art hearing aids, they didn't really solve the problem. For one thing, they required a mechanical sophistication most ninety-year-olds do not possess.

At board meetings the Vincent Astor Foundation's president began to mishear or totally miss what was being said. More than once what she misheard led to hurt feelings. Occasionally she would lose the thread of an argument and, when she failed to respond to a question or take part in the ensuing discussion, Linda Gillies would step in. After one such intervention, the president bided her time in public and then lashed out at her director in private. Linda Gillies had the presence of mind to immediately apologize and Mrs. Astor instantly forgave her. Even in the old days, when the two of them were first working together, Brooke Astor had occasionally shown a flash of anger, but, back then, her vexation would soon blow over. Now the flashes of anger were coming more frequently and with what appeared to be considerably less provocation. For the first time, there were periods when it could be said that relations between the Foundation's president and its director were strained.

Later, Linda Gillies would say that she had come to understand that she had only made matters worse by trying to take up the slack. To Brooke's eyes it may have looked as if her director was getting beyond herself. While Brooke Astor might be grateful when Linda quietly took over more of her day-to-day duties, she didn't like being reminded in front of other people that she was not quite as capable as she had once been. Or to hear that Linda had ideas and opinions of her own. She had begun complaining to friends that Linda was constantly quoting her husband, Arch. At the same time, she had taken to saying that Linda kept pressing her to get her to commit to projects north of 178th Street. Arch Gillies's politics, which had always been far to the left of her own, had never been a problem in the past. And she had never been loathe to venture north of 178th Street. How much any of this really troubled Brooke Astor it's hard to say. Certainly her reservations about Linda's more recent enthusiasms could pass as a plausible justification for the surprising action she was about to take.

Brooke Astor had long been on record as saying she wanted the Foundation to shut down at her death. Even as recently as 1992, she had been quoted in a symposium published in *The Chronicle of Philanthropy* as saying she had no plan for the Foundation to survive her. Having recently turned ninety, she gave no indication that she had any wish to close the Foundation in the immediate future. Certainly she saw no need to close it as long as she felt she could make a difference. But three years later, when she could sense her grasp loosening and there were no indications that she would be dying in the near future, it was becoming increasingly apparent that her plan, as she had originally conceived it, would not prove workable.

Back in 1986, when the Foundation began to cut back on its total annual spending, the board, along with its president and director, had agreed to also cut back on operating expenses. No one was fired, but as various staff members resigned, died, or retired, no effort was made to replace them. Gradually a support staff long considered remarkably modest for an active foundation shrank to two, one secretary and one bookkeeper. By falling back on an ability to quickly master new computer software especially designed for organizations like the Vincent Astor Foundation, Linda had managed to compensate for this slow but steady shrinkage while actually enlarging the Foundation's reach. Even though the Foundation was giving away less than $2 million per year, thanks to the increasing number of grant recipients and Brooke Astor's increasing fame, the Foundation remained very much in the public eye.

Brooke Astor had always been a practical woman and, as such, she could see she had few options if she wanted the Foundation to shut down at her death. She could continue to serve as president, with her director gradually taking over most of the duties that had until now been a reliable source of personal satisfaction. Or she could stay on as president and immediately cede power to one of the two candidates who appeared to be best qualified. There was Linda Gillies of course. And there was her son, Anthony Marshall, who since 1979 had not only served on the Foundation's board but also held the positions of vice president and treasurer.

While Tony Marshall could be counted on to take a special interest in any grants proposed for the Wildlife Conservation Society (the successor organization to the New York Zoological Society), the Museum of Natural History, or the Seaman's Church Institute, at board meetings he was by no means one of the more articulate or innovative participants. The one area where Tony had made his influence felt was in his role as treasurer, where he took an active interest in the daily operating expenses of the Foundation. Unlike his mother, Tony had never been notably generous. And once he was put in charge of overseeing the money to maintain the Foundation's Park Avenue office, he kept a sharp eye on the budget.

Anthony Marshall and Linda Gillies had always had a perfectly cordial working relationship, even though the two were very different in outlook and temperament. So far, they had each been able to get along by going their separate ways. Small as the Foundation was, it still afforded them ample space in which to manage this. Tony, whose primary concern was overseeing his mother's investments, had a separate office next door. In addition, his responsibilities rarely, if ever, overlapped with Linda's. But if his mother's powers continued to fail, the lines defining their respective responsibilities would have to be redrawn. Furthermore, once there ceased to be a strong mediating presence, things might not go so smoothly.

The fact was, Brooke Astor had no intention of ceding her foundation to anyone. Partly it was a matter of control. Moreover, with time, she and the Foundation had become one and the same in both the public's mind and her own. Joan Davidson, head of the Kaplan Foundation, had worked with Linda Gillies on quite a few projects during the eighties. As Joan Davidson saw it, there would be no Vincent Astor Foundation without Linda busy behind the scenes ensuring everything ran smoothly. But Linda never saw it that way. She believed that in some way she was like Raymonde, who, by dressing Mrs. Astor as a star, helped Mrs. Astor assume the role she was born for—one that for many years she played to perfection, while doing a lot of good.

With no background in the field of philanthropy, Linda Gillies, like Brooke Astor, had turned out to be a natural. Physically attractive and possessed of great personal charm, she had proven to also be an excellent office manager and a model of efficiency. Of the two women, however, Brooke Astor was the one with the phenomenal memory. Always she could be counted on to recall a new name or a telling detail and then retain it for months. Even after she turned ninety and had increasing trouble hearing, this continued to be true. Then one day, as Brooke Astor and Linda Gillies were setting out in the car and Linda started to review the folder for one of the key organizations they had agreed to visit, it became clear from Mrs.

Astor's silence, and the expression on her face, that she had no idea what Linda was talking about.

The two women managed to get through that day's round of on-site visits without any further awkwardness, but early the following Monday morning, soon after she arrived at her desk, Linda received a phone call from the Foundation's president saying she'd be in the office around noon. Although Mrs. Astor usually remained up at Holly Hill until Monday morning and then went straight to the hairdresser's, Linda's assumption was that she simply wanted to follow up on some problem they had discussed the previous week. But Brooke Astor had something more pressing on her mind. Without any preliminaries, much the way she'd broken the news of little Astor's death, she announced to Linda that she had decided to shut down the Foundation. By the end of the following year she intended to close its doors, distributing virtually all of the money she and Linda had been carefully husbanding over the past decade. "It was a tremendously courageous thing to do," Linda would later say of this decision.

Seen in one light, it *was* tremendously courageous. Rather than turn in a performance she feared was becoming less than adequate, Brooke Astor was stepping down from a platform that had always suited her perfectly. By closing the Foundation, she would be walking away from a job that for more than thirty-five years had given her days shape and meaning. She would be relinquishing one of her greatest pleasures and also the source of most of her power. She would be giving up the role that set her apart and defined her. A role that made her more than just another Mrs. Astor. But this decision can also be seen in another light. By making a clean break, Brooke Astor was ensuring that no one, however well meaning, would ever scrap her original plan or change her foundation's direction.

Of course this was not a reason she could give voice to in public. Just as she could not admit the job was becoming too much for her. Instead she offered up something that might make perfect sense to most people.

She said that she wanted to use the years that were left to do some of the things she'd never had the time to do before. She suggested that by walking away from the very thing she liked to call Vincent's greatest gift to her—a gift that had called forth reserves of discipline she credited with turning around her life—she was also buying her freedom. From now on she would be at liberty to make her own hours and travel, to see friends and family, whenever and wherever she wished.

However, before Brooke Astor was able to take advantage of her new freedom, there was a good deal of work to be done, both by her and by Linda. The board had to be told. An official announcement had to be made to the press. And of course all the publicity attending this announcement would result in a deluge of fresh appeals. The needs of organizations that had depended on the Foundation for support had to be considered. Final grants had to be awarded. Numbers had to be reconciled. Files had to be closed. Decades of records had to be sifted and sorted and readied for the New York Public Library, where they would eventually be made available to researchers at the Brooke Russell Astor Rare Books and Manuscripts Reading Room. None of this would be easy. But if there were any tears, they were shed in private. Once Brooke Astor made up her mind, there appeared to be no second thoughts.

In January 1997, a small committee of the board met for the first time to determine what would need to be done to in effect close down the Vincent Astor Foundation by the end of the year. After some discussion, the committee decided that in making grants it would be best if the Foundation followed certain guidelines, all of them in keeping with its long-standing policies. First, with rare exceptions, grants would be made to organizations and institutions in New York City; second, education would be a top priority, particularly programs that provided books to the city's schoolchildren and their families; third, special attention would be paid to organizations working with African Americans, especially those in Harlem; fourth, the bulk of the grants would go to organizations that had been funded in the past. And, finally, to ensure that all of this unfolded smoothly it was decided that the entire board would meet twice during the coming year, in April and then in October, to consider for final approval grants recommended by the Foundation's president and director.

After a decade of moderation, the Vincent Astor Foundation suddenly had more than $24 million to give away in the space of a single year. To the Foundation's last big bout of spending Brooke Astor brought her old zest and enthusiasm. Once more all eyes seemed to be turned in her direction. She might not be able to avoid being treated as a public monument but at least she had the pleasure of receiving, while she was still very much alive, tributes long associated with memorial services and glowing obituaries.

At the end of December 1997, having made hefty grants to the city's "crown jewels" and dispersed almost all of its remaining resources as wisely as possible, the Foundation closed its doors. One of the largest grants—$5 million dollars—went to the New York Public Library to pay for works of poetry and fiction to replace the many books that had once filled the now depleted shelves of its eighty-five branch libraries. Another $5 million dollars went to establish an Astor Center for School Libraries, based at New Visions for Public Schools, to provide not only much needed books for the city's schools but also library renovations, conferences, and technical assistance.

A follow-up grant of $140,000 went to New York University for the Astor Fellows Travel Program for New York City public school teachers; and $250,000 went to the Partnership for the Homeless, toward Furnish a Future. The Landmarks Conservancy received $500,000 to complete the porches for the houses on Astor Row. And $250,000 went to the Animal Medical Center to establish the Dolly and Maisie Fund, a special fund within the SAVE program. And $50,000 went to Rockefeller University, toward the construction of a pedestrian bridge across York Avenue at Sixty-third Street, which would make it safer for the university's staff and students, as well as their families, to cross this busy intersection.

Three of the follow-up grants are of particular interest. A $1 million grant went to the Women's Housing and Economic Development Corporation (WHEDCO), constructed within the shell of the old Morrisania Hospital in the South Bronx, a short distance north of Yankee Stadium, situated between Jerome Avenue and the Grand Concourse. The dream child of Nancy Biberman, WHEDCO was an ambitious complex boasting well-designed subsidized housing for low-income women and their families; fully equipped classrooms to provide job training for neighborhood women; an enormous state-of-the-art kitchen; and a brand-new day care center to host a Head Start program. Space in the kitchen would not only be used to provide nutritious meals for the small children at the day care center but be made available, for a modest fee, to anyone in the neighborhood starting up a catering business.

Nancy Biberman's vision—which depended from the start on the active collaboration of various neighborhood organizations as well as the support of the Bronx borough president—had taken years to assume anything like concrete form. Though very different in scale and scope from an old-fashioned settlement house, what Biberman was hoping to build could be seen as a contemporary version of just such a community center. The old hospital building had been standing empty for almost twenty years. Squatters and vandals had compounded the ravages brought by two decades of neglect. The cost of even a modest renovation was going to be considerable. But Nancy Biberman was attempting something far more ambitious than that. Funding was going to have to come from both the public and private sectors. Here, LISC (the Local Initiatives Support Corporation)—a financial clearinghouse set up by the Ford Foundation, to facilitate funding for worthy projects in low-income areas—would prove to be invaluable.

Eventually, in 1994, Nancy Biberman got control of the site along with an immediate $1 million commitment from the Cuomo administration in Albany in low-interest loans. After receiving that commitment, she was promised a matching $13 million equity investment, raised through the federal low-income housing tax credit program. But that November Mario Cuomo lost his bid for reelection to George Pataki, and it looked as if WHEDCO would lose its state financing and the matching federal investment. Then, in April 1995, Brent Staples wrote an editorial in *The New York Times* describing the long abandoned Morrisania Hospital as "majestic" and calling its "impending refurbishment a cause for celebration." Taking care to make note of the recent agreement under Mario Cuomo to provide state financing, he went on to say, "The Pataki administration would be wise to honor that commitment."

Finally, in January of 1996, with the blessing of a politically savvy George Pataki, workmen broke ground. One rainy morning that March, Brooke Astor stopped off with Linda Gillies and one of her dogs on her way to the country. The contractors were still hauling debris from the building and Nancy Biberman, who had a memory of a dog sitting in the backseat but no memory of Linda, later recalled how she went to meet her distinguished visitor's car at the site's one functioning entrance—a side door, on the ground floor, where the Head Start center was going to be. It was raining very hard by then and the ground was muddy. Biberman recalled Mrs. Astor saying to her driver, "'Would you get me my sneakers." While the driver opened the car's trunk and fetched the sneakers, two of the contractors working on the project put up a gangplank made out of boards. "It was muddy, muddy, muddy, and slippery," Biberman remembered. "Each contractor took her by the arm and I held the architectural renderings and I walked her into the ground floor, where the day care would be. There was no going upstairs. Inside, I'm showing her the renderings and talking talking talking and she's looking around. Then she says to me, 'You know, dear, I'm ninety-four years old and I've never had a face-lift.' What she said was hilarious but it was totally appropriate. What she saw when she looked around was a building getting a face-lift."

Over the years Brooke Astor had become a master of finding exactly the right words for any situation. If the words she chose were not entirely fresh, no matter. The Foundation's director was not likely to give her away. Or even think twice about it. The entire WHEDCO adventure seemed to please Brooke Astor. And when she stopped by on her own some months later—this time on her way back from the country—the day care center was almost ready to open. While she was delighted with all that had been accomplished, one aspect of the new center seemed to particularly impress her: "In the classrooms were these teeny tiny toilets," recalled Biberman. "She couldn't get over it. We spent ten minutes talking about the little toilets. She fixated on that one thing. I thought afterward that being a woman of her age and social class, this was something she never would have seen."

In 1996, the Vincent Astor Foundation gave WHEDCO $25,000—not an enormous grant by any means but one that gave Nancy Biberman reason to hope there might be more grants in the future. But that December, when she read in the paper of the Foundation's closing, those hopes were dashed. The way she remembered it, after letting the bad news settle in, she called Hildy Simmons, who was in charge of grant making at Morgan Guaranty Trust and one of WHEDCO's first funders. Did Hildy think she should ask for a final grant and, if so, did she have any idea what size grant she should ask for? Ask for $1 million, Hildy Simmons replied. Finally concluding that she had nothing to lose, Nancy Biberman wrote a one-page letter asking for that amount, to be used to establish a special reserve fund.

Not everyone remembered events unfolding in quite this way. Linda Gillies believed she may have called Nancy Biberman, suggesting that she submit a proposal. And Hildy Simmons had no memory of suggesting $1 million. Linda believed she may have talked to Hildy Simmons at some point about whether WHEDCO was set up to handle a grant of any great size. One thing is certain: when it first came time to seriously consider giving a final grant to WHEDCO, Linda Gillies was prepared to remind Mrs. Astor of their first visit. But in fact Mrs. Astor was the one who brought up the subject when they were going over the list of organizations that had received money in the past. The original impulse came from the Foundation's president, Linda Gillies recalled. "She mentioned 'that big place in the Bronx that we went to.' She didn't remember the name, but she remembered she liked it and she wanted to give more money." With the director's support and the president's enthusiastic endorsement, the board saw fit to give Nancy Biberman the entire sum she requested. Forever after, Nancy Biberman would credit Hildy Simmons with being her fairy godmother, not fully appreciating the fact that she'd had three fairy godmothers working on her behalf.

A final grant of $250,000 was set aside for the Greenwich Village Society for Historic Preservation to cover the cost of constructing and installing a handsome wrought-iron fence around the Jefferson Market Garden, a community garden the Foundation had helped establish and then maintain on the site of the old Women's House of Detention. In 1974, the Foundation had given $6,000 for five years on the condition that the neighborhood would contribute a matching $6,000—which they always did, thanks to the garden's founders, who sent out mailings soliciting donations from the community but were not above sitting in the garden with a cigar box to collect money from any likely passersby. Back in the seventies the Foundation had continued to take a strong interest in community gardens, but by the late eighties housing for the city's homeless had become a more pressing concern. Every so often, though, when she was on her way to visit a site down near the tip of Manhattan Mrs. Astor would ask her driver to make a detour, so that she and Linda could check on how the garden was coming along. To keep out trespassers—drug dealers or homeless men and women who saw it as an ideal place to spend the night—a chain-link fence had been erected around the garden. While Brooke Astor hated the fence and all it represented, she had taken great pleasure in watching the garden first meet and then surpass her most optimistic projections. But, then, unlike most such places the Astor Foundation supported, this community garden enjoyed two striking advantages—not only a vocal and knowledgeable group of supporters but also a location in a world-famous and increasingly prosperous Manhattan neighborhood.

Another of the final $1 million grants went to the Metropolitan Museum of Art "to endow the holiday party for the Museum's staff and volunteers"—a lavishly catered luncheon, replete with music and caroling, held shortly before Christmas. While Brooke Astor had long believed in the saving power of beautiful surroundings, she believed, above all, in the importance of people. From her earliest days as one of the museum's trustees, she had enjoyed a special relationship with its staff—not only the director and principal curators but the librarians, conservators, ticket takers, and guards. Many of the guards she knew by name and one of them had become a friend. Back in 1993, when the museum no longer had the funds for the staff's annual Christmas party, the Vincent Astor Foundation had contributed $25,000 to cover the cost. With inflation, the cost of the party had risen. But thanks to subsequent grants from the Foundation, Christmas had continued to be celebrated by everyone who worked in any capacity at the museum's main building with a deluxe event in the towering glass pyramid housing the Temple of Dendur.

In 1993, on the heels of that first grant, Brooke Astor had become the first museum trustee to attend the big Christmas party. Dressed

32. Patience,
Mayor Koch,
Brooke, and
Vartan Gregorian

33. Vartan Gregorian
and Andrew Heiskell
(Sara Krulwich / New York
Times / *Redux)*

34. Barbara Walters, Tom Wolfe,
Brooke, and Liz Smith, 1988

35. Marshall Rose

36. Brooke Astor and Paul LeClerc

37. David Rockefeller and Brooke Astor receiving the Medal of Freedom, with Tony Marshall in background

At the Astor Court. 38. (top) Philippe de Montebello, Brooke Astor, and Wen Fong. 39. (bottom left) James Watt and Douglas Dillon. 40. (bottom right) Annette de la Renta

41. Brooke Astor and
Ashton Hawkins
(Bill Cunningham / New York Times /
Redux)

42. Brooke Astor and Linda
Gillies, at the Foundation's
last Christmas party, 1997

43. Brooke Astor with John
Richardson

44. Entering the hundredth birthday party with David Rockefeller and William Astor

45. With Kofi Annan, David Rockefeller, and Nan Annan

46. Tony and
Charlene
Marshall

47. Mr. and Mrs. Philip
Marshall, Brooke Astor,
and Alec Marshall

48. Brooke Astor, Boysie,
and Philip Marshall

49. Brooke on Tussie, at the opening of Wild Asia, Bronx Zoo, 1977

in a red suit she might wear to any special luncheon that season of the year, she had been escorted from one large round table to another by Vice President for Operations Dick Morsches, all the while making it a point to greet every one of the ten people seated at each of the forty packed tables and wish them a merry Christmas. At some point a new crowd of revelers would arrive and she would make her rounds again. "It was *hard work*," recalled Morsches. "But she was able to put everyone at their ease." Taking a break from this hard work, she joined a choral group organized by Ken Moore, the head of the Musical Instruments Department. "They got better and better with time," recalled Morsches. "Brooke just loved that. She danced and sang along. Afterward, we went up to have lunch in the Trustees Dining Room. I really was tired, but she was just as happy as could be."

In the ample and imposing but not necessarily convivial space housing the Temple of Dendur, Brooke Astor had been given a chance to experience something not unlike what she had hoped to achieve with her "outdoor living rooms." From then on she made it a point to fund and attend the big holiday party, sometimes accompanied by Dick Morsches, sometimes by Ashton Hawkins or Philippe de Montebello or her son, Tony. One Friday afternoon on her way to her place in Connecticut, Annette de la Renta stopped by dressed for the country, only to hear later, when she and Brooke were alone together in private, that next time something less informal might be preferable.

Brooke Astor might keep a pair of sneakers in the trunk of her sedan, but she did not dress down for any public occasion, even when it was no more than making a brief stop at a South Bronx construction site on her way to Briarcliff Manor. For all that skirts and sweaters might figure large in her country wardrobe, she did not deem them appropriate for an official luncheon. Certainly she would never consider wearing pants or jeans.

When the big holiday luncheon fell on a Friday, Brooke Astor, too, would head for the country. She might return to her apartment for a few minutes, to freshen up and pick up her dogs, but like Annette de la Renta, the stylish younger woman she treated as a beloved daughter, she was sure to get back into her car and put the city behind her. While the city was where she happily conducted her work for the Foundation, her time at Holly Hill was no less important to her. There, over the course of three days, she was able to spend long hours out of the public eye—swimming in one of her two pools, taking brisk walks with her dogs, and reading as much as her heart desired. There she was also able to concentrate on her writing. Or to entertain a handful of friends at a quiet Sunday lunch.

All along Brooke Astor had been leading two lives. Sometimes they overlapped and occasionally they were mutually exclusive, but each life would have been more than satisfying for a woman half her age. For all that the Vincent Astor Foundation provided a focus for her days, she had never let it interfere with her other interests. During the thirty-seven years she served as the Foundation's president, she had also served on the boards of virtually every important cultural institution in the city. But no less impressive was the fact that she had produced five well-reviewed books and a substantial number of articles as well as having three of her poems recently taken by *The New Yorker*.

Without the Foundation to keep her busy, Brooke Astor would have more than enough to occupy her. She would be able to devote more time to her reading. She would be free to become an even more active member of the book group she had started with Carter and Susan Burden back in 1984, which met six times a year and gave her a chance to make the acquaintance of various characters in literature, some of whom elicited such an emphatic response from her one might almost believe that they, too, were in the room. She would be able to spend time with friends she didn't see all that often as well as friends of the heart like Annette. To take even more ambitious walks in the country with her dogs. To devote more time to yoga. To spend a greater portion of the year traveling. To stay months in London instead of only several weeks. To spend more time with her family. And to gradually retreat from the public eye.

But old habits die hard. In 1996, just as she was beginning to sense her powers were seriously waning, she had agreed to a request from Graydon Carter, the editor of *Vanity Fair*, to write a series of essays on manners with the hope that they could be made to fit together and published as a book. In 1998, one year after the Foundation's official closing, Brooke Astor didn't do all that much traveling, but she appeared to be as active as ever. She continued to turn up regularly in Bill Cunningham's photographs in the Styles section of the Sunday *Times*—most often attending a benefit for some organization she had always taken a personal interest in. She continued to swim and take ambitious walks in the country. She continued to take part in her book group and to serve in an emeritus capacity on the boards of Rockefeller University, the Metropolitan Museum, and the New York Public Library.

But four years later, as Brooke Astor approached her hundredth birthday, the long walks in the country had given way to long drives with Chris Ely, her butler at both Holly Hill and Cove End; the swimming had stopped almost entirely; and a decision had been reached by the book group to quietly disband rather than continue without her as an active member. As Mrs. Astor herself would have been the first to tell you, nothing—not even a living monument—can be counted on to remain forever the same.

Ten

A FULL LIFE,
1996—2001

Life is a lonely game to be played out alone.

By the time Brooke Astor shut down the Vincent Astor Foundation, many of the small organizations the Foundation had funded had either disappeared or come to bear little resemblance to what they had once been. Some changes were for the better. Others were not. Certainly New York was not the same city it had been in 1960, when she had set out to make it a better place for the people who lived and earned their living there. The Women's House of Detention was hardly the only old building to succumb to the wrecker's ball, although it may have qualified as the dreariest. Pennsylvania Station, an architectural wonder, had been demolished before concerned citizens could rally in sufficient numbers to save it. Imposing brick and limestone buildings had given way to glass towers, while tree-lined blocks of three- and four-story houses had been leveled by developers who immediately replaced them with cost-effective high-rises. The city's famous skyline had been transformed. Some might say it had lost its distinctive character. Even the Empire State Building had ceded its place as Manhattan's tallest skyscraper to the World Trade Center.

During Brooke Astor's thirty-seven-year tenure as the Astor

Foundation's president, New York had weathered two blackouts, the threat of a race riot in Harlem, the Vietnam war, a near bankruptcy, two long garbage strikes, a shrinking tax base, several economic recessions, and the loss of its position as a major manufacturing center, while coping with deteriorating schools, cracked sidewalks, lengthening welfare rolls, a high jobless rate, and an escalating homeless population. All of this had taken a toll. But even when its services were under siege or faltering, the city itself remained surprisingly resilient. Every building might not necessarily be safe and every citizen might not be totally reliable, but, taken together, they promised to be capable of withstanding any serious assault.

On September 11, 2001, any illusion of invincibility vanished forever. Brooke Astor was just back from her summer in Maine, when, one after another, two hijacked planes flew into the twin towers of the World Trade Center. She was not watching television when the towers came down. But later that day she watched as Rudy Giuliani, the one mayor she had never much cared for personally, rallied a shaken populace, much the way Winston Churchill had during the battle of Britain, with words that seemed to reflect not only what everyone felt at that moment but also what everyone needed to be reminded—words that were simple and direct and made no bones about how bad things were, but offered the promise that, if every New Yorker pitched in, the city could weather this terrible disaster and even end up stronger than ever. It was the sort of approach she herself had once used back in the seventies, when the city was in desperate financial straits.

The mayor's stirring words had the desired effect. Within days New York's luxury stores were removing metal shutters from their doors and its restaurants and theaters were back in business. After putting in place temporary security measures, the city's schools, museums, and libraries all reopened. Although they might receive an occasional bomb threat, most of the schools and libraries were soon back to normal. But the city's restaurants and shops as well as its museums and theaters continued to remain almost empty.

Suddenly there were no tourists with deep pockets. And native New Yorkers showed no inclination to take their place. The city's inhabitants felt better eating in their own kitchens, within easy reach of the television. They felt uncomfortable buying anything that wasn't necessary. They felt no desire to set foot in any tall office building. They had no wish to venture into Midtown, unless they had to go there to earn their living. Natural as this response might be, it was anything but salutary. The immediate effect on the city's economy was devastating.

That September, Brooke Astor was ninety-nine years old. Like most New Yorkers, she was horrified by what had happened. Perhaps because she herself was beginning to feel vulnerable, she took 9/11 especially hard. A few people she knew had quietly slipped away to well-appointed homes situated at a safe distance, and she herself could have easily fled to Northeast Harbor or holed up in her place in Briarcliff Manor. But she wasn't a Marine commandant's daughter for nothing. She chose, instead, to keep to her time-honored fall custom of spending four days a week in the city. On the face of it, she was well insulated from the immediate damage. She was living with her two dachshunds, Boysie and Girlsie, in a comfortable Park Avenue apartment, with friends and her son close by and a staff to look after her.

Always she had seemed content with her single state. Indeed she had chosen it. She had never lacked for escorts or lacked for parties, scheduling as many as three or four parties a night—in the old days for the sheer variety and now for the guarantee that before she'd come upon too many unfamiliar faces or had her fill of voices pitched so low as to be practically inaudible, it would be time to make her good-byes. At least old friends knew enough to speak up. Unfortunately, that fall, with parties everywhere put on hold or canceled, she sometimes found herself with nothing to do after six. Any plausible invitation was beginning to merit serious consideration. One night, lingering with a special friend over a quiet dinner at the apartment, she confessed to the friend—who happened to have been born half a century after she was—that she dearly wished the two of them could marry, just for the company.

Back in June 1996, two weeks after her triumphant stroll with David Rockefeller in the South Bronx, Brooke Astor had sat for an interview with Eileen Simpson, the author of many critically acclaimed books, including *Poets in Their Youth*, and also a trained psychotherapist. The interview was said to be part of a series Simpson was doing on aging. It was set up by Linda Gillies, who was becoming increasingly concerned about Mrs. Astor. The interview, which was held at teatime in Mrs. Astor's library, was never published. In it Mrs. Astor talks about her fears that she is losing her memory and credits this loss to a bad fall she'd had the year before. To help with her balance she has taken up yoga and begun working with a physical therapist. That had helped with her balance, but nothing seemed to help with her memory—even some shots a doctor at Baden-Baden had administered the previous summer.

The woman who first breezes in from a lunch at Le Cirque with the editor of *Vanity Fair* doesn't seem at first to have much cause for concern. She's happy she's had the three poems taken by *The New Yorker*, a longtime dream of hers. Throughout the interview she remains seated with her back straight and her legs crossed neatly at the ankle. She says the piece she is to write for *Vanity Fair* will be on flirting, but she credits her success in life not to flirting but to discipline. Even a successful social life requires discipline, she says. If she herself is tired from her lunch, she makes every effort not to show it. Her manner is gay, her outfit beguiling, and her complexion so smooth and unwrinkled, Eileen Simpson finds it impossible to believe her protestations that she'd never had a face-lift. Her secret recipe to keep her skin from sagging is to massage her cheeks as she prepares for bed at night, with a gentle upward motion of her fingertips, she confides as she gives an impromptu demonstration.

Beneath all the frivolity, however, Eileen Simpson senses an undercurrent of sadness. The memory problems Brooke Astor is having are truly upsetting to her. Physically she is also less strong than she was only a year ago. "I get depressed about that," she says. She speaks of friends of hers who are taking Prozac, but she says she has no wish to resort to such a measure. "I don't like the false gaiety that comes with it," she says. Eileen Simpson, who is more than twenty years younger than Brooke Astor but old enough to understand both Brooke Astor's dilemma and her response to what is happening to her, goes on to note, "[T]here are undoubtedly subjects she would not like to talk about. To admit to taking an antidepressant for someone of her generation and training would not be easy."

When Eileen Simpson asks her if she is ever lonely, Mrs. Astor's response is immediate. "Oh, I've had beaux," she says. "Faithful ones. We've gone dancing together. I love to dance. Last week I went dancing twice." When asked how she manages to get through all the benefits and parties she attends, she says, "One of the most tiring things is to stand on a long receiving line wearing high heels. But I don't stay late. I leave by ten or ten-thirty." When asked what advice she'd give a young woman, she answers, "Be nice to everybody. Don't hold grudges. Stay away from people you don't get on with. If they cross your path, greet them civilly, but move on." The interview, which was to take a full hour, ends on a high note with the two dachshunds rushing in from their walk with the housekeeper and Brooke's getting up to prepare to leave with them for the country.

In October 2000, Brooke Astor was able to sustain the image of a woman undiminished by age when she was quoted in the *Times*, along with three other active New York women in their nineties, on the benefits of a hectic social life. In this article she had credited her longevity not only to her nonstop partying but also to the two mornings a week she practiced her modified form of yoga. In the article no mention was made of the fact that she had broken her hip in June 1998 or the fact that afterward she had taken to using a walking stick to help keep her balance. If nothing else, it slowed her down: most of her falls were owing to the fact that she insisted on trying to walk at the same fast pace as she always had. In the city she tended to treat the stick as a fashion accessory. In the country, she was more inclined to regard it as a cumbersome afterthought. Unfortunately, she had suffered so many spills her walking in the country had to be strictly curtailed.

At Holly Hill and Cove End, she had come to rely increasingly on her butler, Chris Ely—a young Englishman in his thirties who had once served as a footman for the Queen of England and also worked as a butler for Elton John's manager. With Chris she would take long afternoon drives and when she wasn't feeling up to a drive, the two of them would spend the afternoon examining the snapshots Chris had taken of her favorite spots. Sundays at Holly Hill she made it a point to attend the eleven o'clock service at the Episcopal church down the road. After church, she almost always went over to David Rockefeller's for lunch. Sometimes—though not as often as she once had—she would have Chris drive her all the way to the de la Rentas' in Connecticut, to have lunch with Annette and Oscar.

In the autumn of 2001 Brooke Astor's picture appeared with some regularity in the paper, almost always on the society page. The one big exception would be in December, when she accepted an award from the Carnegie Foundation. If sometimes her frankness could be stunning, it was generally offset by her charm. And if sometimes she suffered from lapses in memory, she was always the first to point this out. There was no question, however, that for her family and for most people she depended on she was getting harder to deal with.

Tony Marshall, who himself was fast approaching eighty, was having an especially hard time of it. Since 1979, when he had returned from his post as ambassador to Kenya, he had been managing her investments. Now he was in charge of virtually all her money. Already back in 1993, she had agreed to have Tony share power of attorney with her Sullivan and Cromwell lawyer, Henry "Terry" Christensen. From the trust Vincent had set up she was receiving something like $2 million a year. But according to Tony, owing to inflation, her income simply didn't go as far as it once had. She was hardly poor, but she had three large establishments to maintain and a substantial staff to support and she simply didn't have the resources at her command that she'd once had.

One way Tony sought to cut expenses was by not replacing the caretaker at Holly Hill when he was felled by a stroke and having Chris, the butler, assume most of those responsibilities. Another way was to cut back on the number of gardeners employed at Holly Hill, a property of less concern to him than Cove End, where he and his third wife spent long stretches of time during the summer. As Brooke's old friend Louis Auchincloss has been known to observe, "It's the gardeners that can kill you." This fact was not lost on Tony. Selling off a painting or a piece of jewelry might help meet expenses for the time being, but it didn't solve the underlying problem, as he was quick to point out.

Tony Marshall chose to tell his mother that there was a pressing need to cut back on expenses. Unfortunately, matters weren't helped any when she couldn't quite hear, or always remember, what has just been explained to her in painful detail. But there was more to Brooke Astor's current difficulties with her son than that. Brooke had never had much use for Tony's first two wives, but his third wife, Charlene, was a source of intense personal embarrassment. In the summer of 1989, while still very much married to his second wife but staying alone with his mother at Northeast Harbor, Tony had fallen in love with a married woman twenty years younger than he was.

From Brooke Astor's point of view, her son could hardly have chosen worse. Not only was this woman the mother of three children but she was the wife of Paul Gilbert, the minister at St. Mary's-by-the-Sea, the Episcopal church where Brooke regularly attended Sunday morning services. She had introduced Paul Gilbert and his wife, Charlene, to local people she believed could be of help to them and had welcomed the couple to her home. Indeed she had treated Paul Gilbert himself as both friend and confidant, phoning him late at night on more than one occasion when she had something distressing she needed to discuss. From the start she had regarded him as some-one she could trust.

Northeast Harbor was a small New England village. Even when swollen with summer visitors, it never lost its fundamental character. That was part of its charm. But that was also part of what made Tony's sudden infatuation with the minister's wife such an embarrassment. There was no way for the two lovers to slip away for a quiet unre-marked tryst. No way to hide the scandal. There were too many keen-eyed observers. Too many attentive ears. For both all-year residents and summer visitors this surprising attachment provided fodder for endless speculation. A perfectly ordinary mother of three, notable for nothing more than the fact that she happened to be the wife of the St. Mary's minister, had snagged the son of one of the village's wealthiest and most respected citizens. Compounding the embarrassment was the fact that the son happened to still be married to another woman. Before the year was out, Charlene Gilbert had filed for divorce and moved to an apart-ment in New York, leaving her two youngest children behind with her husband and leaving $550 in their joint savings account.

"I cannot go to church anymore," Brooke confided to friends stay-ing with her. Of course she did go to church, walking the entire way from her house at Cove End, holding her head high and keeping a brisk pace and taking her customary seat in a front pew where she could be sure to hear every word that was uttered by Paul Gilbert during that morning's sermon. And, while she was schooled sufficiently in the ways of the world to understand that this would hardly squash local gossip or make amends for the pain caused by a member of her immediate family, she also made it a point to show her support of St. Mary's and its wronged minister by making a sizable contribution to the church vestry.

When Anthony Marshall, finally having secured a divorce from his second wife, married Charlene Gilbert two years later, Brooke Astor had some cause to be grateful. She attended the quiet service at St. Thomas's in Manhattan and then took the happy couple out for a lunch at La Grenouille. At least their union could now be treated as officially sanctioned. To Charlene she might make every effort to say what was both correct and fitting. To the world at large she might say "Charlene makes Tony happy." That, after all, was only good manners. But the damage had been done. And as time passed and she understood that she and Charlene had very little in common, the mask of politeness began to slip every now and then. In an effort to make amends—or at the very least smooth things over—she might then give her new daughter-in-law some brooch or bracelet Charlene had expressly admired. And that might make everyone feel better for a while. "Money is like manure," as she had always said. Generosity had always come easily to her. And, after all, there was no need to see that much of Charlene and Tony. Throughout his earlier marriages her son had never figured large in her social life.

All his adult life, whenever he happened to be in New York, Tony Marshall might be found, either on his own or with his current wife, at one of his mother's cocktail parties or official dinners or seated at one of the large round tables she paid for out of her own pocket at some major charity benefit. Occasionally you might find Tony Marshall and his current wife at a birthday celebration, but rarely did you see them at a sit-down dinner at the apartment and almost never when the table was set for ten.

One chooses one's friends; when it comes to family, one has no choice. But one has an obligation to make the best of it. That, too, is good manners. On the other hand, there are limits. Brooke Astor might love her son and support him financially to the extent she believed was appropriate or necessary—she might even give generously to the Republican Party when it was in power and lobby for him to have an ambassadorship—but that didn't mean she had to embrace him as an intimate. With Charlene as his new wife, she seemed disinclined to alter this stance in the slightest.

At Cove End, Tony Marshall had always been welcome to come visit with his wife and family. After the divorce from his first wife, he would still bring his sons. Once the twins were in their twenties, they all began staying in the guest cottage with the gambrel roof and water view. The cottage had several bedrooms and looked to Philip Marshall to have been decorated by his grandmother. Certainly it was cozier than the main house. With the addition of great-grandchildren, this arrangement made sense. The fact was, the main house wasn't all that large. With the advent of Charlene, there was no reason to make any adjustment in the nature of the Marshalls' accommodations. But Charlene's needs were very different from those of Tony's two previous wives. After all, she had left behind friends and family in Northeast Harbor, with whom she might wish to spend extended periods of time.

The good thing about the cottage, or even the two smaller cabins, was that they made it possible for guests to go their own way during the day and then meet up in the house for dinner. Now the cottage made it possible for Tony and Charlene to stay on for weeks at Cove End while never playing a part in its social life. Later, Liz Smith would remember a long festive weekend spent in the main house with George Trescher and Brooke in the late 1990s, marked by at least one formal dinner party, with Tony and Charlene hovering about somewhere on the premises. "Sort of like ghosts. Around, but not in Brooke's real line of vision. She was good at ignoring them."

No one likes to feel powerless. And no one likes to feel she can't manage without assistance. Tony wasn't the only one close to Brooke Astor having increasing difficulty pleasing her. For many years she had relied on Raymonde, her French maid, to oversee her wardrobe and also do her makeup, taking Raymonde with her to London, Palm Beach, and Baden-Baden. More than one friend has gone so far as to suggest that such chic as Brooke possessed was owing to Raymonde's ministrations. Raymonde had always done a fair amount of editing of her mistress's wardrobe—not only when laying out her outfits for the day but also when quietly returning purchases made on some spontaneous shopping expedition. Always theirs had been a complicated relationship. From the start Raymonde had refused to converse with her mistress in French, much as Brooke tried to encourage it. When Brooke assayed a question in her native language, Raymonde made it a point to respond in English. (At the same time, within Brooke's hearing, Raymonde felt free to respond to French conversational sallies from Nancy Pierrepont or Rosamond Bernier.) Occasionally there had been blowups. Even at the best of times relations had rarely been smooth.

Finally, in the summer of 2001, Raymonde announced she was retiring to Marseilles. During the spring, not long before Raymonde's announcement, Jolee Hirsch, Brooke's pretty and popular social secretary, had left to work for George W. Bush in Washington. After Jolee's departure, social secretaries had come and gone with dismaying frequency. Alarmed by what they glimpsed, some friends began to keep their distance, or withdraw completely. Others, like Annette de la Renta, Schuyler Chapin, Vartan Gregorian, and David Rockefeller, continued to remain close by.

One of the reasons Brooke Astor could not pack up and leave the city that fall was that the following March she would be celebrating her hundredth birthday. A series of events had been planned in anticipation of this big event. On November 11, she was to be honored as the sole Lion at the New York Public Library's annual Literary Lions dinner. A couple of days later she was to receive an award from the Marine Corps, a branch of the military that had always enjoyed a place close to her heart. And, in December, she was to receive a special medal from Vartan Gregorian at a luncheon ceremony planned by the Carnegie Foundation. Of all these celebrations the one at the Library was the first, the biggest, and the most demanding. At the Carnegie Foundation there would be other people honored along with her, while the award from the Marine Corps would be presented in front of a relatively modest gathering at the Union League Club. But the Library was expecting hundreds of guests.

As always, George Trescher had overseen all the planning for the big Library event. Peter Jennings had been slated to preside as master of ceremonies and his name was prominently listed in the program. That morning, however, the city had received another terrible shock, when a giant plane taking off for the Dominican Republic from Kennedy Airport immediately lost power and crashed into a street in Belle Harbor, a quiet beachside community in Queens. Everyone on board the plane had been killed on impact. Homes on the ground were destroyed, although mercifully the casualties were not anything like those at Ground Zero.

Inevitably, the first thought was: terrorists. No major networks could afford to give cursory coverage to an incident with such horrifying implications. And by the end of the day, when it was becoming increasingly apparent that the crash might owe nothing to sabotage but was more likely to have been precipitated by a structural weakness in the plane's rudder, Peter Jennings, in his role as chief anchor, was still presiding over the unfolding story from the ABC news desk. Once it was clear that there was no need to cancel any big parties that night, the playwright John Guare, who was already playing a key part in the program, agreed to take Jennings's place.

Ordinarily the big November celebration honoring Brooke Astor at the Library would have been a black-tie event, very much like the one at the Union Club three years earlier when she had received the Edith Wharton Award. But in keeping with the mood that fall, the dress code that night was business attire. The crowd was subdued. This was nothing like the big extravaganzas of the eighties or early nineties. The events of September 11 had rendered such opulence unthinkable.

What September 11 had shown, among other things, was how fragile the fabric of the city actually was—dependent not only on its government and great businesses but on the courage and, above all, the generosity of its private citizens. Already city revenues were down. To offset a sudden $1.2 billion deficit, drastic cuts would have to be made in the following year's budget. It was only a matter of time before key services would be curtailed. Inevitably the city's cultural institutions would be prime targets. Indeed by the end of the month the branch libraries would be facing a 10 percent cut, making it likely that they could have to shutter their doors on Saturdays.

Making her way through the throng of well-wishers on the arm of David Rockefeller, Brooke Astor appeared fragile but unfailingly gracious. In her fitted red suit she was easy to spot. Cocktails were served in the main hall, now called Astor Hall. Dinner was in the Celeste Bartos Forum, where slides were projected on the large room's curved walls, providing glimpses of New York's most photographed, if not necessarily most photogenic, hands-on philanthropist. At dinner John Guare read a prepared text giving an overview of her life. Her friend Liz Smith read three of her poems, with "Discipline" figuring large. Brian Bedford, a new friend and one of her favorite actors, was to follow them, reading selections from *The Tempest*.

But before Brian Bedford had a chance to begin his reading from *The Tempest*, David Rockefeller had taken Brooke's arm and helped her from the table and then quietly escorted her from the room. Some tables had still not finished their main course when it became apparent that the guest of honor was not going to return. Later, friends joked that David Rockefeller had rushed Brooke out the door so that he could get home in time to watch his favorite television program. But those close to the two of them knew better. David Rockefeller understood perfectly well the importance of this occasion and Brooke Astor's role in the evening's program. He would never act on his own wishes or preferences unless he believed that their leaving prematurely would be best for everyone.

Until the sole Literary Lion's abrupt departure, the celebration at the Library on November 11 resembled many celebrations in the past. Once again Brooke Astor was being honored. Once again her name was enough to ensure a sizable turnout. Once again her presence served as both a prod and a reminder: New York was always going to need men and women with the vision and energy of Brooke Astor. If there was something bittersweet about this celebration, it was hardly surprising. Now, when the city needed her more than ever, there was good reason to believe that it would never see her like again.

Eleven

TIMING IS EVERYTHING, 2002–2006

Self-pity is the most ignoble of emotions.

David Rockefeller had insisted on giving the big party to celebrate Brooke Astor's hundredth party. Back when she had officially turned ninety, 2,000 paying guests had eventually joined her at the Seventh Regiment Armory, which had been fitted out with masses of flowers, giant hammered metal trees, and thirty-one enormous crystal chandeliers. Among other things, the armory celebration had been a benefit for Osborn Elliott's Citizens Committee for New York. No less important, it had provided Brooke an occasion to dance late into the night.

Osborn Elliott had very much wanted to celebrate his old friend Brooke's hundredth birthday with another big fund-raiser—this time an enormous tented party to take place in Shubert Alley, in the heart of the Theater District. At a lunch the previous spring, he had persuaded her to tentatively agree to this plan. By the fall, however, she had changed her mind, much to his chagrin. Here again David Rockefeller had interceded on her behalf, by convincing her a small gathering would suit her better.

The party to mark this big birthday was to be something very different from what Osborn Elliott had envisioned. First, the dinner would be a private affair. Second, it would be declared off-limits for reporters and photographers. Third, it would be attended by no more than fifty close friends. The dinner would be held in the play house at Pocantico Hills, the Rockefeller compound in Westchester. George Trescher would, as usual, keep an eye on publicity and overall planning. Sean Driscoll, whose Glorious Food had catered so many of Brooke Astor's parties in the past, would take care of the dinner arrangements.

Sadly, certain close friends, like John Mason Brown and Mab Moltke, who had featured prominently at parties in the past, would be missing. Some friends, like Susan Mary Alsop, simply weren't up to attending. And two dear friends, Brendan Gill and Jack Pierrepont, both of whom had played important roles at her ninetieth birthday party, had died in the interim. Both men could be counted on to enliven any party they attended. And for many years she had numbered both among her favorite younger friends.

For Brooke Astor there were close friends and then there were "friends of the heart." Brendan Gill and Jack Pierrepont were "friends of the heart." One might also call them "kindred spirits." Having stayed young in spirit far longer than anyone has a right to, both men had loved parties almost as much as Brooke did. Both could be counted on to enliven the dreariest social occasion, but both also had a serious side.

Brendan Gill, a gifted writer and longtime *New Yorker* staff member, could always be relied on to come up with an apt turn of phrase or amusing quotation and also shared Brooke's unwavering love for the city. Like Brooke Astor, Brendan Gill had come to New York as an adult and fallen in love with it. As a founding member and sometime president of the Landmarks Conservancy, he had more than once enlisted her aid in some down-to-the-wire struggle to save one of its great architectural treasures from a wrecker's ball. Some of the best magazine profiles of Brooke Astor were written by Brendan Gill, who, for her big ninetieth birthday, had provided the text for the small book that was printed to commemorate the occasion. To certain friends she allowed as how she wished he hadn't referred to the circumstances in which she had been raised as "modest," but by 1997 she had forgiven this lapse sufficiently to sit for a long and detailed profile Brendan was writing for *The New Yorker*.

Brooke Astor had first gotten to know Brendan Gill in the late sixties; but she had known Jack Pierrepont since he was an unruly little boy intent on disrupting the exercise class held in the dining room of his mother's house in Bernardsville. The small brat had grown into a courtly and charming man about town, who happened to share Brooke's special interest in the Bronx Zoo and her abiding fondness for Northeast Harbor. In time he had served with distinction not only as chairman of development for the Wildlife Conservation Society and president of the Knickerbocker Club but also as a dedicated board member of the Vincent Astor Foundation.

Brendan Gill's widow, Brooke took care to acknowledge at his big Town Hall memorial service—but that was merely a bit of mischief making. Ann Gill had never played a part in her life. Jack Pierrepont's widow, she continued to see a great deal of, particularly during her summers in Maine, but by then relations were not quite what they had once been. Nancy bored her, she one day confided to Louis Auchincloss. Left to her own devices, Nancy Pierrepont was anything but boring. In Brooke's company, however, she tended to be on her best behavior. Complicating relations, she was also Brooke's sometime decorator.

The cause of any falling off in their friendship was complicated, but it seems to have predated Jack's dying and to have owed something to an incident that, temporarily at least, tainted relations with both Pierreponts—an unhappy financial transaction stemming from an honest misunderstanding. Jack Pierrepont had acted as a go-between for the sale of Brooke's Maine camp, August Moon, by passing along to another summer resident, Susan Lyall, an asking price Brooke had mentioned casually in conversation. At lunch one Sunday he told Lyall the price was just over $1 million. According to Lyall, after she agreed to the asking price, Brooke Astor walked the land with her, making it clear that she wanted her to have it at a good price because she believed she would take good care of it. When the two women returned to Cove End and Tony was informed, he demanded an extra $800,000, saying that what Lyall had agreed to was the asking price before taxes and certain fees were paid. In the end, Susan Lyall paid just over $1 million for the camp and Mrs. Astor toured the property one last time with her, making sure everything was in place. But a mistake had been made.

Parting with August Moon would have been painful for Brooke Astor, no matter how little profit she cleared. The camp was her creation. Her sanctuary. Her retreat. Once she had been forced to give up driving her own car, the camp had lost much of its allure. All the same, to actually part with the camp marked the end of an era. Anyone associated with this sale was at risk. Even so, her natural inclination was to forgive and forget. With time all might have been forgiven, but then Jack Pierrepont failed her by finally growing old. In his sixties, suffering from two arthritic knees, he had chosen to have both joints replaced and continued to dance with her at parties and benefits—laughing with Louis Auchincloss, after a particularly strenuous night of dancing, about whether it was possible that their old friend Brooke might have had a "back lift." Retired, he had devoted more time to his painting. Faced with the inroads illness was making on his body, he had always soldiered on and even made light of any disability. But, finally, after he was diagnosed with brain cancer, he retreated to his New York apartment, where Nancy saw to his care as best she could and Brooke was not inclined to seek him out. He just stopped talking, she would later say.

Brendan Gill, on the other hand, had been spared such a fate. For him there had been no serious falling off. Just a gradual slowing down. As his life changed direction, he and Brooke had less reason to see each other. Within days of Brendan's death a "Comment" piece with his byline ran in *The New Yorker*. For most friends and acquaintances his death came as a shock. But Brendan—who had always managed to catch the last train home to Bronxville, no matter how much serious partying he had been doing—had been battling prostate cancer for some time. "Brendan always knew when to leave a party," his close friend Margo Wellington later observed.

Because Brooke Astor no longer had an experienced social secretary working for her, David Rockefeller's staff was delegated to make up the guest list for her hundredth birthday. Early on, the staff ran into problems when it became apparent that fifty invitations would not be sufficient. You couldn't possibly leave out the heads of the city's great cultural institutions, for instance. A call was placed to Washington and Jolee Hirsch was consulted, and another fifty guests were added to the list. But even to keep within this limit many longtime intimates had to be left out. Louis Auchincloss was never invited. Nor was Arthur Schlesinger. Or Linda Gillies. Or Douglas Dillon. Some exclusions were pure oversight. Some were owing to slights real or imagined. And some were owing to Brooke's preference for the company of young people. Inevitably, with the passing years, a good many of her younger friends had grown too old for her. Certainly Jolee Hirsch, who had made a success of the job in part because she was young and pretty and naturally outgoing, had always been aware of this. In the end the guest list—which managed to seem at once selective and arbitrary—would have done the first Mrs. Astor proud.

With David Rockefeller's party fast approaching, Brooke Astor still had not found anyone to adequately replace her French maid. She did, however, have a lovely blue ball gown designed for her by Oscar de la Renta. In the days leading up to the party she gave interviews to a select group of journalists—most notably, Alex Kuczynski from *The New York Times* and Liz Smith from the *Post*. These two interviews were conducted over tea in the red lacquer library, where she had always enjoyed meeting with friends over cookies and little sandwiches and where she could now count on having a reasonably good chance of hearing what was being said to her.

All over the country, as well as in New York, the big birthday received extensive coverage. It was an event. Without exception, the pieces written were tactful and admiring—depending for the most part on highlights from a very long and very public life. If the *Times* piece chose to dwell on her saying she'd never had a face-lift, that was not Brooke Astor's fault. And if the paper of record chose to publish a list of invited guests, that was not her fault, either. Inevitably such a list could only cause hurt feelings. Indeed rumor had it that when one famous guest—a man who had actually been invited—noticed that his name was not on the list, he immediately made his displeasure known in no uncertain terms.

For the big party, friends and family flew in from all over the world. Brooke Astor's two surviving nieces, Romana McEwen and Emily Harding, were to be there. So was Viscount William Astor, another favorite relation, the long-haired hippie she had once tolerated and then come to cherish as a handsome middle-aged man. Her two grown grandsons, Philip and Alec Marshall, were present for the occasion, both also looking strikingly handsome. And while the press might be barred from the party, certain members of the working press, like Barbara Walters and Liz Smith, did attend in their capacity as friends.

In her specially designed blue gown, the guest of honor looked radiant and, as always, rose to the occasion, even though she'd had a bad fall recently. Walking into the party she spotted her Maine friend Nancy Pyne, and when Nancy threw up her hands and gave her hips a little jiggle, she responded in kind. The little speech she gave that night at dinner was everything that it needed to be. From the start she had seemed genuinely pleased by all the attention. And indeed early on, when she asked William Astor to escort her from Holly Hill to the party and then to lend her his arm for her grand entrance, she had gotten up to a bit of mischief. Tony might have expected that he would be taking his mother into the party, even though David Rockefeller was to be her official date for the evening.

At the dinner Brooke Astor had David Rockefeller on her left and Kofi Annan on her right. With her at the round table were the de la Rentas, along with Barbara Walters, Lord Astor, and Nan Annan. When dessert was served, she circled the room on David Rockefeller's arm, visiting with the guests seated at the nine other round tables. Later, she would have photographs of these brief exchanges to pore over with her butler, Chris. Occasionally a friend would look Brooke's way and catch her swaying ever so slightly to the music the small band was playing. One friend spotted her taking a couple of steps with David Rockefeller, but that was all. This time there was no possibility of even a single long dance with Freddy Melhado. No occasion for him to appreciate how strong she was. Even so, she appeared to be having a good time.

The following Monday Brooke Astor was honored at a luncheon at the Metropolitan Museum of Art, attended by the members of its President's Council as well as certain members of the full board. Once again her official escort was David Rockefeller. A few days earlier there had been a birthday luncheon at the New York Public Library, where she'd chosen, as always, to celebrate with librarians rather than with members of that board. All of these events received extensive coverage in the press.

By the spring of her big birthday New Yorkers were happy for the distraction. Resilient as always, New Yorkers were once again giving parties and going to the theater. There was no reason to stay close to home unless they felt so inclined. One night in May, Brooke Astor joined John Hart and Brian Bedford for dinner and the theater. The two men had decided to take her to see Elaine Stritch perform in her critically praised and highly personal one-woman show. On the face of it, this seemed like a good idea. One amazing survivor was being taken to meet another. The seats were excellent, but it was clear from the moment Elaine Stritch took the stage that Brooke was restless. Two things were going on. She couldn't hear much of what Stritch was saying and what she did manage to hear she didn't much care for. "Cunt" and "fuck" were not acceptable words for conveying strong emotion. To her ears they sounded vulgar. No less important, she was put off by the way Elaine Stritch was dressed. To get up on a stage in front of hundreds of people wearing nothing more than a long white shirt, black tights, and black high heels showed a lack of respect. She was ready to leave after the first act. Unfortunately, there was no way of locating Marciano Amaral, her driver.

During the second act, Brooke sat much of the time gazing at her lap and fiddling with the clasp of her handbag. When Stritch sang "The Ladies Who Lunch," Brian Bedford glanced in Brooke's direction, but she did not seem to take offense. She may not have heard Stephen Sondheim's words or caught their meaning. Or she may not have taken the lyrics personally. Over the years she had done her fair share of lunching, but as president of the Vincent Astor Foundation she had never had any cause to see herself as some frivolous socialite. After Stritch's performance ended, Brian Bedford went backstage alone and John Hart saw her home.

Back in the old days most of Brooke Astor's lunches had taken place at the Four Seasons or at the Knickerbocker Club, in the company of men. At the Knickerbocker, she could pick up the check gracefully if need be, but at the Four Seasons there was the pleasure of dining in a room full of the city's rich and powerful and having them stop by to pay their respects. Of late, though, she had been finding it increasingly difficult to negotiate the long walk to her Four Seasons table—even when she made use of the freight elevator to bypass the stairs and enter through the kitchen. One time Ed Koch, the former mayor, discovered her, looking somewhat lost, making her way down the hallway that led to the building's side entrance, and, over her protests, insisted on helping her to the door and then out to the sidewalk, where he waited with her until her driver pulled up. More and more she was lunching at the Knickerbocker, where the staff made a great fuss over her and where she felt protected and safe. And more often than not, she was lunching with women—not only with Annette de la Renta or Barbara Walters but new friends like Dorothy Cullman and Florence Irving, who shared her zest for philanthropy and were helpful and understanding when, on occasion, she let slip some of the things that were troubling her.

Recently, she confided, she had given Charlene a lovely bracelet and her daughter-in-law had never bothered to thank her properly with a note. Worse, Charlene had reportedly taken the bracelet immediately to Christie's to have it appraised. Thanks to her, Tony and Charlene now had their own car and driver. But the more that she gave them, the more they seemed to want from her. Furthermore, Tony kept nagging her about expenses, telling her she had to cut back.

Finally before her big birthday, she confided to her friend John Hart that she'd agreed to let Tony sell the beautiful Childe Hassam *Flags* painting over the library mantel, undertaken just as America was entering the First World War—the painting that Brendan Gill had described in their last interview as being "exhilarating" and "full of high hopes." Tony had said that he could get good money for it. And with that money she would be able for some time to continue living the way she always had. It was a shame to have to part with the painting, but she seemed to have little choice.

Friends, never quite sure what to believe and increasingly aware that Brooke's powers were failing, listened and tried to offer words that might provide some comfort. One year after the big birthday, when Brooke complained to Liz Smith that Charlene was stealing her jewelry, Liz Smith found it hard to credit. " I just chalked it up to 'geriatric paranoia' and I even said to her that I didn't feel that could be so." Around that time Liz Smith stopped making an effort to see Brooke Astor, having gotten the impression from Brooke's close friends that she wouldn't know who she was anyway. Liz Smith was not the only one to fall away. Making it doubly difficult to keep in touch was the fact that the social secretaries now responsible for screening calls kept turning over in such rapid succession they never had a chance to get a proper grip on the job.

For the Childe Hassam painting Tony got $10 million from a dealer who soon sold it again for double that price. Tony himself took a $2 million commission. His mother had paid $172,000 when she bought the painting in the early seventies, so even with Tony's commission she was clearing almost $8 million before taxes.

Still, Brooke continued to worry about expenses. Sometimes longing to buy herself a new outfit but not quite daring to jeopardize her finances, she would stop by the Astor business office at 405 Park to talk to Alice Perdue when she knew Tony wouldn't be around. When she asked Alice Perdue if she had sufficient funds to cover such an extravagance, Alice would always say, "Mrs. Astor, you can buy dozens of outfits and not have to worry for twenty years." Alice Perdue, who ran the business office, was hoping to reassure her, but she was also telling the truth. Brooke would go on to a lunch with friends and a bit of shopping, relieved and happy, but by the time Tony once again brought up the need to cut back on expenses a few weeks later, she would have forgotten what Alice Perdue had told her and panic would begin to set in.

Of course, she had never been as wealthy as the world at large believed her to be. The Foundation, with its generous and much publicized grants, had contributed to the mistaken impression that she had a great fortune at her command. She was no longer "the little sister of the rich," but by no means did she have anything like the money Laurance and David Rockefeller had. Or relatively new philanthropists like George Soros and Bill Gates and Richard Gilder. Or even Jayne Wrightsman. The Rockefellers were certainly aware of this.

On the other hand, Brooke Astor had funds sufficient to maintain her for many years to come, in the style she had first set in her early years as a widow and then made her own. The interest she received annually from the trust that Vincent had set up for her continued to bring her some $2 million a year. At her death, in keeping with the explicit terms of Vincent's will, which gave her "power of appointment," the principal would go to several major nonprofit institutions of her choosing. Originally her plan had been to give the money through the Foundation; now, with the Foundation closed, she would be giving it directly. Tony had done well with her personal investments. (In 2006, when pressed to explain his actions, he would say that he had seen to it that his mother now had investments worth $82 million.) At his mother's death, Tony would benefit from a trust she had set up to ensure that her son would enjoy a comfortable income during his lifetime. At his death, though, that principal would go to a few of the city's major cultural and scientific institutions—what she liked to call its "crown jewels."

To more than one friend Brooke Astor had quoted with a little laugh the words of Andrew Carnegie on the pernicious effect of leaving large sums of money to one's descendants and then added, "Tony would not be happy if he heard me say this." So while her son stood to benefit from her death, he would not be getting the kind of money any uninformed observer might imagine. Furthermore, at Tony's death, his wife would cease to receive any money from her mother-in-law's estate.

As Brooke Astor approached her hundredth birthday two close male friends who cared deeply about her both observed that it might be a blessing if after this big celebration Brooke went to sleep one night and failed to wake up. If that had indeed happened, things might have turned out more or less the way she'd planned for them to— although the beautiful *Flags* painting that she had more than once promised to the Met would have not been part of the estate she left.

Instead, Brooke Astor went on to participate in the various celebrations in her honor and then to spend that summer with her two dogs in Maine—receiving far fewer visitors than she had in the past and inviting virtually no one to stay over, except for Tony and Charlene, who as always went their own way. Once again, her butler, Chris, oversaw the running of Cove End. But there was no unsupervised swimming in the lovely pool she'd had built after selling her camp and no long walks with Nancy Pyne or Nancy Pierrepont. Such walking as she did was restricted to the grounds of the property. And whenever guests were invited for tea, Chris made sure she was provided with a slip of paper with their names, to prevent any confusion on her part during their visit.

The summer of 2002 would be her last summer in Maine. Late in the spring of 2003 she broke her hip. Back in June 1998 she had broken the same hip leaving a big event at the Museum of Natural History and had astonished her nurses with her quick recovery. When Minnette Christie, the nurse who saw to her care at Holly Hill, brought her to the indoor pool for her first session of physical therapy, much to her horror, Brooke Astor immediately began swimming laps, with no ill effect. Then, when it came time for her to take her first real walk, she insisted on setting off across the grounds of the property. This time, however, the break was more serious, requiring two subsequent surgeries and a long convalescence in the hospital. Owing to the extended periods under anesthesia or the seriousness of the trauma or simply to her advanced age, she failed to bounce back.

That December, however, Brooke Astor felt well enough to join Sean Driscoll for their annual pre-Christmas lunch. Usually the two of them had lunch at a restaurant of Driscoll's choosing—Jean

Georges, for instance, or the Café des Artistes—where she would invariably have to cope with well-wishers, whom she would greet politely even when she failed to recognize them. This time, to protect her privacy, Sean Driscoll chose to have their lunch at the offices of Glorious Food, where in front of the fireplace a small table was set for three. He invited Bill Cunningham, her favorite photographer, to join them. In addition, he enlisted her favorite waiter to do the serving and then remain at her side to ensure that she had everything she needed.

The lunch was a mixed success. Sean Driscoll had picked Brooke Astor up at her apartment, where a Polaroid shot had been taken in the hall, to remind her later of what she had done that day. A nurse had accompanied the two of them in her car, but stayed downstairs with the driver. At lunch, Sean Driscoll sat on her right, by her good ear, and Bill Cunningham on her left. For this occasion she had donned all her finery—including the Medal of Freedom she'd been given by President Clinton, which was held in place on her jacket by a jeweled panther—but she was not the same woman she had been a year earlier. What saved the lunch was the photographs Bill Cunningham had brought with him—photographs he'd taken of her over the years. "She would focus on the pictures and tell little stories," recalled Driscoll. She'd say, 'Was that a Bill Blass I was wearing?' Bill would turn over the photograph, to check what he'd written there, and then he'd say, 'Yes, Mrs. Astor, it was.' But at the same time she didn't always seem to really know who I was or who Bill was."

At the end of the meal, when it was getting to be time to leave, Brooke Astor couldn't find her pocketbook. Hard as they looked, no one could find it. Finally, Sean Driscoll sent the waiter downstairs to see if it might be in her car—which it was. "After the waiter handed her the pocketbook, Brooke began to search inside until she fished out her American Express card. I had trouble convincing her to put the card away. She wanted to pay for the meal." It was Sean Driscoll's belief that having the waiter there made her mistake his place for a restaurant. But, no matter the cause, her confusion was undeniable. That was the last pre-Christmas lunch they would share.

In 2004, two years after the big birthday party, there was a picture in Bill Cunningham's column showing Brooke Astor looking far from her best, cutting a birthday cake with her son and daughter-in-law hovering over her, but looking straight at the camera. By that time Douglas Dillon and Laurance Rockefeller were dead, as was Eileen Simpson. Nancy Pierrepont had died quickly and unexpectedly from cancer. Brooke Astor, on the other hand, persisted in lingering on, even as her presence gradually faded from view. At the same time, Tony and Charlene Marshall were becoming more visible—primarily as successful investors in the theater, where with David Richenthal, an experienced Broadway producer, they were instrumental in putting on a Tony Award–winning revival of *Long Day's Journey into Night* and then helping bring to Broadway *I Am My Own Wife*, which also won a Tony Award.

To the second awards ceremony Charlene Marshall wore her mother-in-law's famous emerald necklace, an astonishing choice not lost on any of Brooke's old friends who happened to be watching on television. This was the necklace she used to tell Mab Moltke she wished to be buried in. The very same necklace that years later, when death no longer seemed a remote possibility, she let it be known she wanted to go to Annette de la Renta. All in all, it seemed an unfortunate choice. Or, at the very least, one that indicated that the wearer no longer cared what anyone thought. No matter what eventually became of the necklace, it would have been fitting to wait for its owner's death.

By the winter of 2005 few of Brooke Astor's old friends were being permitted to see her. Annette de la Renta made sure to stop by at least four times a month. If possible she would stop by on her way out for the evening, so Brooke would have a chance to see what she was wearing. Florence Irving came to visit in the afternoon as often as she could manage (but nowhere as frequently as Annette), sometimes bringing with her James Watt or Dick Morsches. Most old friends had fallen away long ago, but those who hadn't, like John Hart, were now being turned back by a social secretary who answered the phone. Mrs. Astor, they were told, wasn't in any shape for visitors. In time she was left almost entirely to the care of nurses and the household staff, with occasional visits from her doctor.

At Holly Hill, though, she still had Chris Ely. And in New York she had Marciano Amaral, whom she had made promise he would stay with her until her death and who continued to stay on in an apartment reserved for him on East Seventy-second Street and to see to it that on a beautiful afternoon she had a chance, even in winter, to be out doors—driving her to the Met, where he had permission to leave her car by the fountains in front of the museum's main entrance and then helping her into the wheelchair he had brought along in the trunk. In winter he would bundle her up in a heavy blanket so she'd be warm, and then take her for a long walk in the park, where she would have a chance to again see her beloved trees, as well as any children who happened to be sailing their toy boats in the stone basin designed for this purpose or exploring the nearby statue of Alice in Wonderland. Mrs. Astor had her good days and bad days, but Marciano had noted that whenever her son came to visit her Mrs. Astor would tuck her head down and appear not to understand a thing he was saying to her. "She was reacting the way a small child would and it worked against her," he would later say.

In January 2005, Tony Marshall fired Chris Ely and closed Holly Hill. That September, upon returning from his Maine vacation, Tony fired Marciano Amaral and Alice Perdue, telling the latter that her computer skills were no longer adequate to run the Astor business office. Both felt that they, like Chris, had been let go because they were loyal to Mrs. Astor. Whether or not this was so, Tony was acting as though he believed his mother would not notice any difference in the care she was receiving. Yet, when Marciano went to tell Mrs. Astor that her son no longer wanted him to work for her and he was going to have to leave her after all, tears ran down her cheeks.

David Rockefeller had managed to get Tony Marshall to reopen Holly Hill the summer of 2005. Word had it that he accomplished this feat by threatening to embarrass Tony publicly by bringing Brooke up to Maine, to stay with him in Seal Harbor. Brooke Astor stayed on through the early fall in the house where more than once she had said she wanted to end her days—albeit without Chris to take her for drives or help her recall all the things in the neighborhood she loved to keep track of. But the following summer Holly Hill remained shuttered. This time Tony argued that his mother had to stay in the city to undergo radiation for a skin cancer on her face that could not be left untreated. Leaving his mother unattended was something else again. While some of her friends wondered if, given her advanced age, a punishing course of radiation was really necessary, Tony made plans with Charlene to spend most of their summer in Maine, sailing up the coast to Northeast Harbor in a million-dollar yacht with three staterooms he had bought the year before.

For some time, Annette de la Renta, David Rockefeller, and Brooke Astor's grandson Philip had been alarmed by the increasingly spartan conditions Brooke Astor was living in and also by what they were hearing, either directly or indirectly, from disaffected and fired staff members—not only from Chris Ely and various nurses and maids who believed Mrs. Astor was being neglected but also from Alice Perdue, who was concerned about checks she had been asked to write and also about changes in the way the Astor office had been doing business—starting in the early summer of 2003, soon after Mrs. Astor broke her hip the second time, and gaining momentum in February 2004, when Terry Christensen, the Sullivan and Cromwell attorney who handled Mrs. Astor's legal affairs, was fired.

Because she frequently wrote and entered Mrs. Astor's checks, Alice Perdue could see that large sums of money were being invested in Tony Marshall's Broadway projects.

Terry Christensen not only had a power of attorney with Tony Marshall but had been listed with him as co-executor of Mrs. Astor's most recent will, which had been drawn up in the spring of 2002. However, in May 2003 Tony Marshall had written a first check to Francis X. Morrissey Jr., a lawyer he was bringing in to help with estate planning. In January 2004, G. Warren Whitaker, a well-regarded estates lawyer at Day, Berry and Howard, was also brought in.

All along Tony Marshall must have been counting on his mother's friends' perfectly natural desire to protect her from any undesirable publicity. No one wanted the world to know how fragile she had become. And for a long time their wish to keep private all that was happening to Brooke Astor worked to her son's advantage. Finally, in July 2006 Brooke Astor's grandson Philip went to court to ask that his father be removed as her guardian, with JP Morgan Chase Bank temporarily taking over responsibility for her financial well-being and Annette de la Renta taking interim responsibility for her care.

In his appeal to the court Philip Marshall said that his father had "turned a blind eye to [his grandmother], intentionally and repeatedly ignoring her health safety, personal and household needs, while enriching himself with millions of dollars." Three of Mrs. Astor's friends filed affidavits in his support. Annette de la Renta said, "Because of the failure of Ms. Astor's son, Anthony, to spend her money properly, the quality of life of Ms. Astor has been significantly eroded." David Rockefeller said, "I am concerned about her welfare and hope that Guardians are appointed to look after her needs." Henry Kissinger joined in, saying, "I believe that Annette de la Renta would make an excellent Temporary Guardian of the Person for Mrs. Astor, and an excellent Permanent Guardian of the Person."

By going to court they risked revealing how bad things were. But by going to court they also saw to it that Brooke Astor was properly cared for. Tony Marshall was temporarily removed as his mother's guardian and within little more than a week Brooke Astor was back at Holly Hill, with Chris Ely to look after her and a favorite cook making her meals.

The legal battle that ensued provided fodder for both *The New York Times* and the tabloids for the rest of the summer and into the fall and early winter. It was immediately revealed by Alice Perdue that almost $1 million of Mrs. Astor's money had gone to underwrite the production company that had invested in those two Tony Award–winning Broadway hits. It was also revealed that in the spring of 2003 Brooke Astor had signed over her Maine estate to her son, who had then gone ahead and signed it over to his wife. On the heels of these revelations came the news that, back in the mid-1990s, Francis Morrissey had been suspended from the New York State Bar for two years for mishandling a client's escrow account. Furthermore, he had a reputation for winning the confidence of elderly millionaires, who then saw fit to leave him hundreds of thousands of dollars and sometimes even millions in their final wills.

In the face of these embarrassing revelations, Tony Marshall protested his innocence. What his mother's friends were doing was simply "bad manners." His mother, he continued, would be appalled by this. Immediately some of his famous friends, like Mike Wallace and Martha Stewart, rallied to his side. They knew him to be a loving son and a gentleman. Never had they witnessed him behave in a manner that was anything but affectionate and appropriate.

In the tabloids, which searched out every detail of her relatively impoverished first marriage, her ensuing divorce, her high-handed way with the help, and her penchant for economizing on her mother-in-law's cosmetics and medicines, Charlene Marshall was cast in the role of Lady Macbeth. As various concerned observers who preferred to remain nameless weighed in, the consensus seemed to be that if anyone was at fault it would appear to be Tony's third wife, a full twenty years his junior.

If this was indeed the case, there was no written evidence. Unlike Lady Macbeth's hands, Charlene Marshall's remained, in every respect, clean. Like her husband, she expressed nothing but indignation. But as Chase and Brooke Astor's court-appointed attorney sifted through the records in the sealed Astor offices, it was increasingly apparent that, starting in 2003, Tony Marshall had redirected property and money worth many millions of dollars—almost always to the advantage of his wife. Francis Morrissey, who was also to benefit handsomely, had been named, along with Charlene Marshall, to take Terry Christensen's place as an executor of Mrs. Astor's will—a will that had been changed significantly with the addition of three codicils.

The first codicil had been prepared and witnessed by Terry Christensen in December 2003, the same month that Brooke Astor was having lunch with Sean Driscoll at the offices of Glorious Food. According to the *Times*, "Under the first codicil, 51 percent of the Vincent Astor Trust would go to a fund run by Mr. Marshall, enabling him to distribute the money to charities."

The second codicil, dated January 12, 2004, not drafted by Terry Christensen, named Tony Marshall as sole executor of his mother's estate and gave him outright all the money that was left after various bequests had been paid, thereby doing away with the trust she had set up to maintain him in comfort during his lifetime.

The third codicil, dated March 3, 2004, instructed the executor to sell Mrs. Astor's real estate holdings as part of the estate rather than giving them to Tony Marshall at her death. The expense of selling the property would become a tax deduction for the estate.

Vincent Astor's will had given his wife "power of appointment" over the principal of the trust that was to support her during her lifetime, but the understanding was that she would be giving this money to charities of her own choosing. If this first codicil did not violate the letter of Vincent Astor's will, it did go against his intentions. For years Brooke Astor had been promising substantial sums of money from that trust to various city institutions. The second codicil ran directly contrary to what Brooke Astor had been saying about inherited wealth. And, as was her custom, she had made her intentions known to various parties. She had planned for her money, after Tony's death, to go to benefit the people of New York.

"Don't die guessing," Brooke Astor liked to say, and this bred-in-the-bone curiosity—this wish to see and savor everything that came her way—had stood her in good stead until she turned one hundred. It had made it possible for her to regard everyone she met as worthy of her attention. It had made it only natural for her to appreciate the dreams as well as the needs of the men and women she was trying to help with the foundation she'd remade in her own image. Clear-sighted and practical, she had taken the measure of anyone who came her way and then acted accordingly. If she made mistakes on occasion, her judgment remained remarkably reliable. Until her late nineties, the same could be said of her timing. Like her friend Brendan Gill, she had always known when to leave a party. Then, toward the very end of her life, when old age began to overtake her and she was passing the point where it might have been possible to control what was happening to her, she had lingered on—long enough to see a full century, but perhaps longer than was wise.

EPILOGUE

I did not attend any of Brooke Astor's big birthday parties in 2002 but I did join Mrs. Astor and Florence Irving for lunch that spring at La Grenouille, a restaurant she and Laurance Rockefeller had favored back in the seventies when they were seeing a lot of each other. Although she hadn't been there in some time, she immediately recognized the handsome son of the old owner and greeted him. She told him how much she had always admired the flowers. Later, she invited him to visit her again in Maine. For this occasion she had dressed in a cream-colored tweed suit with a matching hat and gloves. The hat had a little brim and a touch of veil that was particularly flattering when her face was in profile. The lunch had been set up in part so she could tell me some of the stories Florence felt I should hear. But that day she didn't feel like telling old stories.

I was seated to Brooke Astor's right, beside her on the banquette, by her good ear, with Florence across from her. In some ways it was reminiscent of our first meeting. In other ways it was totally different. When she was complimented on how well she looked, she said that was because she was feeling better than she had the last few weeks. She'd been a little depressed and then she'd thought to make an appointment to have her hair colored. There was nothing better for lifting the spirits, she said, touching a honey-colored tendril visible beneath the brim of her hat. Next, she turned to me and asked what

I thought of our president, George W. Bush. She wasn't making idle conversation. I knew she liked it when people had something to say for themselves, but I also knew she was a Republican. "I guess he's doing a good job," I said, hedging, and was instantly ashamed of myself. "I'm not so sure," she said with the sort of emphasis that guaranteed a laugh. She wasn't making a joke, however. She let me know that with an emphatic nod of her head.

At lunch that day Brooke Astor had an appetite. She ate all the Dover sole Florence had ordered for her and finished most of the crème brûlée. Before coffee was served Florence brought out an envelope of snapshots from the birthday luncheon at the Met and passed them across the table to her. "Too much makeup," Brooke said, handing me a picture and pointing to the big red blob on each of her cheeks. She was right.

Before we left the restaurant, Brooke Astor said one more thing that stays in my mind. As we were getting ready to leave the table, she warned me to be careful at tea or her dachshund Boysie would try to steal my cookies when I wasn't looking. I remembered she'd warned me about the same thing the previous fall when I'd gone to the apartment for tea. Boysie was naughty. He was also Brooke's favorite and had spent much of my visit wedged in beside her on the sofa. Indeed it seemed to me that I had spotted her passing him one of her own cookies when she thought I wasn't looking. She must have read my mind. As she gathered up her gloves, she let me know just how important Boysie had become to her. She said, "Boysie jumps on my bed in the morning and won't stop barking until I get up."

One afternoon in the winter of 2002, Louis Auchincloss spoke to me of the qualities that made for a great philanthropist. He said, "To spend is easy, even pleasant; to give, at least wisely, involves sweat and even tears."

Later that winter, Kent Barwick, head of the Municipal Art Society, tried to define just what it was that made one of the society's founding benefactors unique. "I don't think you could have been Mrs. Astor at any period of time other than the last part of the twentieth century," he said. "It's like the Woolworth Building, which is wonderful partially because it's an overlap between a modern skeleton—the construction and elevators—and elaborate handcrafted surfaces. It took thousands of years to refine the skills that produced the mosaic work and the carving of the woodwork in the lobby. A decade later a skyscraper wouldn't be able to have that kind of work anymore."

Nelson Aldrich, who had read *A Midsummer's Night's Dream* to Brooke Astor's mother and had time to study the daughter at close hand at several dinners, later put it somewhat differently: "None of the women I know are willing to use their power as easily as she has been able to. But the basic character is one I recognize from the women I grew up with in Boston. These women were one generation older than Brooke. These Brahmin women—especially after the husband had passed on—came into their own. They had extraordinary curiosity and enthusiasm for the world, perhaps because they had been sealed off from the world. They kicked over the traces. Of course there were differences. Brooke Astor was self-taught. And she liked men."

Vartan Gregorian saw her as possessing still another quality found in an older generation: "In the past—in the nineteenth century or so—it was not your money that bought your friends. It was your brain, your ability, your creativity. She's one of the last of that era. She exposes you to all kinds of people. She puts you down amongst them. She does not invite to her home anybody she does not like. Of course sometimes she makes mistakes."

David Rockefeller saw this openness to all kinds of people as being fundamental to her nature. And having been with her in all kinds of places, he spoke from firsthand knowledge. "The most remarkable thing about Brooke Astor is that she devoted so much of her time to helping New Yorkers from every way of life. Most important, she treated everyone with respect—as if she was meeting with Queen Elizabeth, whom she knew quite well."

"With Brooke it is a personal response," said her friend Barbara Walters. "But it is also the personality she has. She is very kind. She is also very witty and likes being slightly wicked. She will tell a story about some man she was sitting next to at dinner who was trying to impress her. This man said, 'Mrs. Astor, how many lovers have you had?' And she said, 'That's how I count myself to sleep.'"

The response from Brooke Astor could on occasion be a little wicked. But it could also be breathtakingly practical, according to Susan Burden, who came to know Brooke Astor well after Brooke and her late husband, Carter Burden, started their reading group back in 1984. "During the early days of the group, Renata Adler walked into Brooke's living room just having adopted her son and Renata was *very* thin. Renata's thin anyway and she had lost tons of weight. As she walked into the room, her skirt fell off. Literally. Brooke didn't miss a beat. She took Renata back to her room and began pinning her skirt so it would stay up. Brooke loves being the focus of attention, but she has a way of looking out for people."

"She knew another world and came from another world," said Annette de la Renta, who many felt was the person Brooke loved best in this world. "But she is curious about everything and sees every-thing. Discipline, I think, is the key to her. She certainly lived by that. She'd say to me, 'Annette, I'm not sure I can do it.' Or 'Annette, I feel dreadful today.' But she's like a dalmation at a fire. She can be really sick and not feeling well, but when people are expecting her, there she goes."

"She has great style," said Brian Bedford. "I know an awful lot of talented people, but I know very very few people who have tremen-dous style in their lives. Wasn't it Oscar Wilde who said, 'I put my tal-ent into my work and my genius into my life'?"

"With the reading group or dinner parties," recalled Susan Burden, "you'd get the feeling she wanted you to stay. She wanted to hold on to you. When she was having a good time, she didn't want the night to end." At the same time, she was ready for the next adventure. "She had no fear of small airplanes," said Annette de la Renta. "She'd get into a mosquito. She has zero physical fear. She'd have been with Lindbergh if he'd asked her."

"After my wife passed away, Brooke was very gracious and would invite me to dinner parties," said Marshall Rose. "We'd go out with Bill Blass, she and I. Bill was a single man; I was a single man; she was a single woman. One night I was at Mortimer's with Bill and Brooke. The food at Mortimer's was awful and the service was worse. Bill left and I walked Brooke home. As we were walking, she said to me, 'If I were only fifty years younger.' I look back and I say, 'If I were only twenty-five years older.'"

By the time 2006 drew to a close, the presiding judge had cleared Tony Marshall of elder abuse, as far as his mother's person was concerned, but JP Morgan Chase continued to express serious concern about his handling of her financial affairs. There were some worrisome discrepancies. So far, the most striking was the error in reporting the purchase price of the Childe Hassam painting by some $5 million, thereby saving Brooke Astor more than $1 million in taxes.

In October, Tony Marshall agreed to permanently relinquish his role as his mother's legal guardian. He and his wife also gave up their roles as his mother's executors. (Early in August all ties had been cut with Francis Morrissey.) Both parties agreed to drop the court case and wait for the various issues to be resolved after Mrs. Astor's death, should her court-appointed executor choose to pursue them in surrogate's court. As part of this agreement, Cove End had been removed from the possession of Charlene Marshall and transferred back to

Brooke Astor's son. Cove End, along with a painting by Andrew Wyeth and a grandfather clock, had been placed in escrow to be part of the collateral against future claims against the Marshalls. In addition, the settlement required Tony and Charlene Marshall to pay $1.35 million—$850,000 within the next ten days and $500,000 by July 1, 2007—to Chase to cover late penalties and interest relating to Mrs. Astor's tax returns.

Back when Alice Perdue had been helping run Mrs. Astor's office, Tony Marshall one day suggested to her that because he had no brothers or sisters no one would care what happened with his mother's will. On this point, he proved to be badly mistaken. Having shown himself ready to sacrifice one strong woman for the benefit of another, he was now left to face the consequences.

In October 2006, Annette de la Renta was named as Brooke Astor's permanent guardian. It had been Mrs. Astor's often stated wish that she be able to live out her days at Holly Hill. Now that Annette had seen to it that she was safely settled in the place she had chosen to be, she once again had Boysie and Girlsie for company and a staff that put her needs first. She had rooms that were fresh and bright—far brighter than they had been back in the fall of 2002, when Tony had sold the lovely *Flags* painting and then persisted in doing everything possible to keep cutting back on expenses. Both of her grandsons were now free to visit her whenever they wished to. Close friends had begun to make appointments to see her, proving more than ready to make the hourlong trip from the city, if only for the chance to take her hands in theirs and once again tell her how much she meant to them.

AFTERWORD

On Monday, August 13, 2007, little more than a year after the court battle erupted, Brooke Astor's life came to an end. That Saturday night, when it had become clear she was dying, Tony Marshall paid a final visit to her bedside and, according to his own account, held his aged mother in his arms. Annette de la Renta, who had seen to it that Holly Hill was once again a fitting residence for Brooke Astor, was the last one to spend time with her. Separately and privately, Tony and Annette both bid farewell to a woman whose wishes each professed to know best and whose interests each was prepared to fight to protect.

Back in the summer of 1992, not long after she'd turned ninety, Brooke Astor had composed a letter containing precise instructions for her funeral, ranging from a list of designated pallbearers to her preference for a service using the 1928 edition of the Book of Common Prayer. "I have had a wonderful life" was the inscription she'd later chosen for the stone to be laid over the grave site alongside Vincent's, where she was to be buried. On balance, it could be argued that Brooke Astor did have a wonderful life. At least up until the very end. Certainly this was the tack taken by the front-page obituaries and the radio and television tributes that ran immediately upon her death.

Within days, however, the court battle was back in the news again.

On August 15, lawyers for JP Morgan Chase and Annette de la Renta caused a stir by asking Justice Anthony A. Scarpino Jr. of the Westchester County Surrogate's Court to jettison the 2002 will entirely, along with its problematic codicils, and replace them with a will drawn up in 1997, the year Brooke Astor closed the Foundation. By the terms of the 1997 will, the Metropolitan Museum of Art was bequeathed the Childe Hassam *Flags* painting; Linda Gillies was given two small pins and a $100,000 legacy; and Charlene Marshall received a ruby-and-diamond pin with matching earrings, as well as one long fur coat and one short one and the right to stay on as a paying tenant at the Seventy-ninth Street duplex where she was now living, should her husband predecease his mother. In both wills Tony Marshall would inherit all his mother's real estate, but in 1997 he was to receive only $2.5 million outright plus an annual income of five percent, not seven percent, generated by a trust made up of only half the money remaining after all bequests had been made. If the court chose to honor the 1997 will, the city institutions Brooke Astor had supported stood to benefit by as much as $60 million.

Like any good party, a successful funeral bears the imprint of those in charge. Of course it is difficult, if not impossible, to put into effect plans that are fifteen years old—particularly when many people slated to take part are themselves dead and those still living have become your sworn enemies. Even so, his mother's funeral promised to be the one occasion on which Tony could honor her wishes and also occupy center stage. Without question it had been his mother's wish that her service be held at St. Thomas Church on Fifth Avenue and Fifty-third Street. It is far from certain that she would have set the time for 2:30 on a summer Friday afternoon, when everyone with a house in the country is hoping to beat rush-hour traffic. Nor would she have waited to the very last minute to announce that the funeral was open to the public.

Before the service, Annette had eighteen people to lunch at her apartment—not only David Rockefeller but also Brooke's two doctors and their wives, Chris Ely, Brooke's two nurses, the Henry Kissingers, and Philip Marshall, along with his wife and two children. One way or another, all had been of particular help to Brooke Astor during her last year.

David Rockefeller and Annette de la Renta, like many friends who had been on Brooke Astor's original list, had difficulty deciding whether to go to her funeral or stay home. Not knowing what kind of reception they'd get, Linda Gillies had made the trip down from Maine and Alexandra Isles had come in from Connecticut. Only on Thursday did John Hart receive a phone call from Charlene inviting him to come sit in the VIP section, a designation he found a bit odd for a funeral. By the time Linda got a similar phone call, she was no longer home to receive it. Earlier in the week, having received no formal invitation from the Marshalls, Philippe de Montebello and James Houghton, the Met's director and board chairman, had decided not to attend. Paul LeClerc, head of the New York Public Library, had agreed to serve as an honorary pallbearer, although the Library, like the Met, had already hired a major law firm to represent them in Westchester.

Perhaps it was all the predictions by the media of a great turnout of mourners. Or the haphazard way the invitations were delivered. Or the fact that it was midsummer. Or the fear certain people had that they might be pointedly snubbed by the Marshalls. Perhaps it reflected the fact that anyone who wasn't famous or expensively dressed or who failed to come across as someone who had every right to be there was summarily directed to a side entrance and ushered upstairs. Whatever the reason, whereas Annette's dining room had been full that afternoon at lunch, once you looked beyond the section reserved for special guests, you saw many pews in the main body of the church were half full or unoccupied. (*The New York Times* would report the next day that half the church's 1800 seats remained empty.)

The psalms and hymns that afternoon had all been chosen by Brooke Astor. The two presiding clerics were well known to her as were two of the three men who went on to speak about her. David Rockefeller, the first to speak, was not even listed on the program, owing to the fact that only at the last minute had he decided to come. Halfway through the service, David Rockefeller made his way to the lectern. At this point in his life he was an experienced eulogist, well aware of what was called for on such occasions. But at the end, after sharing with the mourners his memories from a longtime association with his good friend Brooke Astor, he made no mention of her son. Instead, he spoke of visiting her at her Westchester estate with "her dear and loyal friend Annette." When he had finished, he walked down the aisle to the pew where the de la Rentas were seated with the Kissingers and slipped in beside them.

David Rockefeller was immediately followed by Tony Marshall who spoke first of the "special bond" he had shared with his mother and the special times the two of them had enjoyed in the company of his wife Charlene. After reading a poem by his mother—a poem that she had originally wished to have read by Jack Pierrepont, Laurance Rockefeller, or Nancy Pierrepont, all now dead—he picked up where he had left off, giving that "special bond" a special twist. He wanted everyone to know that while Brooke Astor's friends and the people of the city had lost someone who meant a great deal to them, his loss was far greater. His voice quavering and his eyes welling with tears, he told them, "I've lost my mother."

Michael Bloomberg, the third speaker, having played no part in the controversy surrounding the deceased, was free to honor her memory in any way he pleased. While he would go on to touch on specific things she had done for the city, he seemed most at ease when speaking of the many reasons Brooke Astor shared a unique historical perspective with his ninety-eight-year-old mother. "They came from an era before the Internet, before television, even before David

Dinkins and Ed Koch were in knee pants," said Bloomberg, giving the two former mayors present their due while having a little fun at their expense. It was an impulse Brooke Astor herself would have understood and might well have appreciated that afternoon at St. Thomas's when fun was not much in evidence.

On the steps, leaving the church just behind Linda Gillies, you could spot Paul LeClerc, Randy Bourcheidt, and Gregory Long—all of whom had come to appreciate Brooke Astor's special qualities while collaborating with her on projects benefiting literature or the arts. Just ahead of Linda were the talk-show host Charlie Rose, who at one time had been very close to Brooke Astor, and Whoopi Goldberg, who had not been close to her at all. Whoopi Goldberg had no doubt come out of loyalty to the Marshalls. Philip Marshall, who felt no such loyalty, stood outside on the sidewalk with his wife and two children. Asked by a reporter how he felt, he said, "Relieved."

Philip Marshall, like Annette de la Renta and David Rockefeller, would not be going on to the private reception the Marshalls had planned at the Colony Club. Linda Gillies, on the other hand, did make it to the reception and noted that the club's big ballroom seemed to have been reserved with the idea that there would be more than just a smattering of people. Those friends from the old days who made it to the ballroom—Rosamund Bernier and John Russell, for instance, and Tom and Suzie Coolidge—stayed for a while to chat but didn't linger long.

By the end of September, when the New York Public Library and the Metropolitan Museum had held their own memorials for Brooke Astor, Boysie and Girlsie were happily settling in on a farm in Vermont and Tony Marshall was facing legal action on two fronts. In Manhattan, a grand jury was meeting, seeking to determine whether his actions and Francis Morrissey's had in fact been criminal. In Westchester, the judge was deciding whether to permit Annette de la Renta and JP Morgan Chase to go from serving as Astor's guardians to serving as co-administrators of the estate, or to reject their petition and accept her son's two candidates. He was also trying to decide what to make of a letter dated December 26, 2000, written by Tony Marshall to a neurologist treating his mother, expressing "serious concerns" about her mental condition and quoting her as saying, "I feel I'm losing my mind." (Certainly, the letter appeared to make a persuasive argument for falling back on a will written prior to that date.)

The Library memorial—which made a point of emphasizing Brooke Astor's considerable gifts as a writer—was held that September in the Celeste Bartos Auditorium. This time, Tony had no control over the event. Indeed, he was not invited. He did attend the Friday night memorial at the Metropolitan Museum, which was open to the public and which kicked off a special Brooke Astor weekend. At the Grace Rainey Rogers Auditorium, he and Charlene sat in the front row, just off the right aisle, almost directly under the podium. Unless you looked twice, you were not likely to notice them. But from where he sat, Tony could hardly fail to hear every word uttered by Philippe de Montebello and Lord William Astor, both of whom made special mention of the devoted attention Brooke had received from her good friends David Rockefeller and Annette de la Renta and then made no mention of him.

Later that fall, however, Tony Marshall had the satisfaction of seeing one of his candidates for co-administrator, Judge Howard Levine, take Annette de la Renta's place. (Annette, for her part, let it be known to friends that she was relieved to be removed from a position that had left her subject to a barrage of lawyers' letters. By all accounts, Howard Levine was qualified for the job and well respected, and, no less important, JP Morgan Chase would remain in place.) Tony could also derive some satisfaction from a decidedly sympathetic article in *New York* magazine that finally gave him a chance to present his side. He had little time, though, to savor these triumphs.

On the Monday after Thanksgiving, he received a summons from the office of the Manhattan District Attorney ordering him to appear in court the following morning, where the presiding judge would be handing down a criminal indictment.

"Bad Heir Day" proclaimed the *Post*'s Wednesday front page—a perfect headline as well as a perfect caption for the accompanying photograph, which showed a disheveled and windblown Tony Marshall on his way to the courthouse to be arraigned. It was not a flattering photograph. But it was not unfair. More than one person in the courtroom Tuesday morning had noted that suddenly Tony had aged twenty years. And no wonder. Already his fingerprints had been taken. His passport was to be lifted. Bail was to be set for $100,000.

As he sat facing the judge, behind a long wooden table, Tony Marshall had been read an eighteen-count indictment accusing him of conspiring with Francis Morrissey to take advantage of his mother's "diminished mental capacity" in order to steal artwork worth millions of dollars while bilking her estate of many more millions. If convicted of the first count, which charged him with scheming to defraud in the first degree—most egregiously when persuading his mother to sell her Childe Hassam *Flags* painting by convincing her that she desperately needed the money and then taking a $2 million commission—he could be spending twenty-five years in prison. To all eighteen counts he pleaded not guilty.

"We'll be all right," Charlene was heard to reassure a visibly shaken Tony, the morning of his arraignment, after she hurried over to embrace him. But there was just so much she could do to guarantee this. And, of course, whatever happened to Tony, she would be all right. No one could accuse her of any criminal wrongdoing. Worst-case scenario: If Tony was slapped with a steep fine and then sent to jail and the Westchester court went on to decide in favor of the 1997 will, she would still end up a rich woman.

That Friday, Francis Morrissey, just back from Europe, was

charged with being part of a conspiracy to defraud a vulnerable Brooke Astor. In addition, he alone was charged with forging Astor's signature on the third codicil to the 2002 will. Unlike Tony Marshall, he entered the courtroom wearing handcuffs. But he, too, had his bail set at $100,000. And he, too, pleaded not guilty.

Although facing the gallows may focus some minds wonderfully, the prospect of a jail sentence seemed to have the opposite effect on Tony Marshall. First, he turned in an expired passport and, when confronted, explained that it was the only passport he possessed—apparently forgetting that within the past year he had used a new passport to visit Turks and Caicos. Suddenly he was being called a scofflaw and a flight risk. But, worse, that Saturday he was accused by the *Post*—which featured a photograph of his mother's barren, leaf-strewn grave site on its front page—of continuing to treat his mother badly, even now that she was dead. Where, the accompanying article asked, was the handsome headstone supposedly destined to rest alongside Vincent's? The best response Tony could manage was to have someone call and say that he'd simply forgotten to sign the necessary paper. The headstone was ready. The delay did not signify neglect or a lack of respect. It was nothing more than an oversight.

At his arraignment, Tony Marshall had been ordered to return to criminal court on January 30th. When this court date was pushed back an additional month, he was receiving, among other things, more time to recover his balance. Another man might have used this time to come to some accommodation with all the city organizations lined up against him. But six months after Brooke Astor's death, the Park Avenue apartment stood shuttered and Chris Ely remained at Holly Hill, keeping the property in order, while awaiting some decision as to its future. With time passing and no settlement in the offing, legal costs were rapidly mounting. At some point stiff tax penalties would be incurred.

The trouble was that Tony Marshall showed every sign of being a man who believed he was innocent. A year and a half after Philip had first asked to have him removed as his mother's guardian, Tony Marshall continued to see nothing wrong in what he had done. Instead, he blamed the gossip of disaffected servants, the greed of the charities, and the jealousy and social ambitions of certain of his mother's friends. But, above all, he blamed his son.

Philip Marshall, who stood to gain no more from the second will than he had from the first, was certain of one thing: He did not want his father to spend his remaining years in jail. When he'd first petitioned the court, it had never occurred to him that anyone—much less his father—had been systematically stealing large sums of money. For the moment, the only comfort he could take was his belief that all the publicity given his grandmother's sorry plight might encourage others who suspected elder abuse to speak out. On this point he and Annette de la Renta were in complete agreement. Annette, coming upon a *Times* article in late January titled "Manhattan Doctor is Accused of Fleecing Mother out of $800,000," was moved to read that the two women who brought their suspicions to the district attorney "had been emboldened" by all the news stories they'd read about "the Astor case."

It was some comfort to those close to her to look forward to a time when the actual court case was settled and the only reminder would be future occasions when Brooke Astor's final public performance would be credited with turning a harsh spotlight on still another problem in need of solving. But it was no less comforting and definitely more heartening for friends who cared about her to look back to a time when another kind of abuse had played a crucial part in her life—a time when, stuck in a marriage to a man who beat and humiliated her, she had taken her first steps out into the great world and set about turning herself into a serious writer.

In *Footprints* Brooke Astor had mentioned almost in passing how as an unhappy young wife she'd summoned up the courage to ask a

Vogue editor she was sitting next to at a Bernardsville luncheon if she might attempt to write some book reviews for her. She'd noted that these reviews, written in the form of a letter to a friend "Anne," were the first the magazine had ever run. Apart from this distinction, she didn't appear to think they merited much attention. "Girlish" she called them. Now, thanks to a suggestion by Paul LeClerc—who'd located and then passed along several of her *Vogue* reviews—Robert Silvers was able to provide those attending the Library memorial with a close look at this "girlish" reviewer, who already in her twenties was prepared to take on the likes of Sinclair Lewis, declaring his *Elmer Gantry* to be nowhere near as good as his *Main Street* or *Babbitt*.

"Not only is the book less well written, the theme itself has stumbled over the heights of Realism and into Freudian depths," wrote an intrepid Brooke. "Babbitt was not a person of great intellect, or great feeling, or great virtue, but he was the epitome of a type, and one could laugh with him, and at him, and condone his faults." Had Miss Madeira read this review, she might have smiled at the brio and sheer nerve of her former pupil, while Mabel Russell, who had pulled Brooke from school far too early, might have felt a stab of envy. Even Edith Wharton, had she chanced upon a stray copy of the magazine, might have looked forward to one day, in the course of her travels, meeting up with "Anne's" lively and amusing but surprisingly shrewd young friend.

BIBLIOGRAPHY

Aldrich, Nelson W., Jr. *Old Money: The Mythology of America's Upper Class.* New York: Knopf, 1988.

Astor, Brooke. *The Bluebird Is at Home.* New York: Harper & Row, 1965.

———. *Footprints.* New York: Harper & Row, 1980.

———. *Patchwork Child.* New York: Random House, 1993.

Chernow, Ron. *Titan: The Life of John D. Rockefeller, Sr.* New York: Random House, 1998.

Cowles, Virginia. *The Astors.* New York: Knopf, 1979.

Fox, James. *Five Sisters: The Langhornes of Virginia.* New York: Touchstone/Simon & Schuster, 2000.

Gill, Brendan. *Tallulah.* New York: Holt, Rinehart & Winston, 1972.

Gratz, Roberta Brandes. *The Living City.* New York: Simon & Schuster, 1989.

Gregorian, Vartan. *The Road to Home.* New York: Simon & Schuster, 2003.

Heiskell, Andrew, with Ralph Graves. *Outsider Insider.* New York: Marien-Darien Press, 1998.

Homberger, Eric. *Mrs. Astor's New York: Money and Social Power in a Gilded Age.* New Haven: Yale University Press, 2002.

Hoving, Thomas. *Making the Mummies Dance.* New York: Touchstone/Simon & Schuster, 1994.

Israel, Lee. *Miss Tallulah Bankhead.* New York: Putnam, 1972.

Kaplan, Justin. *When the Astors Owned New York:* Viking, 2006.

Kavaler, Lucy. *The Astors: An American Legend.* New York: Dodd, Mead, 1968.

Lewis, Alfred Allan. *Ladies and Not-So-Gentle Women.* New York: Penguin, 2000.

Lucey, Donna M. *Archie and Amelie*. New York: Harmony, 2006.

McCarthy, Kathleen D., ed. *Lady Bountiful Revisited: Women, Philanthropy, and Power*. New Brunswick, N.J.: Rutgers University Press, 1990.

Morris, Charles R. *The Cost of Good Intentions: New York City and the Liberal Experiment*. New York: Norton, 1980.

Nielsen, Waldemar A. *The Big Foundations*. New York: Columbia University Press, 1972.

Ostrower, Francie. *Why the Wealthy Give*. Princeton, N.J.: Princeton University Press, 1995.

Rockefeller, David. *Memoirs*. New York: Random House, 2002.

Sinclair, David. *Dynasty: The Astors and Their Times*. London: J.M. Dent & Sons, 1983.

Thomas, Lately. *The Astor Orphans: A Pride of Lions*. Albany, N.Y.: Washington Park Press, 1999.

Varney, Carlton. *The Draper Touch*. New York: Shannongrove Press, 1988.

The Vincent Astor Foundation, 1948–1997. New York: Vincent Astor Foundation, n.d. [c. 1998].

Wharton, Edith. *A Backward Glance*. New York: Touchstone/Simon & Schuster, 1988.

Wilson, Derek. *The Astors: 1763–1992*. New York: St. Martin's, 1993.

ACKNOWLEDGMENTS

In this age of hyperbole, when one can find even the most lackluster celebrity being touted as remarkable, Brooke Astor truly deserves all the accolades she has received. From the start she *was* unique. She was also tireless. From the time I set out to examine her life and accomplishments in November 2001, I have been reminded of her energy time and again. This book about her would not have been possible without the help of Linda Gillies and the early cooperation of Mrs. Astor and her son, Anthony Marshall. During the months preceding and following her big hundredth birthday, Mrs. Astor's charm remained considerable. For the time she gave me I will always be grateful. Linda Gillies, who served as the director of the Vincent Astor Foundation from 1974 until its closing in 1997, continued over the years to be a wise and reliable guide, one whose responses to my questions about Mrs. Astor and the Foundation were jargon free, invariably fair, and never for an instant boring.

Louis Auchincloss was the first friend of Mrs. Astor whom I interviewed, and the last. Without him, this book would be sadly diminished. At the same time, I owe much to the memories and insights offered by Renata Adler, Brian Bedford, Susan Burden, Annette de la Renta, Sean Driscoll, Everett Fahey, John Hart, Ashton Hawkins, Florence Irving, Roxana Robinson, Charles Ryskamp, and Robert Silvers.

In the five and a half years since I started work on this book I have interviewed almost one hundred and fifty people—not only Mrs. Astor's friends and acquaintances but men and women who got to know her through her work as president of the Vincent Astor Foundation. To the following individuals, some of whom are no longer alive, I am indebted for the many details that provide depth and color to this portrait of Mrs. Astor: Lady Virginia Airlie; Nelson W. Aldrich Jr.; Winthrop Aldrich; Joe Armstrong; William, Viscount Astor; Marciano Amaral; K. K. Auchincloss; Kent Barwick; Laurie Beckelman; Rosamond Bernier; Tom Bernstein; Roland Betts; Nancy Biberman; Bob Bickford; Randy Bourscheidt; Preston Brown; Robert Caro; Schuyler Chapin; Henry (Terry) Christensen; Evie Clarkson; Dr. William Conway; Thomas Coolidge; Stephanie Copeland; Lord Cranbourne; Dorothy Cullman; Joan Davidson; Gordon Davis; Suzanne Davis; Jimmy Davison; Philippe de Montebello: Irene Diamond; William Dietel; Douglas Dillon; David Dinkins; John Dobkin; Catherine Dunn; Andrew, Duke of Devonshire; Deborah, Duchess of Devonshire; Jacqueline Drexel; Catherine Dunn; Elly Elliott; Osborn Elliott; Jason Epstein; John Fairchild; Father John Felice; Liz Fondaras; Wen Fong; Dr. Philip Fox; Howard Friedman; Ellen Futter; Peter Gates; Richard George; Richard Gilder; Robert Giroux; Barbara Goldsmith; Roberta Brandeis Gratz; Vartan Gregorian; John Gross; Paul Gunther; Albert Hadley; Emily Harding; Kitty Carlisle Hart; Leda Hayashi; Robert Hayes; Dru Heinz; Andrew Heiskell; Jolee Hirsch; Thomas Hoving; Marnie Imhoff; Jay Iselin; Alexandra Isles; Dwight Johnson; Penny Kalk; Elizabeth Kasowitz; Dr. William Kaye; Horace Kelland; Henry Kissinger; Ed Koch; Eleanor Lambert; Kenneth J. Lane; Paul LeClerc; Joshua Lederberg; Adam Lewis; Gregory Long; Susan Lyall; Romana McEwen; Fern Mallis; Richard Manson; Ann Marcus; Philip Marshall; Joyce Matz; John Meaney; Frederick Melhado; Richard Morsches; Nancy Newhouse; Bill Nimkin; Peggy Nichols;

Rodney Nichols; Ivan Obolensky; Peter Paine; Gilly Palmer; Alice Perdue; Charles Pierce; Karen Phillips; Howard Phipps; Dr. Guy Pidgeon; Nancy Pierrepont; Robert Pirie; Betty Prashker; Nancy Pyne; Nancy Reagan; Lydia Redmond; Jim Regginato; Fergus Reid; Marjorie Rice; John Richardson: David Rockefeller; Laurance Rockefeller; Elizabeth Barlow Rogers; Elizabeth Rohatyn; Felix Rohatyn; Marshall Rose; Arthur Ross; Francis Russell; John Russell; Molly Salisbury; Betty Kelly Sargent; John Sargent; Alexandra Schlesinger; Arthur Schlesinger; Christopher Scholz; Helen Scholz; Joel Sesser; Frederick Seitz; Hildy Simmons; Liz Smith; Peter Stanford; Serena Stewart; Beth Straus; Frank Thomas; George Trescher; Helen Tucker; Sidney Urquhart; Anna Glen Vietor; James Watt; Betty Wallerstein; Barbara Walters; Margo Wellington; Alison West; Thorsten Wiesel; Tony Wood; and Kathryn Wylde.

During the years I have been working on this book, many people have been of help to me. First of all, I would like to thank the Corporation of Yaddo for a gift residency, which made possible the writing of an outline and rough draft in the fall of 2005.

There would have been no book, however, without my editor, Starling Lawrence, who encouraged me to undertake this project, responded to my first draft with enthusiasm, and then went on to read and edit every chapter as the book was written, offering the sound counsel of a first reader who happens also to be a writer. Much credit is due also to Molly May, his assistant, who came to this project in its final stages but did everything possible to make things go smoothly. No less important was the careful attention provided the whole staff at W. W. Norton, especially Nancy Palmquist, but also Anna Oler, Don Rifkin, and Louise Brockett.

My agent, Amanda Urban, was the first to see that Mrs. Astor and I might make an interesting match and then did her best to make sure that everything would work out for the best.

Never would I have been able to finish this book on deadline without Trent Duffy, who kept me steady over the years, while serving first as a resourceful researcher and unrelenting fact checker and, finally, as the manuscript's clear-eyed copy editor. I also owe much to Asha Schechter, who provided able and much needed assistance as the photo researcher for this book.

I want to thank Jeanie M. James, the archivist at the Metropolitan Museum of Art, and Harold Holzer, senior vice president for external affairs. I'd also like to thank Peter Johnson, David Rockefeller's associate, for doing his best to assist me with permissions and photographs. And I want to give a special thanks to Michael Hechtman and Laura Harris of the *New York Post*, who made available to me folders of Astor-related clippings housed in the newspaper's library. I appreciate the help of Rebecca Brooks at the Madeira School for providing a transcript of a 1997 interview with Brooke Astor.

I am indebted to the staff of the Dutchess County Surrogate's Court in Poughkeepsie, New York, for providing access to a sampling of Vincent Astor's wills as well as invaluable documents relating to the 1959 court hearing.

I am especially grateful to the staff of the Brooke Russell Astor Rare Books and Manuscripts Reading Room at the New York Public Library, who, over the course of several years, made available to me countless boxes containing the clippings and folders that form the Vincent Astor Foundation's extensive archive.

I greatly appreciate Barbara Shiers's volunteering to retrieve from New York Surrogate's Court Charles Marshall's will, along with his father's, and the time she then took to provide me with a clear understanding of just what had been inherited by his widow—the estate's assets as well as its debts after death duties had been paid.

As always, friends and family have done much to make possible the writing of this book. First of all, I would like to thank Ann Thorne for her encouragement and advice. In addition I want to thank Sally Arteseros, Sheila Biddle, Elisabeth Biondi, Joel Conarroe, Florence de Dampierre, Mickey Friedman, Angeline Goreau, Mary Gordon, Duncan Hannah, Molly Haskell, Michael Janeway, Billy Kiernan, Bannon McHenry, Thomas Mallon, Honor Moore, Jerry Orbach, Sarah Plimpton, Alison Rose, Jeannette Watson Sanger, Benjamin Taylor, Lily Tuck, Patricia Volk, LuAnn Walther, Sam Waterston, Wendy Weil, Brenda Wineapple, and Beverley Zabriskie. In addition, I am thankful for all the help I received from the late Edward Tuck during the early stages of this book.

Finally, I want to thank my husband, Howard, for his continued support, as well as for never uttering one complaint during the long hard autumn of 2006.

ILLUSTRATION CREDITS

1: Metropolitan Museum of Art, Gift of R. Thornton Wilson and Orne Wilson, 1949 (49.4). Photograph © 1981 Metropolitan Museum of Art. 2, 3, 5, 8: From *Patchwork Child* by Brooke Astor, copyright © 1962, 1993 by Brooke Astor. Used by permission of Random House, Inc. 7, 32, 36: Collections of the New York Public Library, Astor, Lenox, and Tilden Foundations. 9: Courtesy of Christopher Scholz. 10, 28: Courtesy of Annette de la Renta. 11: John Springer Collection / Corbis. 12, 16, 20: Bettmann/Corbis. 13: Oscar White / Corbis. 14: Herbert Gehr / Time Life Pictures / Getty Images. 15: Cecil Beaton / © Condé Nast Archive / Corbis. 17: Courtesy of Serena Stewart. 18: Courtesy of the Cecil Beaton Studio Archive, Sotheby's, London. 19: Philip Marshall Collection. 21: Horst P. Horst / Condé Nast Archive / Corbis. 22: Associated Press. 23, 30: Courtesy of Louis Auchincloss. 24: Marty Reichenthal / Associated Press. 25: Philippe Halsman / © Halsman Estate / Courtesy of the Rockefeller Archive Center. 26: Courtesy of the Rockefeller Archive Center. 27, 42: Courtesy of Linda Gillies. 29: Courtesy of Charles Ryskamp. 31: Courtesy of Ronald Reagan Library. 33: Sara Krulwich / *New York Times* / Redux. 34: Richard Corkery / New York *Daily News*. 35: WireImage / Getty Images. 38, 39, 40: Courtesy of Department of Asian Art, Metropolitan Museum of Art, New York. 41: Bill Cunningham / *New York Times* / Redux. 43: Don Pollard / Courtesy of the Metropolitan Museum of Art. 44: Mary Hilliard / Courtesy of David Rockefeller. 45, 47: Mary Hilliard. 46: Michael Albans / New York *Daily News*. 48: Philip Marshall Collection. 49: Burt Glinn / Magnum Photos.

INDEX

Index